he Uses of Cultural Studies

The Uses of Cultural Studies

A Textbook

ANGELA McROBBIE

SAGE Publications

London ● Thousand Oaks ● New Delhi

First published 2005

 SAGE Publications Ltd
1 Oliver's Yard
55 City Road
London EC1Y 1SP

SAGE Publications Inc.
2455 Teller Road
Thousand Oaks, California 91320

SAGE Publications India Pvt Ltd
B-42, Panchsheel Enclave
Post Box 4109
New Delhi 110 017

British Library Cataloguing in Publication data
A catalogue record for this book is available from the British Library

ISBN 1-4129-0844-2
ISBN 1-4129-0845-0 (pbk)

Library of Congress Control Number: 200409954

Typeset by M Rules
Printed in Great Britain by TJ International, Padstow, Cornwall

Contents

Acknowledgements

This is a textbook and it is fitting that I offer my deep thanks to some of my former students who have, over the years, become friends and colleagues. These include Isaac Julien (from our time at Central St Martins College of Art and Design), Alev Adil and James Barrett (on the MA course at Thames Valley University), Boris Ewenstein, Caspar Melville, Yeran Kim, Bakri Bahkit, Mira Levinson and Vrajesh Hanspal, among many others at Goldsmiths College, University of London. I would also like to thank my North London friends and neighbours, Paul Gilroy and Vron Ware, Denise Riley, Charlotte Brunsdon, Sarah Thornton, Mica Nava, Stuart Hall, Lucy Bland, the Winston family and Bill Schwarz. I am indebted to Paul Du Gay, Sean Nixon, Larry Grossberg and, of course, my daughter Hanna Chalmers. I have truly appreciated the input, support and extraordinary intellectual stimulation of all my Goldsmiths colleagues and specific assistance from Richard Smith and Zehra Arabadji. Special thanks to Yinka Shonibare for permission to use his work for the cover design and thanks also to Sage editor Julia Hall.

Further Materials I originally appeared in *Theory, Culture & Society* 19 (3), 2002.

Further Materials II originally appeared in *Feminist Review* no 75, 2003. Reproduced with permission of Palgrave Macmillan.

Introduction: Privilege and Delight

Writing a textbook like this requires, above all, thoughtfulness about the students who one hopes will read the book. That is, the process of writing is undertaken to foreground pedagogy, and to take into account the role of the teacher as someone who is invariably constrained in terms of time and resources and who is forever looking for ways to enlarge upon the curriculum, and to provide students with the means by which they can pursue particular interests in more depth without getting lost or straying too far from the starting point of what is usually called course content. My main topic in this book is contemporary cultural theory and its uses in amplifying our understanding of a wide range of everyday social, cultural and political practices. In recent years, teaching at Goldsmiths College in London, I have noticed how exceptionally keen and eager students are to absorb and understand key writers like those whose work I engage with in this book. These students are often frustrated by what they perceive as their own weaknesses when they find themselves struggling with unfamiliar terms, with new vocabularies and with the much wider intellectual context which the writers themselves inhabit. In an inter-disciplinary academic environment, students have to learn how to draw limits on what they can realistically engage with, across diverse fields of intellectual activity. And there are also more limits on time than was the case some years ago. Nowadays undergraduate students usually have to undertake paid part-time work. Under these circumstances they cannot afford the straightforward pleasures of getting lost for days at a time in the library, and they are anxious and fearful when they find that work they know to be important is also even more demanding than they imagined. My aim here, is not, however, to try to deliver a quick fix, or a step-by-step guide to cultural theory. Ideally I would like to help students to grasp the importance of this body of work, without being intimidated by it. It is not my intention then to offer a short cut; instead I would like to lead students through a number of themes found in each of the theorists I deal with, and then

I would like them to see how these feed into and shape the field of cultural studies, not as a tightly defined discipline but as a shifting terrain, a site of dispute and contestation.

The model I emulate here is one which dates back to the late 1970s and early 1980s when the Open University in the UK gave the fledgling subject 'cultural studies' an enormous boost by developing a unit in Popular Culture with the unexciting name U203. The distance learning techniques of the Open University require that a good deal of effort is put into preparing course materials, from large unit guides, to set texts, and additional edited collections as well as television and radio programmes. U203 was a milestone event for the future of cultural studies. It presented students with a substantial range of theoretical work from Barthes and Foucault to Lacan, Althusser and Gramsci, while also providing large numbers of case studies and more concrete material, including Eco's study of the *James Bond* novels, Dick Hebdige's analysis of youth culture and my own work on *Jackie* magazine (Waites et al., 1982; Bennett et al., 1981). Of course this teaching material was the outcome of the effort of many people. But what I try to hold onto here, is the accessibility without simplification which characterised U203, and the connection made between cultural theory and various forms of cultural practice. The format I adopt is to present lengthy chapters on six cultural theorists, at the end of which there are extended notes on a topic drawn from the world of political or popular culture, or the arts, which has a particular relation to the work of the cultural theorist, illuminating and complementing the writing, but also, itself, being illuminated in return. In addition, at the end of the book I include two review essays each of which deals with more recent work by Bourdieu et al. (1999) and Butler (2000c).

It is important to draw attention here to the influence which various forms of neo-Marxist theory have had on the formation of cultural studies from the mid 1970s onwards. While to those over the age of 35 this might seem self-evident, to a younger generation it is often perplexing, something which, unless they have academic training already in Marxist-influenced social science subjects, is simply a mark of a bygone era, a time of intellectual and political fervour, a time when it seemed possible to draw on a materialist, class analysis of the whole social world, and make sense of it accordingly. The question is, how much of Marxist theory needs to be available to students of cultural studies today to allow them to understand the historical and intellectual context of more recent cultural theory? Ideally I would always want to preface a course on contemporary cultural theory with a number of lectures on Marx, and then on Adorno, Benjamin, Althusser, Gramsci, Laclau and Mouffe, and Stuart Hall. For the purposes of this book I have attempted to highlight, where appropriate, the precise way in which the authors I consider here look to and are influenced by Marxist theory, while also challenging some of its underlying principles. In Chapter 1 on Stuart Hall I examine an earlier co-authored article on political communications. This is a piece which offers a different way of carrying out media analysis from what was established in sociology and mass communications at the time. It was also a bold and risky endeavour. The bibliography shows just a handful of texts, the article considers in detail one single television programme. Hall et al. might as well be saying, this is how it can be done, with only Gramsci and Althusser and Roland Barthes hovering in the background. Hall brings the reader with him as he experiments with the possibility of analysing a television text. By this means he also proposes a way of understanding the relation between media, politics and ideology.

In the chapter on Hall I also track his well known analysis of the Thatcher government and the wider political culture it brought into being, and here too we find a loose, improvised yet also accessible style in Hall's writing. Many of the essays on Thatcherism were first published in a magazine with a much wider readership than exists for academic texts. In both the media work and also in his writing on the Thatcher years Hall analyses what he calls a 'complex unity' which emerges as a distinctive modality of power. For Hall this means that power works most effectively through articulation, through making connections across diverse and divergent fields, through a kind of stitching together process which consolidates power by means of negotiation, concession, sometimes reaching for consensus by means of tactical retreat. But this can also be a principle for the left, especially once the idea of the over-arching unity of class, and the relinquishing of other differences in its favour, is abandoned. This kind of thinking continues in more recent work where he participates in debates on multi-culturalism. How do we live together and acknowledge differences? Only when there is, yes, a horizon of universalism which expects of us all that we bow to the rights of others to pursue their differences, not in hermetically sealed ways, but rather within a framework of intersection and overlap so that the possibilities for democracy (always unfulfilled) are opened up and extended by this 'complex unity in difference'.

Paul Gilroy's work also proposes a number of themes, the political urgency of which is overwhelming. Over the years they keep drawing his attention; these are the questions of nation and nationalism, belonging and unbelonging, restless diaspora and the utopia of being beyond race. In Chapter 2, I use the term 'black and not-black' to describe the movement in Gilroy's writing, this reverberates because it signals his own 'double consciousness', the necessity of occupying blackness to counter the historical power of racialising discourse and the yearning to be beyond blackness and to live in a world where such a notion, such an observation about a person, that he or she is black or white, is insignificant, and totally unremarkable. Music is the form which Gilroy draws on most heavily to develop his arguments. It provides an incredibly powerful soundtrack to his writing; the complexity of jazz rhythms, the flourishes, the screams and the cries of James Brown, the heavy bass lines of George Clinton's Funkadelic sound, the volume and the profusion and the endless inventiveness of black diasporic musics is what makes Gilroy marvel at such outpouring and it replenishes his own jaded spirits in the face of the negation of his political aspirations. His own entanglement with music such as this, its existence as a lifeline and a space for safeguarding a history and acting as an archive, also provides him with a space for his own habitation. The affects of music and the intensity of these sonic experiences provide Gilroy with a kind of pre-figurative imagining of what might be other than what is.

In Butler, who is already so written about that it is daunting to enter into the arena of Butler scholars, my aim in Chapter 3 is to extrapolate a few key themes in her work and knit these together so that they illuminate for readers some of the key dynamics of sex and gender in contemporary culture. These include, in my view, a new form of gender retrenchment which comes into view, one which seems to take on board the existence of gay and lesbian sexuality, and which also acknowledges gender fluidity and thus the degrees of enactment or performativity which underpin the daily practices of masculinity and femininity. On the basis of this recognised fluidity, there are produced, within the immensely powerful and also inventive terrain of consumer culture, entertainment and popular culture, any number of consolidated codings of sexuality which combine novel aspects of sexual difference with emphatic 'gender normativity'. By absorbing and even celebrating gay and lesbian sexual desires, new representations of sexuality appear all the more able to enforce what it is to be 'a real girl' or 'a real boy'. There is a lot more work to be done on this area, and students might well want to consider such renewed normativities in more detail, and with this the subtle but heightened levels of social constraint inscribed within the popular narratives of our times, for example, television programmes like *Sex in the City, The OC, Will and Grace, Queer as Folk*, and also in the mainstreaming of soft porn magazines like (in the UK) *Zoo, Nuts, Loaded* and so on. Butler's inventiveness for the purposes of this textbook lies in three areas. First is her engagement with feminism as it was, and as it might become, in the light of her revising of the previously agreed distinction between sex as given and gender as learnt. Second, there is her re-examination of Freud's understanding of bisexuality and Butler's own account of gender melancholia, and third, there is, of course, her theory of performativity. The close attention given by Butler to everyday political events and processes coincides with a melancholic strand in her writing. There is recognition of the full array of forces which are formidably resistant to a radical sexual politics and to a politics of kinship which do not, inevitably, privilege heterosexual reproduction.

Homi Bhabha's writing usually produces levels of anxiety among students on the basis of its dense, ornate, digressive and unconventional style. I attempt in Chapter 4 to clarify and contextualise. I suggest that one of the keys to this difficulty is that Bhabha himself is an experimental writer, and that the concepts which he creates are also activated in his texts; indeed they provide his writing with form by means of a post-colonial critique of literary and aesthetic formalisms. Bhabha's (anti-) formalism is based on his efforts to write into being the 'third space', to 'move beyond' and also to activate the idea of 'time lag' so that our comfortable western sense of time and viewpoint are overturned, or at least disrupted. In this chapter I concentrate on those aspects of Bhabha's writing which are more directly connected to cultural studies. First, there is his political engagement with class and his argument about how it must give way to multi-culture and to notions of community including those created by migrants and post-colonial artists. Second, I focus on his understanding of post-colonial agency (and cultural translation). This he claims is to be found in writing, art and in the distinctive cultures produced in the borderline negotiations of diasporic peoples as they find themselves drawn towards the cosmopolitan urban centres. Third, I examine one of Bhabha's most brilliant essays where he dissects the racial stereotype drawing on Foucault, Said, Fanon and produces from this dissection a new understanding of the prevalence and ubiquitousness and repetitiveness of this form on the basis of the troubling gaze with which the racial other, subjugated into apparent mimicry of the dominant culture, looks back at the colonising powers. The requirement as inscribed within the fixed boundaries of the stereotype, that he or she be 'more than' in order to be 'less than', offers enormous potential for understanding racial representation across popular culture.

Pierre Bourdieu, who died in January 2002, left behind him a legacy of sociological work the value of which is still to be fully appreciated, at least in the UK. That such prolific studies were produced by this one person who surely must have written night and day, and quite relentlessly, is not just admirable on the basis of the contribution to knowledge, but also itself a kind of act of love, that is love for the social sciences and for the possibility within this field of offering specific ways of understanding how the social world operates so as to shore up power in the hands of already privileged groups. Bourdieu was antipathetic to cultural studies, but this does not reduce my admiration for him; ideally I would like to have been able to persuade him otherwise, but even still his contribution to cultural studies remains outstanding. I outline in detail the differences between his account and those found in cultural studies, I also trace through the incredible significance of his concepts of field and habitus, and I then show how his analysis of taste allows him to develop a sharp understanding of how the realm of consumer culture is a key site for the reproduction of social inequalities and thus for the strengthening of the status quo. In that section I focus on the role of education in the transmission of cultural capital and the function, as Bourdieu sees it, of the new cultural intermediaries whose roles in the service sector (as for example 'lifestyle gurus' and other similar occupations) produce a kind of widespread and popular 'goodwill' to those social arrangements which are in fact predisposed to act in hostile ways towards the very people who are the subjects of this kind of illusory self-improvement.

The chapter on Jameson allows attention to be focused on Marxism in relation to culture and politics. Once again I extract from the work themes which are useful in relation to an imagined dialogue. Looking back at his magisterial article, in what is now 20 years after publication, we are able to see how utilised his account of postmodernism was as a means of creating heavily inter-textual cultural artefacts which permitted even greater degrees of space for reception and reading by diverse readers and audiences than had been the case before. In effect, Jameson's analysis has shaped the sensibility of university-educated cultural producers from the late 1980s onwards, or at least this is my claim. With the help of Jameson's remarkable analysis of postmodernism, young media and cultural producers and indeed artists were provided with a perfect formula for creating forms inflected with irony, pastiche and knowing self-referentiality. Already Quentin Tarantino and David Lynch were working in this vein, but academic postmodernism (shorn of the Marxist critique) provided substantial cultural capital to graduates in media and cultural studies as they looked for work in media and culture industries. By these means, television also reinvented itself to reach younger and more sophisticated audiences. This is apparent not just in Lynch's *Twin Peaks*, but also in series like *Seinfeld* and *The Larry Sanders Show* and also *The Sopranos* and *Six Feet Under*. In the UK the influence is most visible in television, where youth audiences are being targeted. It is most obvious in the pastiche shows based on recycling and the injecting of irony into old, out of date, programmes using high levels of audience participation and ribald humour and sexual innuendo against garish, plastic sets and featuring 1950s-style band musicians.

The many chat shows which follow this kind of postmodern recipe (from *Graham Norton* several nights a week on Channel Four to *Jonathan Ross, Johnny Vaughan* and others) demonstrate how it has become the norm to revive, in a knowing manner, this form which in the past seemed to embody the very idea of popular television. By these means the banality of entertainment could be offset by the role of script writers and producers enchanted by the possibilities postmodern theory gave for reinventing television as simulacra. Jameson's work, against the grain of its own Marxism, had an incredible allure and appeal for a post-Marxist culturally oriented generation for whom media and popular culture are omnipresent and for whom (prior to Sept 11th 2001) the western world, although responsible for enduring inequalities and injustices and despite being in many ways a fearful place, was not perceived of as a place of war and strife and militarisation. Possibly more so than the other theorists in this book, Jameson's analysis of postmodernism has influenced readers beyond the confines of the academy. These populist readings of Jameson ignored his own repudiation of postmodern eclecticism and the proliferation of styles and instead took his writing as a kind of legitimation for producing playful and celebratory cultural forms. In fact I avoid the debate on cultural populism in this book and I also avoid in the Jameson chapter the protracted debates about postmodern culture, preferring to concentrate on two related topics: the idea of cognitive mapping and the challenge to Jameson by post-colonial critics, notably Spivak and Bhabha. Both these issues are central to cultural studies in relation to the politics of globalisation and post-colonialism. Where Jameson still seeks a sense of eventual class unity, Bhabha and Spivak insist on the necessity of fragmentation, on new 'third spaces' for thought and for cultural activity. If Jameson seems to speak from a secure seat of power, the Marxist inside the western liberal academy, his post-colonial critics question the basis of this authorisation. It may be apposite to conclude this introduction by pondering the authorisation to speak or write, as I do here, in a teacherly mode. One cannot be unaware of the changes which are transforming the life of the university, and yet the role of pedagogue, and the space and freedoms which that role still permits, is one of privilege and delight. And finally, the title of this book suggests a dimension of usefulness or value which cultural studies can bring to our understanding of the world in which we live. It is this capacity which has led me here to focus on the work of six leading cultural theorists.

1

Stuart Hall and the Inventiveness of Cultural Studies

GUIDE TO THE CHAPTER

Media–Politics–Ideology 1

In this chapter I extrapolate from the full range of Stuart Hall's work in order to concentrate on three exemplary moments. These are the moments of television (mid-1970s), the 'authoritarian populism' of Thatcherism (late 1980s), and multi-culturalism (2000a, 2000b). I provide both an elucidation of these texts and also an account of their inter-connectedness, despite the years between them. The first of these marks the time when Stuart Hall was focusing on the media, in this case television, and was exploring the possible usefulness of Althusser's theory of ideology for understanding the day-to-day practices of political communications, in particular the relation between the media, the state and politics. This was also the period of Hall's work when an explicitly Marxist analysis was most prominent. There was an overriding concern with how in an advanced capitalist society, the underlying class relations of power only became apparent in the 'last instance', for the reason that the big ideological institutions possessed their own autonomy. Their operations appeared to be quite disconnected from the economy, its modes of production and the organisation of labour. This autonomy and an ethos of neutrality served the capitalist order all the more effectively, with conflicts between spheres, for example, between journalists and politicians, producing an illusion of separate interests, while in reality masking the consensus or unity in regard to those fundamentally capitalist elements of the existing social order, which must, at all costs, be protected, secured and reproduced. Hence the use of the term 'complex unity'. The very terms by which these institutions conducted their daily operations were so naturalised that they became the means by which those millions of people who came into contact with such spheres, (mis)-recognised and (possibly) understood the world. To the extent that institutions like the press or television perpetuated themselves according to routine practices based on professional and technical codes and conventions, they also reproduced the very structures of the capitalist society.

The article, 'The "Unity" of Current Affairs Television', was first published in the *Working Papers in Cultural Studies* series by the University of Birmingham, Centre for Contemporary Cultural Studies. This was an in-depth examination of a pre-election edition of the UK BBC television programme *Panorama* broadcast in October 1974 (Media Group, 1976). The article shows how at Birmingham in the early 1970s a research object (that is, the single programme) was constructed as a collective undertaking.[1] Although the field of political communications was already established in British and American sociology, Hall et al. look instead to the French Marxist philosopher Althusser and the Italian Marxist Gramsci, to other Centre for Contemporary Cultural Studies work, and to official documents and reports produced within the broadcasting industry. Only one sociological text is referred to, Stan Cohen and Jock Young's *Manufacture of News* (Cohen and Young, 1973). Hall et al. take issue with existing academic work on this kind of topic. They part company from the 'conspiracy thesis' where 'programming is depicted as the public voice of a sectional but dominant political ideology' (Hall et al., 1976: 60). This implies top-down control in a mechanistic and absolutist way. There are also problems with the 'displacement thesis' which sees broadcasters as holding power largely in their own hands as television finds a more autonomous role for itself (ibid.: 60). This disavows the complexity of the subtle intersections and ongoing, if distanced, relations between media and state. And likewise there are many problems with the 'laissez-faire' thesis. This posits television as a kind of window on the world, a medium which merely reflects on events. Hall et al. propose a starting point which considers that television 'never deliver(s) one meaning' (and here we see the influence of Barthes (1972) and his claim about the inherent polysemy of meaning), but rather offers a range of meanings, where there is nonetheless a preferred meaning to which the viewer is guided or directed. The delivery of such a preferred meaning is the benchmark of success for what is understood to be good television, but the production of such a preferred reading is the outcome of extremely hard work on the part of the programme-makers. Ideological work of this sort is also labour, and this requires the gathering and selecting of items for inclusion, and organising these while also implementing certain technical and professional codes of practice. The right nuance of meaning can never be assured; there is always the potential for breaks, disruptions and leakiness. Moment by moment there is very deft footwork going on, so that the desired outcome is secured.

Far from there being a conspiracy between broadcasters and politicians to pull the wool over the eyes of viewers and electorate, (the crude left analysis), Hall et al. suggest that in such a complex society as our own, the relation between television and state is one of relative autonomy (following Althusser's famous (1971) essay on the 'ideological state apparatus'). Broadcasters and journalists operate according to their own professional encoding practices and are not answerable in any direct way to the politicians, even when they are working for a state-funded organisation like the BBC, except in the last instance. The 1976 article examines in detail the nature of the relation between media, the state and politics at a critical time when what seems to be at stake is the unity of the country itself. Hall et al.'s approach (one followed through subsequently in Hall's own work) is to bring together a historical contextualisation of the socio-political climate of the time, with a structuralist reading of a key text (in this case *Panorama*), as a means of producing an understanding of how ideology operates within the terrain of ordinary television, in this case an unexceptional (if lively) pre-election edition of a familiar current affairs programme. Underpinning the lengthy analysis is a claim that a single programme can indeed play a key role in the production of a certain kind of common sense about the terms and conditions through which the political is conducted within a mass media environment. This then justifies what we might describe as a micrological approach to questions of media (as signifying practice) and power.

Many of the issues covered in the article are directly relevant and familiar today. Stuart Hall was considering a moment when the BBC found itself under close scrutiny. There was a good deal of discussion about broadcasters having too much power, there were claims that the BBC focused unduly on comment and analysis when it should be simply reporting. These criticisms were directed towards current affairs programmes for the reason that current affairs values required wide knowledge and expertise. The journalists were expected to 'signpost their knowledgeability', and provide insight in an authoritative manner. This depth of analysis routinely applied to various topics made the politicians nervous or jittery, as Hall et al. imply.[2] This anxiety was in turn connected with the various concerns about national unity and the perceived dangers emanating from nationalists and others. At a time of great political strife in Northern Ireland and in the run up to an election, a good deal was at stake in regard to public opinion. A series of industrial disputes had challenged the Tory government and forced an election in February of 1974. The second election of that year was called as the Labour government attempted to secure a better majority.

Alongside the confrontations with the trade unions, and the ongoing conflict in Northern Ireland, there were also challenges from the Welsh and Scottish nationalists as well as the fraught question of entry into Europe. The edition of Panorama broadcast three days before the election with the title 'What Kind of National Unity?', provided the authors with an ideal opportunity to examine the means by which controversial issues were tackled on air and how a satisfactory outcome was sought on behalf of all the parties involved.

Case Study: *Panorama*

The analysis draws on semiology to examine the programme sequence by sequence, and to show how a combination of codes, visual and verbal, lexical and kinesic produce a whole programme with a unified 'communicative structure'. According to the norms and conventions governing this genre of television, current affairs content is 'encoded'. The ideal is for the decoding moment (that is, the moment of reception) to confirm the successful encoding as a kind of transparency effect. This is sought by means of orchestrating a particular combination of levels of connoted meaning, so that the viewer easily registers this over-all preferred meaning. In the edition of *Panorama* this preferred meaning is, first, that there is a win for the Labour Deputy Leader Jim Callaghan on the basis of his successfully taking command of the television debate, second, an overall win for the prevailing norms of parliamentary democracy as a two-party system, and third, a win for the programme itself wherein its own 'complex unity' somehow alludes to or connotes that of the country as a whole and is thus a comforting microcosm.

The encoding process requires what the authors describe as ideological work, 'each level makes its own kind of sense but each, in the television discourse is incomplete without the other. Thus the moment when the two are brought into alignment with each other is the moment when the sense of a particular part of the process is completed, by the over-determination of one system on another' (Hall et al., 1976: 66). What the study is aiming to describe is the connotational meaning as it has been 'ideologically inflected and structured' by the broadcasters (ibid.: 67). The term 'prefer' indicates how meaning is not entirely fixed, and the term ideology indicates the presence of a political intention in the attempt to achieve successful encodings. The segments of the programme comprise a kind of jostling for position by media and politicians alike, within, however, the contours of a 'prestructured topic'. This topic is constructed through an assumption about the British parliamentary system being normatively a two-party rule, which is seemingly under threat but is, however, invoked and confirmed by the organisation of the programme. 'On the underlying Unity the broadcasters assume a consensus' (ibid.: 75). This assumption of consensus is what Hall et al. perceive as critical to the ideological process. The textual analysis tracks the process whereby control of the topic shifts, within these constraints, from the first half of the programme to the second, through the visual and verbal combination of elements. The most important part of the programme is the live debate between Jim Callaghan (the Labour Deputy Leader) and his fellow contenders David Steel (Liberal) and William Whitelaw (Conservative). The analysis shows how a slip by the presenter, where he gives away something of his own (apparently Liberal) political preferences (by using the word 'dogma' to describe a Labour position), allows the slightly aggrieved Callaghan to then take control of the way the subsequent debate develops. Callaghan comes up with a Labour strategy for unity (the social contract with the unions) which he is able to pose against the threat to unity and to parliamentary democracy itself.

Hall et al. then follow Callaghan's interventions where he ignores or abandons 'preferred conventions' and 'gestures his way into a commanding position'. 'To appreciate the importance of Callaghan's gestural acts it must be pointed out that he and Whitelaw are afforded symmetrical space' (ibid.: 86). He gets away with taking command because of the 'precise nature of the balance between the media and politics in current affairs television . . . especially at election times'. The 'transparency effect' requires both the politicians to abide by certain media rules while the media 'guard against the charge of selectivity or bias by . . . presenting the politicians "live" or "in their own words" thus creating a seemingly neutral space' (ibid.: 87). The relation between media and politics is therefore akin to that between the seemingly neutral state and politics. If the state is then the 'organiser of hegemony' Hall et al. concur that the media too works hegemonically. The preferred reading of the programme is one in which Callaghan appears to win the debate, but is it because of the breach by the presenter? The authors argue it is also because Callaghan, with his skillful performance, abides by the rules of the programme but then, in the aftermath of the slip by the presenter, is able to take advantage while also showing off his expertise as a consummate speaker and hence natural political leader. During the minutes of live debate the operation of the media rules do indeed guard against bias in that all participants are given more or less equal time and space. What is confirmed, then, in the programme is the good health and unity of the parliamentary system as such. *Panorama* (and implicitly the BBC) is therefore the custodian and 'guardian of unity'. The problems the programme is concerned with are those 'which have registered with . . . the established Parliamentary parties'.

The ideological effect of television in this instance is to make the parliamentary form of the state a 'natural, taken for granted formation', and the 'power to define' means being able to flag the various leads and topics. Ideology is not then 'a media trick', but a set of structuring devices which provide the frame for all that is seemingly open and apparent, which in turn becomes a hallmark for a particular definition of politics. The conventions of balance and neutrality in current affairs are such that they ensure the reproduction of the 'structure in dominance'. This is the crux of Althusser's argument about the ideological state apparatuses – their relative autonomy enables them to reproduce the prevailing conditions of political power. But this is no easy task; social reproduction requires extremely hard work, hence the careful navigation through awkward moments. Since underlying and motivating politics and the state are issues of class struggle and contestation, the ideological effect of media is to restore and maintain existing class relations. But this is never completely achieved; there are always new possibilities for disruption. The ideological work of the media is to safeguard the terms by which politics defines itself, and to ritualistically and repetitively invoke these so as to ward off alternative or competing definitions as to what constitutes the political. The weak points in the process of transmission where the preferred meaning is never entirely secure are also the points for other more radical possibilities to emerge. This is where meaning could be made to be other than what it already is.

Media–Politics–Ideology 2

Looking back at this article, almost 30 years after publication, there is a great deal that could be said about the inventiveness of cultural studies.

In many ways I take it to be paradigmatic of Hall's own *oeuvre*, including the co-authorship. But what is most noticeable about the article is that it is truly work in progress. If the doing of ideological work in the context of the single episode of *Panorama* required hard labour as the authors argue, this too can be seen in the article itself. Unlike some of the better-known articles by Hall on politics and media, this one reveals the marks and even untidiness of its own construction, in an almost Brechtian way. The authors do not attempt to conceal the way in which they seem to be testing the waters of media analysis, to see how well their reading of Althusser and Gramsci stands up when transplanted into the heartland of the British media and the day-to-day workings of the UK political establishment. They also seem to be assessing how well the 'Ideological State Apparatuses' (ISA) essay works, not through a crude application of cultural theory to cultural practice, but by providing an analysis which elucidates, step by step, the theory of ideology. The authors make a compelling case for this approach being much more substantial than the content analysis approaches of media sociology at the time. They attempt to show just how much is at stake in the space and time of a single television programme and thereby make a claim for the micrological politics of meaning. Far from being a relatively unimportant piece of broadcasting when measured against issues of ownership and control of big media corporations (the political economy approach), the authors give an account of the relations between media texts like this one, and the state and politics. The article is not a finished polished object or perfect academic artefact, and by the standards of mainstream social science research it probably falls short precisely because rather than rehearsing its methodological underpinnings, it gestures instead to possibilities for further work (on audiences and reception for example) and it bears the stylistic marks of an intervention drawing on Marxist theory rather than a piece of scholarship respectful of existing sociological work in the field.

The 1976 article also sets a course for the various studies which followed, from *Policing the Crisis* in the late 1970s, to the work on Thatcherism in the late 1980s (Hall, 1988; Hall et al., 1978). It might be said that there is then a particular 'complex unity' in Hall's own work (more on which later). But if we can see the specific agenda of cultural studies being drafted in the course of this article, we might well ask what kind of issues would arise if we were to undertake a similar analysis today? Even if we restrict ourselves to politics in the UK and the British media (that is, holding globalisation of media at bay), the changes have been momentous. The establishment of the new Scottish parliament and the consequences of devolution for both Scotland and Wales provide new meaning to the question of 'national unity'. The break-up of Britain argued for by Tom Nairn (1979) has, to some extent, happened, overseen by New Labour and without political trauma. As Hall's most recent work demonstrates (and as we shall see later in this chapter), anxieties about national belonging and unity continue unabated however, now inflected along the lines of 'multi-culture' (Hall, 2000a, 2000b).

Panorama still exists, though located in a slot in the schedules (Sunday night, after the 10 pm news) considered a demotion from the days when it dominated current affairs television.[3] There is no longer a single primetime current affairs programme on BBC1, nor does current affairs as a televisual category possess anything like the important status it did in the mid 1970s. To a certain extent its remit has been incorporated into the more extended news coverage to be found across all five terrestial television channels. So that 'complex unity in difference' has also undergone transformation. All of the channels now routinely broadcast analysis-oriented current affairs items within the framework of news. Current affairs television has *per se* been sidelined in favour of entertainment and so called 'factual television'. As the number of channels has multiplied, the whole world of television has been transformed. There is greater competition, commercialisation, deregulation and all of these have displaced political television from the centre of the airwaves. Some would argue that the tabloidisation effect has made current affairs sometimes sensational, often led by lifestyle topics or else simply marginal. (*Students might find it interesting to examine the now-standard use of the 'dramatic reconstruction' format in* Panorama *programmes.*) While there is not space here to discuss, in depth, the restructuring of current affairs television, it could be claimed in relation to Hall et al.'s article that current affairs no longer takes its lead for topics from the parliamentary agenda. Instead its remit has widened (perhaps because of the mushrooming of social movements and pressure groups), it is attentive to voices from way beyond the narrow political spectrum and, of course, its concerns are also reflective on the way in which the media more generally is increasingly able to define and shape the political agenda. Any number of campaigns and issues have in recent years moved into the political spotlight against the wishes of the politicians, but with the help of the media.

There has also been a shift in the balance of power between politics and media with the latter assuming a more self-defining, autonomous, assertive and emboldened role. While the nature of the relations between state and BBC remain the subject of continuous interrogations (the license fee, the nature of public service, ratings, unfair competition and so on), it would be harder to argue today that a slip like that made by the journalist, where he revealed his own political disapproval of Labour by using the word 'dogma', would be damaging to the media process and be grounds on air to retreat somewhat from directing the debate. Consider the sarcastic tones of BBC news presenter and inter-viewer Jeremy Paxman and the word 'dogma' would have no such adverse consequences. It is still the case that political journalists are, of course, expected to conceal their own preferences, and it is also the case that there are strict conventions governing the coverage of political items, particularly during election time. What could be argued is that journalists, despite these conventions, are less respectful, more pugna-cious and interrogatory in style, and more importantly that there has been an absorption of the traditional (parliamentary) current affairs agenda into extended news broadcasting. What is left of current affairs is often indistinguishable from lifestyle features and documentaries about aspects of everyday life.

Media–Politics–Ideology 3

There are many other questions which could be posed in relation to the Hall article. Does the Marxist theory of ideology still pertain? If not, how does media studies fare nowadays without the notion of 'complex unity' provided by Althusserian Marxism? The media itself has, of course, fragmented and also proliferated and current affairs no longer occupies the place it once did as the face of public service broadcasting. In these circumstances can current affairs, when and where it still exists, in its distinctive and relatively autonomous way, reproduce the relations of dominance? Critical to this work of reproduction was, as Hall et al. argue, managing to keep the class-based nature of the political antago-nisms which motivated the work of the ideological state apparatuses concealed. This then allowed politics to appear as though it was con-ducted entirely and solely within the terms and conditions set by politicians and media alike. Callaghan was able to present his social contract as a way of maintaining national unity in the face of social and industrial conflict. This in itself required subtle manoeuvres to allow him to appear as the natural voice of national unity, thus temporarily at least solving what Hall later pinpointed as one of the key contradictions of social democracy – having to find 'solutions to the crisis . . .within the limits of capitalist survival' (Hall, 1988). But how does this argument look at a time when class relations are less prominent and antagonistic and have been replaced by other forms of social conflict? Does social democracy continue to be charged with this duty of shoring up a capitalist economy? Or rather is it the case that social democracy is now being reshaped out of all recognition so as to provide even more effective support for an aggressive neo-liberal social order? This is exactly what Hall has recently argued (Hall 2003; see also Extended Notes at the end of the chapter).

We might conclude this section by suggesting, *first*, that as a result of social and political changes, the spectrum of issues for current affairs television has widened, but sadly, only to include more banal everyday issues. This widening process takes place in a context where a powerful media is itself increasingly dominated by entertainment values, which means that current affairs is less prominent. To survive it has had to adapt to the norms of more popular genres. The ascendancy of entertainment and celebrity culture across the airwaves also contributes to a wider process of depoliticisation. This is not entirely unpalatable to New Labour in so far as their strategy of 'corporate managerialism' is also broadly depoliticising in intent. The electorate can be assured that they are in safe hands, they need not be too involved in politics since their interests are being well looked after. Thus the people are free to enjoy *Big Brother* or *Who Wants to Be a Millionaire?* Although the media frequently champions the causes of individual citizens, families and individuals against the politicians, it broadly consents to this de-politicising process by reducing the number and quality of current affairs programmes and documentaries.

Second, we might also suggest that the unity of broadcasters and politicians on capitalism and parliamentary democracy as being the natural mode of government is possibly more entrenched today than ever before, since the demise of Eastern European socialism and the decline of the socialist left as representing a viable political alternative. *Third*, it could be suggested that should the question of unity be posed today, it would surely focus on multi-culturalism. Would there be the same kind of agreement round the table as in the 1976 *Panorama* programme, that multi-culturalism now threatens the unity of the UK? My suggestion would be that a much wider range of views would be solicited, from across the spectrum of lobbies, pressure groups and campaigning bodies, than would have been the case in the past. The question then is, does the mere presence of this pluralised spectrum of opinion tally (or not) with Hall's suggestion that the breaks, the leakiness, the possibility of other unpreferred meanings coming forward can be sites for radicalisation? At one level Hall's own answer would surely be that it depends on how the broadcasters attempt to frame and control what seems like a pluralisation of positions. In addition, the simple presence of more voices from different constituencies need not in itself unsettle the consensual premises of broadcasting. A radical politics of meaning would emerge when new possibilities of meaning around multi-culturalism, for example, were able to challenge more normative understandings within the context of a television debate and when a preferred meaning was suspended or even countered. But does the preferred meaning *per se* still exist as the necessary outcome and professional logic of contemporary current affairs television?[4]

Fourth, we might also suggest that just as underlying class antagonisms were displaced through the framework of consent for national unity shared by broadcasters and politicians alike in the *Panorama* programme, the social antagonisms of race and gender when tackled on television nowadays rarely if ever involve looking at their structural rootedness, nor is there any attempt to examine the consequences of racial and sexual inequities. If anything there is even less emphasis on socio-economic factors and a good deal more focus on individual narratives, on unique stories, or dramatic case studies. Thus, despite the widening of outside agencies and media submitting items deemed newsworthy as current affairs, a narrow logic of consensus does indeed prevail in that there is very little, if any, questioning of the values upon which the basic structures of social and economic organisation are based. The *fifth* and final point is that where there is a tension between consensus and good television, it is from within the changing conventions of what now constitutes lively or even aggressive debate on television, that is, it is inherent to autonomous, though 'in the last instance' contested, televisual norms (see the Gilligan affair described in note 2 and note 5 below). The old rules which framed the gentlemanly debate, that is, a good-humoured knockabout between middle-aged white males, no longer guarantee audience attention and can appear stuffy or boring to the more diverse audiences which the various channels must now chase. The broadcasters have to find ways of producing some regular explosions on air, and they must work hard to represent the fullest range of views and opinions. With New Labour pursuing a 'beyond left and right' pathway and with little parliamentary opposition pushing a different agenda, broadcasters must daily look beyond to the organisations like Christian Aid, Amnesty International, Refuge, Liberty, and Greenpeace to fulfil this contestatory role.

Indeed it could even be argued that on occasion BBC journalists (and their counterparts in the *Guardian* and the *Observer* newspapers) themselves come to occupy a consistent space of opposition (despite the professional codes which require political neutrality) to the consternation of the New Labour cabinet, who are regularly subjected to lengthy and aggressive questioning on the BBC Radio 4 *Today* programme.[5] Overall, however, the possibilities for radicalisation have been dramatically reduced. As television has become more dominated by commercial entertainment values in a context of wider depoliticisation, the overall commonsense consensus is that, of course, capitalism plus parliamentary democracy are the only imaginable forms of social organisation. This is so obvious it does not even warrant further consideration. At the same time political broadcasting itself cannot rely solely on the two parties to provide high-quality political television today, so journalists and editors must look further afield and must encourage critical investigative reporting. Some degree of hope resides in *critique* which in itself upsets the political parties. It is *critique* which punctures the blandness and complacency of consensus and this increasingly comes from the ferocity, pugnaciousness and independence of the journalists on BBC2's *Newsnight,* on Radio 4's *Today* programme, very occasionally on *Panorama* and more regularly on Channel 4 *News.*

Breaking the Spell of the Welfare State: Stuart Hall Meets the Iron Lady

In Hall's writing on Thatcherism the focus is more on culture and less directly on media. The theory of ideology is developed along with Gramsci's concept of hegemony to account for the radical transformation brought about through the Thatcher period. Drawing on the

concept of articulation (Laclau and Mouffe, 1985) Hall shows how dis-
parate elements can be 'stitched together' to produce an entirely new
political vision. The principle of articulation also demonstrates how
ideological strands have 'no necessary class belonging' and can therefore
be made highly meaningful for social groups other than those with
whom they might be associated. This, in turn, is the argument which
allows Hall to undertake his revision of Marxist thinking. First, that
ideologies do not belong to, or have some natural link with, a specific
social class. Second, that in complex societies ideological effort, when it
is set about in as thorough and dedicated a way as it was in the Thatcher
years, can have enormous social impact, it can change society 'as we
know it'. Third, Hall suggests that this change can take place without it
necessarily following the lead from, or working in close relation to, economic forces. Hall continues here in his rejection of the traditional
Marxism which reads all superstructural phenomena as somehow
reflecting in a direct way economic forces which are at the base of the
society and which are the driving force of the society. In highly complex
modern societies the realm of ideas and beliefs and values have their
own materiality and are embedded and activated in practices and institutions. Articulation provides Hall with a specific way of understanding
social change, in that it shows how bundles of meaning can be attached
and re-attached; they can be transplanted and they can, as it were, land
in new unexpected places. New formations of meaning converging
together can adhere, they can become consolidated blocks which then
become the terms by which people understand themselves and the
world around them. If the left can work at this level, and seek to create
its own convergences of meaning, a margin of hope appears, as cultural
practices become possible dynamics in this politics of meaning. The
three key components of Hall's analysis of Thatcherism are: (1) the use
of Gramsci; (2) the concept of authoritarian populism; and (3) the lessons to the left (learning from Thatcherism). The way in which these
each contribute to the inventiveness of cultural studies will be examined
in the sections that follow.

The collection of Hall's writing, *The Hard Road to Renewal* (1988) comprises, in the main, relatively short articles written by Hall from 1978
onwards, many of which appeared in the monthly magazine *Marxism
Today*. The wider and non-specialist readership of this journal means
that the tone of the writing is particularly accessible, even when Hall is
engaging with complex arguments, for example, in his use of Gramsci

to understand the dynamics of the Thatcher government and to revise aspects of Marxist orthodoxy in a bid to renew or modernise the left. The key elements of Gramsci's work which Hall draws on are hegemony, the terrain and duration of struggle and, finally, the importance of the popular. Hegemony refers to the way in which consent on the part of the people or electorate is sought through a sustained attempt to create a new ethics, a new moral order, a new kind of subject. This forcefulness, which is also non-coercive, requires ideological work so that the ground is prepared for a new kind of commonsense. With Thatcherism this entailed dismantling many of the assumptions about the underpinnings of British post-war society, hence the emphasis on 'breaking the spell of the welfare state'. Hegemony is therefore a kind of active reach-out-and-touch mechanism of power, it involves deconstructing some previously fixed positions (for example, working-class support of social housing) and then attaching the same social group to a new and unexpected set of ideas (for example, home-ownership and the property-owning democracy). This requires effort at every level of political society from the think-tanks and university departments, where the ideas are brokered, to the popular media and tabloids who turn these ideas into a popular idiom. The reach mechanism of hegemony, in the case of the sale of council houses, shows the politicians reaching out over the heads of the local authorities, the voices of traditional working-class representation and also moving beyond the socialist principles of collective ownership, and saying to the people, 'this new way of being, this new subject position, is available to you and we now seek your consent to this new kind of society'. Hegemony, therefore, indicates a practice of power and leadership based on changing the whole landscape of popular belief.

Hall's account of Thatcherism is an excellent example of how social transformation can take place in front of our eyes. Hall's analysis, yet again, conveys something of his own effort to trace how such transformation actually happens: these work-in-progress signs are not hidden away, as they would be in a conventionally magisterial work. He focuses on the many manifestations of privatisation as it takes shape within a political culture which has been accustomed to, and proud of, its public sector. In her determination to eradicate traces of the old Labour collectivism, Mrs Thatcher transformed many aspects of everyday life by means of the privatisation of local services, from leisure centres to hospital cleaners, from cleansing departments to public transport. So far did these franchises and tendering out processes enter into the norms and conventions of daily life, that now the very idea of reversing such practices becomes unthinkable. The return to 'council housing'? Unimaginable. Re-nationalisation of the railways? Highly unlikely, despite the high costs to government of bailing out the franchisees. And so on. This is what is meant by the terrain of struggle. As John Berger, echoing Hall, has recently pointed out, what Gramsci also recognised was that these processes are actually constitutive of a kind of revolution.[6] For the left, an equally sustained process carried out at every level of society, would also be a kind of revolution; perhaps this is what is achievable once the telos of 'revolution' is abandoned. Politics is therefore about envisaging long duration, and the terrain is the site for constant intervention. Nothing is ever 'done'.

Gramsci also provides an understanding of the importance of the popular as a necessary site for effecting political transformation. This, above all, was where Mrs Thatcher succeeded as she tapped into popular working-class grievances not addressed by the Left in power in the local authorities and indeed in government. They had been too concerned with bureacracy, they were too happy to stitch up a deal with the 'union bosses' and, as Hall points out, Labour in office has rarely encouraged active participation and grassroots organisation. Thatcher committed herself to freeing the people from the bureaucrats of the town hall, whose policies restricted the choices of ordinary people on important issues like where they wanted their children to go to school, and whether or not they could paint the front door of their council houses a different colour. This ability, to recognise and successfully address the terrain of ordinary life, which under Labour had been governed by statist and monolithic procedures set in place by the extensive field of the welfare state and public sector, which in adverse economic conditions could not deliver what it originally promised, was the basis of the popularity of Thatcherism. Gramsci's writing served also to remind the left that they could not succeed hegemonically without gaining this popular consent and without being open to new ideas and fresh thinking, even if that meant critically examining some of the old points of faith.

The phrase which Hall coined to encompass the 'complex unity' of Thatcherist values was 'authoritarian populism'. This distinctive style of leadership emphasised the need for a new popular morality based on law and order and family values. By defining the dynamics of popular capitalism as inclusive, it too became a moral force. Capitalism was now an economic system, not just for the wealthy or for the affluent middle classes, but also for the ordinary people; they too could become stakeholders (later taken up by Blair) and investors in the newly privatised public facilities, they could own their own house, see it go up in value and recoup the rewards. Democratic populism was another mark of Mrs Thatcher's radicalism. She could plug into working-class grievances about the over-bureaucratised left, the trade unions and the local authorities and she could encourage forms of grass roots revolt by drawing attention to the undemocratic elements and the paternalism of old Labour, thus pulling the ground away from under Labour's feet, through drawing on their own vocabulary. Thatcherism was able to present these ideas as appropriate for a rapidly changing world; she was also a classic 'moderniser'. The idea of popular capitalism was forward looking and had novelty value without totally offending those who wished to uphold conservative traditions.

How was it possible to build up such a force for change? Hall points to the many levels of society to which Mrs Thatcher turned her attention. The universities had academics who, for some years previously, had been developing what seemed at the time unpopular and even unpalatable ideas, for example, Keith Joseph, who was the academic who drew attention to the issue of young single mothers being supported by the welfare state. Hall also points to other figures like head teacher Rhodes Boyson, who became a regular writer for the tabloid press on popular issues like falling standards and the failings of progressive and leftist teachers. There were strenuous efforts across the whole civil society to gain consent for the strong law and order measures that needed to be taken to stop the slide into excessive liberalism and the decline of authority. Authoritarian populism was thus the strongest possible counter to the values and beliefs of the late 1960s, to the left-wing radicalism which developed through the 1970s, and which included new social movements such as feminism and gay rights. These had all contributed to the decline in family values, the failure to punish criminals, the encouragement of dependency on social security, and the discouraging of enterprise (a newly favoured word). This paved the way for a more disciplinary society. By repeatedly drawing attention to 'folk devils' such as trade union militants, social security fraudsters and single mothers who, as the tabloids put it (often drawing on American new right arguments) were wedded to the state, support increased for harsh measures to be taken against these groups.

Mrs Thatcher's discourse was also effective, argues Hall, for its interpellative capacity. It brought new subjects into being by naming them in
a popular language. The concerned parent fed up with too-liberal
teachers. The anxious hospital patient who wanted to have surgery on
the day of his or her choice, in order to get back to work as soon as possible. The fearful owner-occupier who wanted to see 'more bobbies on
the beat'. The upwardly mobile council tenant who wanted to buy his or
her property from the council as soon as possible, and so on. By stitching together these new constituencies in the language of fairness, choice
and modernity there was, as Hall argues, a reshaping of democracy.
The enormous effort put into presenting the electorate with a persuasive
interpretation of how things had come to be the way they were, allowed
the new right to embark on an overhauling of the entire social fabric
with 'unremitting radicalism'. The ideology of authoritarian populism
was able to pull together the traditional moralism of the Tories and
rework it into a new language of competition, standards, and yet again,
national unity. This whole ethos came to occupy a prominence in everyday life quite separate from the success or failings of the economy.
Indeed, unlike the economy during the time of New Labour (1997–),
there were few signs then that unemployment rates would fall and not
many indicators that the much vaunted 'enterprise culture' would ever
amount to anything more than a growth in small one-person businesses.
Yet, despite this, the Thatcher revolution still moved forward.

In these articles Hall is constantly attempting to engage the left with
the import of this 'great moving right show'. Hall pleads and cajoles that
the left might find some more effective way of countering this force. He
sees the left as relying on old sectarian battles to divert its attention
from the inroads being made by the right. He reminds the left of Mrs
Thatcher's incredible popularity, of her ability to somehow get under
the skin of the British through speaking a distinctive kind of common-
sense. And he argues that the left is relying on worn-out economistic
arguments which predict an eventual downfall of capitalism. Claiming
that the left is over-bureaucratic, paternalistic and untuned to popular
sensibilities such as the pleasures of the consumer culture, Hall suggests
that it would nonetheless be possible to reclaim lost ground and find a
way of re-articulating some of the concepts and ideas favoured by
Thatcher. Hall actually picks up on the word 'choice' and proposes that
the left could reclaim this and re-inflect it so as to draw people back into
popular grass roots politics, for example, through having more of a say

on the organisation and running of the local schools or hospitals. That is, choice need not be only understood as part of an individualising neo-right vocabulary, but could conceivably be connected with forging new social democratic kinds of citizenship. The 'transformism' of the Thatcher government allowed it to claim a whole new reality as its own, while the left was not able to offer any credible agenda for the post-industrial society, for a society no longer entirely marked out by identities of class, where people will increasingly be earning their livings in very different ways from the old industrial society and where the electorate will comprise of a diversity of interests and identities. In fact in these last pages of *The Hard Road To Renewal* Stuart Hall is in effect telling (New) Labour how to do it, how to mount an effective intervention across the whole new social landscape, how to win back ideological terrain to a different kind of Labour Party, how to address constituencies such as women and mothers, how to work with academics and with think-tanks and how to re-invent itself as modern.

From Unity to Difference?

There is a 'complex unity' in Hall's own work through, paradoxically, an endless openness, a sense throughout the writing of constant, relentless contestation, a tracking and tracing of the contours of the 'structures in dominance' (also the presence throughout of Gramsci's influence) and a keen, forensic attention to the interstitial spaces that open up within and between the broad strokes of power, and the possibilities for opposition and resistance from within such cracks and crevices. While Hall engages with Foucault, he never wholly inhabits a framework which envisages power, even as it is widely dispersed into biopower, as so all-enveloping, so thoroughly subjectivising, so without the breaks and ruptures which Hall has always perceived and seized upon as sites of opportunity. At the same time there is no hint of a too-easy endorsement of agency, indeed the word barely exists in his vocabulary. Across the work considered in this chapter, there is not a single moment where Hall can be seen to do what cultural studies is often accused of, which is to over-emphasise the capacities for resistance. He does, however, retain a keen interest in cultural practices and this can be seen in many of the recent essays on post-colonial art and photography and on the cultural politics of 'new ethnicities' (see Hall, 1992a, 1992b, 1998b, 1999). Hall does not seek to dazzle his readers theoretically in a way that, especially in the post-Marxist times, many social and cultural theorists do, there is never any display of erudition for the sake of it. Instead a teacherly mode, as well as a thinking-in-progress, a leading of the reader through Hall's own inquiries, as a kind of implicit engagement with an imagined reader or audience, is what produces a body of work which is perhaps more interactive, more dialogic than all of the other writers considered in this book. This pedagogic style is what marks out Hall's writing as political intervention as well as scholarly endeavour, indeed the two are so deeply intertwined as to be almost inseparable. Kobena Mercer has also pointed out that much of Hall's work is characterised by a profound open-endedness (Mercer, 2000). Partly through his role as teacher, partly through the collaborative ventures both at Birmingham and at the Open University, much of the work also functions as a blueprint for further research.

This openness comprises a generous space for others who might be captured by the possibilities of cultural studies. It is this unusual style which leads people to Stuart Hall's work. And when Hall engages with the left and when he comments on cultural studies as a radical intellectual project, there is also a performative dynamic in operation too. He brings these entities, the left, and cultural studies, into being, in this distinctive, intertwined, often quite practical way. There is, however, a more marked theoretical shift in Hall's most recent work. Here we see his earlier focus on the politics of meaning become more decisively influenced by Derrida. While meaning remains the terrain upon which politics is so decisively conducted, Hall is now drawn towards the way in which meaning itself is always haunted by other layers and levels of meaning, there are deferrals from prior meanings, residues and traces hanging, like a cloud, above highly contested terms such as multi-culturalism. This is all the more so when the multi-cultural question poses some of the most important issues for contemporary politics. The multiplicity of uses to which the term is put, from the corporate multi-culturalism of global brands to the pluralist multi-culturalism which, however, requires 'a more communal or communitarian political order' (Hall, 2000a: 210), marks out its contestedness. For Hall the import of the term lies in its addressing how, in non-homogenous societies, 'commonness in difference' might 'be imagined and constructed'? (Hall, 2000b).

The essay 'The Multi-cultural Question' provides Hall with an opportunity to rehearse, again in a way which takes the reader with him, the reasons why multi-culturalism can posit a new kind of political logic by extending and enlarging the capacities for radical democracy. Hall sketches the conditions of emergence for contemporary multi-culturalism, which include the changing global world, the times of post-coloniality, the ruptures brought about by the end of Communism in Eastern Europe, the rampant free marketisation on a global basis, and the defensive new neo-nationalisms also brought into being. Globalisation produces unstable localisms, spaces of proliferating difference, which in turn become the site for 'translations from below'. Neither is there homogeneity within these groupings which emerge, nor is there some kind of intact tradition. There is instead (and in many of Britain's cities) 'communities in translation'. (In the case of the UK, the national unity, so precious to Labour politicians like Jim Callaghan in the *Panorama* programme described above, was, as Hall then also indicated, a good deal less homogenous than was commonly perceived. It was cut across by differences of race and class, region and income, and, we might add, women were still excluded from most institutional aspects of 'national belonging'.) 'Massive forms of pluralisation' have in the intervening years foregrounded, once again, the question of national unity at a political level, and also Britishness or Englishness at a cultural level. If globalisation appears to be a force for cultural homogenisation (under the big brands it brings to diverse locations), it also produces as a counter-reaction a wide range of localisms or indigenisations; these in turn constitute the various forms of difference which more directly challenge assumptions of unity. But 'difference' is both critically related to the 'structure in dominance' of globalisation, and it is also both fluid and without a 'fixed political inscription: sometimes it is progressive, sometimes it is emergent, sometimes it is critical, sometimes it is revolutionary' (Hall, 2000a: 217).

Alongside these processes ethnic minorities are, suggests Hall, making three claims, for 'genuinely universal racial justice, for equal outcomes to the major social and economic processes and . . . also . . . for the recognition of difference' (ibid.: 225). This, argues Hall, is 'the political task which the multi-cultural question confronts'. But the very act of bringing together the demand for both equality and difference 'signals nothing short of the emergence of a transformed political logic' (ibid.: 236). Hall offers a series of useful points in regard to the pursuit of this political logic. Personal liberty need not be seen, for example, as a primary and triumphant western value, but instead it has become, as 'the right for all peoples to live their life from within', a 'cosmopolitan value'. Likewise everyone participates in forms of 'cultural belongingness', thus multi-culturalism poses the question of finding a framework for resolving conflicts between different cultural groups without this requiring the assimilation to a wider norm. He continues, '[t]he specific and particular difference of a group or community cannot be asserted absolutely without regard to the wider context provided by all the others to whom particularity acquires a relative value' (ibid.: 235). That is, if we all recognise the particularity of our cultural values then that requires us to find a wider context beyond these particulars so that others might make their demands. Would this wider context constitute a revised universalism? Hall answers this by reminding us that identity itself is dependent on the relation to others in that (and here he draws on Laclau's psychoanalytical vocabulary) the subject is formed (and exists) through a sense of incompleteness. 'The universal is part of my identity in so far as I am formed, very much, by the lack of those others to whom I'm obliged to relate' (Hall, 2000b). This is to say that we are all the same in that what we lack is also a constitutive part of what we are, even as we disavow it as difference. Others are an integral, necessary part of who we are.

This suggests a differently understood horizon of univeralism. Hall warns against the dangers of using the difficulty this poses as a reason to return to the old Enlightenment ideals which were, after all, 'opposed at every point to difference'. But can the universal become a fluid and emergent terrain of agreement, a space for becoming in difference? An 'incomplete horizon which stitches your particular together with mine'? Universality is rendered a negotiative, open-ended process. It is incomplete because 'it can't be filled in with an unchanging historical content'. It too is formed in relation to the particulars which it repels or excludes; thus as Hall quotes Laclau 'the universal is incommensurable with the particular' but it 'cannot exist without the particular' (Hall, 2000a: 235). It is forced to bend as new demands are put to it. But because there can be no definitive 'content' we have to be willing to resist the attraction of a return to absolutes. The universal becomes a point of obligation, recognition and negotiation. Is this what is meant by commonness in difference? Or, more specifically, can this mark out the means by which there is an extending, deepening, and thus replenishment, of democracy? And is the multi-cultural, as the terrain upon which, in a heightened sense, commonness is now sought, a possible vehicle for pursuing this new democratic logic 'as an ongoing struggle without final resolution' (ibid.: 235)? That this is unrealised works positively rather than negatively (as closure), as a process of politicisation, rather than depoliticisation, and all of its attendant ills. This would suggest, then, that for Hall the multi-cultural question provides the possibility for expansive democratisation, not as an end in itself, as something that can be, once and for all, done and can be completed, but as a condition for the renewal of radical politics itself. This process of enlargement takes place as groups are pulled into the political process by virtue of their demands for recognition, so that many new public spheres come into being, with the effect that democracy is made more open, heterogeneous, a fluid horizon of negotiation.

Let us conclude this long chapter, then, by pondering those interstitial sites of resistance, the eruptions of difference which emerge in the cracks and cleavages which globalisation cannot quite call to order, cannot quite totally hegemonise. My reading of Hall here suggests that the noisy clamour of 'multi-culturalism' as it finds different expressions across a range of cultural sites, in towns and cities across the UK, from the Friday prayers held out in the street outside the now closed Finsbury Park mosque in London, to the drum 'n' bass beats and the ever-evolving sounds of British black music (today Grime, tomorrow who knows?), are indeed themselves negotiative strategies, outbursts and declarations, which push wide open the boundaries of what it is to belong, to become and indeed to be British. The fear that this now (post-9/11) gives rise to, that multi-culturalism has gone too far, and that there needs to be more and better assimilation in the UK, is a means of avoiding confronting and addressing the enduring inequities and the racial injustices which are perpetuated across the terrain of political culture and everyday life.[7] This recent call to national unity, one which is made repeatedly and in various forms by New Labour politicians, implicitly seeks to defuse and contain the emergent politics of multi-culturalism. What Hall is saying is that the heterogeneity of contemporary multi-culturalism provides a new opportunity for opening out across the political terrain discussion about race, ethnicity, history and national identity. But instead of engaging with enduring racial inequalities and encouraging the diversification of public spheres, there is increasingly a move towards closure and containment in the call to assimilation and integration. By these means, the current UK government also finds itself attempting to reverse and negate the undeniable and formidable impact which Hall's writing has had over a period of almost 40 years.

Notes

1   While the original article was authored by the 'Media Group', and in
    a later version by S. Hall, I. Connell and L. Curti, I am taking the
    liberty here of referring to it forthwith as a key part of Hall's pub-
    lished work.

2   One of the most cataclysmic events in contemporary UK politics
    actually took place on the BBC Radio 4 *Today* programme on 29th
    May 2003, just after 6 am, when journalist Andrew Gilligan sug-
    gested that the intelligence dossier compiled to make the case to go
    to war with Iraq had been deliberately 'sexed up' to suggest that
    Saddam Hussein had weapons ready for use within 45 minutes. The
    events which followed this claim and the pressure put upon the
    informant, Dr David Kelly, led to his suicide on 18th July. Although
    the Hutton Inquiry (reporting 28th January 2004) later cleared the
    government of any wrongdoing, the episode represented one of the
    most destabilising to the Blair government since coming to office. It
    also, however, resulted in the resignations of both the Director
    General of the BBC, Greg Dyke, and the Chair of the Governors,
    Gavyn Davies.

3   Ironically, in the wake of the Hutton Inquiry which criticised the
    BBC for falling standards in news and current affairs, it was
    announced in the *Guardian* (29th June 2004: 2) that *Panorama* was to
    be removed from its 'graveyard' slot on Sunday evening at 10.15 pm
    and returned to a new primetime slot. This would 'restore current
    affairs to its proper place and prominence'.

4   Among the many groups and organisations now asked to contribute
    to recent current affairs programmes on multi-culturalism in the
    UK are the Muslim Council of Britain, the Indian Muslim
    Federation, the Muslim Association of Britain, The Islamic Forum of
    Europe, and the Islamic Society of Britain.

5   I am not suggesting that journalists inside or outside the BBC rep-
    resent some sort of coherent political opposition to New Labour. It
    is more that the aggressive, assertive and less editorially prescribed
    style of interviewing and reporting which is now the norm within the
    field of quality UK political communications, is alarming to politi-
    cians. This less-scripted 'freestyle' is what precipitated the Gilligan
    affair. And the findings of the Hutton Report allowed the govern-
    ment to demand that political communications within the BBC be
    thoroughly reviewed.

6   John Berger in an interview for Nightwaves, BBC Radio 3,
    December 2001, argued that in Gramsci's writing there was a prin-
    ciple of hope through the very non-existence of revolution; this
    allowed for recognition that the struggles of the left were the terrain

of revolution, it was not a once and forever thing, but the process of struggle.

7   This recent turn on the multi-cultural question took shape on the pages of *Prospect* magazine in a piece by the editor David Goodhart attracting a good deal of attention across the quality media as fresh thinking and new common sense on the issue post-9/11 (Goodhart, 2004).

Extended Notes

Stuart Hall Meets Tony Blair

In a recent article published in the magazine *Soundings*, Stuart Hall develops one of the most incisive critiques of the Blair government to date (Hall, 2003). This is a virtuoso piece, an accumulation of thinking which connects back to Hall's analysis of the Thatcher years and extends this forward towards the end of the second term of New Labour in office. Hall addresses that aspect of New Labour which resists association with a single definitive programme; the way in which its actions appear to those who still define themselves as on the left, (including backbenchers inside the government, party members, and those outside) as confusing and contradictory. This means sometimes adhering to decent values of tackling 'child poverty', providing good quality child care, and ensuring that pupils leave school with better qualifications, while at the same time pushing all social programmes through within an overarching vocabulary which refutes the values of social democracy and warmly embraces free marketisation. (Even the tackling of child poverty is couched so as to avoid being seen as providing additional welfare or support to the parents of these children . . . as this would smack of traditional welfarism). In the article Hall perceives the scale, the relentlessness, the sheer ambition and the ruthlessness of this project. The New Labour plan is to create a more fully developed mode of neo-liberal governance which complies with the needs and the overall inclinations of the global capitalist economy, by means of a transformed (barely recognisable) social democratic pathway. Hall further recognises that this pathway itself is what New Labour is also dedicated to re-defining; social democracy is in the throes of profound change. Indeed the Blair government, by virtue of its still residual 'old Labour' credentials is better placed than Mrs Thatcher was, to see through the 'modernisation' of now seemingly old-fashioned or antiquated social democracy. There is just enough of the old core values still acknowledged and indeed ritualistically invoked now and again in order that this job of transformation can all the better succeed. And when this gentle touch does not seem to work then the so-called bruisers in the Cabinet (in particular the ferociously eloquent Dr John Reid) can be relied upon to argue the government's way through the most unsalvageable of positions. It is not just that the spell of the welfare state is being broken, its backbone is now being shattered, so that it might not ever recover. Hall also reflects on what he did not so clearly perceive when writing about Thatcherism, which was that it was so deeply intertwined with the changing requirements of the global economy while also changing the political culture of the UK. The post-industrialisation of the UK was taking place hand in hand with the relocating of manufacture and the emergence of an international division of labour; Thatcher's many attempts to kick start 'enterprise culture' were forward-looking ways of introducing ideas of individualisation as a strategy of self-governance, which in turn paved the way for New Labour's endeavours. 'This approach is effective well outside the machinery of the state. Slowly but surely, everybody – kicking and screaming to the end – becomes his/her own kind of "manager"' (Hall, 2003).

Hall's article is a sombre account of the devastation of the social welfare apparatus wrought by New Labour. 'Do not be deluded', he seems to be saying to many of us who struggled hard to find some radical content in the Giddens-inspired Third Way politics (Giddens, 1998). This, in the first term of office, was heralded as a programme which could renew social democracy, deliver resources to public services while also participating in the global economy, and keep the conservatives out of office by maintaining broad-based electoral support for New Labour. Hall now sees just how well Blair et al. have indeed learnt the lessons from Thatcherism, including some of those he himself argued for. There is a degree of uncanniness in Hall's position vis-à-vis New Labour and in particular its 'modernising wing'. The connection is not with Gordon Brown's redistributive and social justice corner of government (tackling child poverty as above). Nor is it with the young men and women of the Treasury schooled in US economic theory and looking to find ways to translate this into policies palatable to the UK electorate. No, the connection is still at what we might describe as the interface of 'media–politics–ideology'. For media read 'spin', for politics read 'modernisation' and for ideology read 'Thatcherism re-invented for New Labour'. Stuart Hall's thinking haunts the contours of this government's office. For those who were in the orbit of *Marxism Today* through the 1980s (Mandelson, policy advisor Geoff Mulgan and policy consultant Charles Leadbeater) some of Hall's lessons have been learnt too well in that they have provided a kind of template for doing what Thatcher did, but only better, particularly in regard to the politics of meaning, the power of language, the possibilities provided by processes of articulation, the moral fervour, the hegemonic reaching into the inner recesses of the popular psyche as shaped by the tabloid press, the stitching together of this with that, in unlikely but effective combinations, and the great gains to be made by trashing and demonising the old left, the feminists, the anti-racists, all of whom, we are constantly reminded, made Labour unelectable during the long Thatcher years. Simply because Hall has been New Labour's persistent public critic and interlocutor prior to, and throughout, their years in office, and because no one could mistake his left-wing voice as that of old (trade union-dominated and largely white) Labour (that is, he has always been 'modern'), and because his writing has also had a performative force of bringing into being 'the left', which it seems merely to describe, Hall's writing occupies a truly significant place in British public life (see also Rose, 1999 for a Foucault-inspired analysis of New Labour, and for an account of the decline of liberal democracy in the US, see Brown, 2004).

The crux of Hall's argument rests on the emphasis in New Labour rhetoric that only the private sector can deliver services efficiently. This single claim, repeated mantra-like as it is applied across the whole range of what once were public services, actively borrows from the language of traditional social democracy (for example, justice, equality and so on) in order to push further forward with privatisation. (For example, the 'opting-out' Foundation Hospitals will provide a better range of facilities and care delivered on a fairer basis for ordinary people than those remaining within the traditional National Health Service (NHS) system.) If the political culture of New Labour is led by neo-liberal principles with a social democratic underpinning, then this weak partner is also in the process of being transformed according to the logic of the free market. But it also remains the weak link which nonetheless provides New Labour with some residual 'labourist' credentials for the party faithful. The way in which this inner core of social democratic principles is eroded is in the accusation levelled against the big institutions of the state that they are failing, inefficient, wasteful, a burden on the taxpayer, that they are anti-democratic in their inability to involve and take into account, in the case of the schools, parental choice and in the case of the NHS, patient choice. Fighting for their very existence, organisations like the BBC, and institutions like the NHS and the universities, are subjected to scrutiny by means of auditing, assessment, targets and league tables, with the effect that the language of the market indeed becomes established as the norm, the everyday vocabulary by which ratings are secured or targets met. As Hall points out, at its most invidious, the NHS as a system, and the principles which underlie it, comes to be understood purely in terms of individual patient experience: 'Is there a bed for me?'

Overall the privatisation of social needs means life-long management of the self. While such a programme can indeed have positive effects (health regimes, exercise, good eating and so on), the culture of self-reliance also sees the demise of values of collective responsibility, care and social welfare. Dependency and weakness become unviable. It is this frenzied governmental activity at the level of what was once 'the social' which is what makes New Labour's particular style of neo-liberalism different from its US counterparts. Active governance, strong, day-by-day, presence in social affairs, seeing through processes of privatisation or semi-privatisation rather than just leaving it to the market, and appointing all kinds of 'tsars' and personal advisors, this is what marks out the terrain of New Labour's busy two terms of office. Hall points to some unity in this complexity. The radical new right forcefulness inside New Labour (manifest in the disdainfulness to, and dismissal of, left and feminist voices, and the 'cosying up' to right-wing politicians like Silvio Berlusconi) makes the alliance with George W. Bush less surprising.

Readers might at this point wonder what the weaknesses are in Hall's analysis; they might also imagine that my own account here is too heavily weighted towards endorsing Hall's writing across the board. In fact I have deliberately avoided invoking the various critiques of Hall's work. His critics and interlocuters are many. My aim has been rather different, which is to air and rehearse the span of Hall's writing by pulling out a number of themes which in my view are the most potent and which show the full force of his contribution, which is simply different from and more than that of an entirely academically oriented social or cultural theorist. But for the sake of a mini-debate, let me raise a few questions. In his writing on Thatcher, Hall frequently addresses 'the left'. What if that 'left' never really was? Or rather maybe there was even more of a need at the time to engage with what the left was, wasn't, or might have been? As Wendy Brown points out, Stuart Hall's writing has carefully and generously avoided the kind of angry sectarianism and the accusations and counter-accusations which have been standard within the activist left (Brown, 2000). But perhaps the cost of positioning oneself in the borderland between theoretical writing and political writing is that at key points for the desired readership, that is, for the left, the pragmatics of the short term rather than the longer term becomes uppermost. More people on what was the old left in its many variations back in the 1970s and 1980s, who were also part of the left addressed by Hall through those years, are now solidly ensconced inside the House of Commons or indeed the House of Lords or are within the orbit of New Labour as policy-makers and advisors, than might be imagined. Did the left itself then take part massively in the 'great moving right show' too? Did those on the left simply say, 'this is what we have to do to become elec- table'? If it is the case that the shift to the right has taken many who were on the left with it, and if there are also those still on the left who have felt the need to make certain tactical concessions, then this means that left- academic endeavours, like cultural studies, must rely more on the academic environment and the university for their continued existence. This in turn will have particular consequences. Voices like that of Hall now have to function as 'productive singularities', and there is a certain loneliness in such distinctiveness.

2

Black and Not-black: Gilroy's Critique of Racialised Modernity

GUIDE TO THE CHAPTER

Introduction

In this chapter I aim to demonstrate not just the extraordinary significance of Gilroy's work,[1] but also the value and importance, indeed
necessity, to the field of cultural studies, of historical work which peruses
the letters and writings, novels and non-verbal forms of communication
of people who have suffered, and recorded by some means, often musi-
cally, the experience of their racial subjugation. This might seem
obvious. But when it is combined, as it is in Gilroy's case, with both careful re-reading of philosophical writing for its conception of non-white
European 'others', a feature hitherto overlooked by scholars inattentive
to the 'racialising' currents which were so critical to Enlightenment
thought, and with an argument which disputes the very category of
'race', a profoundly distinctive oeuvre of work emerges, one which challenges to the core, the body of ideas which have acted as a frame for the
humanities and social sciences in the modern period. Gilroy, like the
black scholars from earlier periods to whom he turns, refuses to dismiss
Enlightenment thinking on concepts like freedom, emancipation and
individual rights, even though his writing is shaped by recognition that
the practice of 'racial terror' was a crucial component of progress,
reason and rationality. Instead, like his intellectual precursors, he prises
from the Enlightenment elements which can be reworked for the purposes of being able to conceptualise freedom from racial inequities.
Recognition of this 'double consciousness' (a concept borrowed from
DuBois), that is, to be simultaneously inside and outside European
modernity, provides Gilroy with a model for his subsequent work.
Indeed his work proceeds through further developments of 'double-
ness', a motif for pursuing what I would describe as a politics of being
black and not-black. His anti-essentialism is deployed against the absolutisms of putting people, or assuming people, to belong in one camp
or another, of ascertaining racial categories and allocating persons
places according to such 'fictional' attributes. Hence his work is con-
sistently open-ended, he imagines a state of being beyond race, he
looks forward to non-national spaces, not so much of belonging, as of
movement, and his preferred terms for such processes are diaspora and
hybridity.

Gilroy's central ideas are already in place in his first single authored book *There Ain't No Black in the Union Jack* and are then developed and further explored in the later work (Gilroy, 1987). Gilroy is attempting to open the world out, to encourage a capacity to think beyond the imagined unity of states and nations which have, as the very embodiments of modernity, been seen as constitutive of a world order. Gilroy sits uncomfortably alongside academics who write more narrowly on race or ethnicity. He is scathingly critical of much of this work. He also shows himself willing to enter into angry disputes with black scholars and activists for whom the category of race remains a recognisable mark of who 'we' are, and who 'we' are not. A feature of Gilroy's style is to confront too easy complicities which lead to closure and racial fixity. But neither is he happy with the slide into a celebratory mode which sometimes accompanies cultural studies work on UK multi-culturalism and its creativities, as though hybridity somehow delivers. His work is marked, then, by a singularity of vision, a relentless argumentative and critical voice.

In the pages that follow I will attempt to track and elucidate the movements of Gilroy's thinking, but I want to flag up some questions, at this early stage. Gilroy's central argument has a double focus: first, to demonstrate the way in which nationalisms have created only suffering and emiseration for those perceived as excluded from soil and blood, and, second, that in finding ways of confronting the full force of their own historical exclusions, black people are in danger of formulating their own black nationalisms. This latter can easily grow out of an understanding of their own culture as separate and distinct. When 'cultural absolutism' emerges, black activists can end up occupying a similar position to right-wing racists: they each want rigid separation, they each want to be able to preserve racial or cultural purity. This same argument is developed to the fullest extent in the recent book, *Between Camps*, where Gilroy describes the commonalities between fascist thinking and the Nation of Islam (Gilroy, 2000). Thus, in asking us to think beyond nation and also to connect ethnic absolutisms with neo-fascism, Gilroy is shaking the foundations of some seemingly progressive political sensibilities which have been developed by black people in recent years. He is also disrupting some of the currents which remain the basis of unifying movements of suppressed black people. To apply Gilroy's thinking globally is to see the world as conflictual on the basis of these desires for purity of ethnicity and nation.

The preservation of cultures and nation states is productive of end-less pain and suffering, but can we envisage an end to these desires? Perhaps the true significance of Gilroy's work is that, like Judith Butler, he marshals great intellectual powers to sustain the imagining of an entirely different political formation, of being beyond race and nation in Gilroy's case (and beyond gender and normative kinship in Butler's case). Of course in Gilroy's writing there is a distinction between nation and nationalism, but power is on the side of the forces which work to unite the two, and the counter forces of transnationalism and 'inter-culture' are invariably fragile. The other question we might ask of Gilroy is, how right is he to attribute a slide towards neo-fascism from the expressions of black neo-nationalism? Are there not great diversities and also some degree of openness within what he would see as a range of essentialisms? Or rather, must more historical and sociological atten-tion be paid to the specificities of these formations before the label of essentialism is cast upon them? How substantial is the support among black people in the UK and also in the USA for the Nation of Islam? Gilroy is alert to the danger that these ideas might be taken up by large numbers of black people. But what evidence is there of this? The per-nicious anti-semitism of Farrakhan and his camaraderie with white supremacists are indeed evidence of right-wing politics within the heart-land of dispossessed black populations, but it is also important to look at the limits of their successes.[2] Gilroy does not consider these more situ-ated kind of questions, though his writing is a good deal more nuanced on these issues than is suggested by one of his fiercest critics (see Chrisman, 2000). Maybe the more significant point is the marked decline of black political consciousness, the even greater polarisation of wealth and poverty, the slide into quietude, the disengagement from participation in democracy, which is as widespread in the UK as it is in the USA.

Marx and Beyond

There Ain't No Black in the Union Jack is a book located within the particu-lar configuration of political debates on race which emerged in Britain in the early 1980s. It appears exactly midway through the triumphant 18 years of Tory government. The book seeks a critical dialogue with the work of figures like Raymond Williams, who embodies the British cultural studies tradition, and yet who envisages identity as requiring long-term attachment to place (that is, rootedness), and also social historians like E.P. Thompson and Eric Hobsbawm, both of whom have found reason to endorse forms of 'left patriotism'. Gilroy debates with key figures of the British left intellectual tradition. He also engages with the sociology of race and with black activists, intellectuals and writers working in the field of race relations. There is another dialogue informing the book, which is with Marxism, in particular, its Gramscian version, which had a profound influence on the development of cultural studies associated with the Centre for Contemporary Cultural Studies in Birmingham. In relation to Marxism there is a debate on the centrality of class with Gilroy opting for the conceptual value of the term 'class formation'. This moves discussion away from classes as fundamental and opposing categories through which history inexorably proceeds, to a field of activities and conflicts where class relations along with other social relations of race and gender are constitutive of the historical moment, in all of its over-determined complexity. In relation to Gramsci, he expresses concerns that the notion of the 'national popular' inscribes within its articulating movements nonetheless a sense of closure, a fixed set of distinctive features which mark out the terrain of nation.

For Gilroy culture exists where human subjects negotiate the social structures they find themselves inhabiting and from this encounter they also create meaning. Culture is the site of meaning creation and action and it is also a historical entity. Culture is a central component of political movement and organisation. The analytic strengths of Marxism and the value of class for understanding the deeper and structural movements of capital means that Gilroy's starting point must be those writers who engage with both race and class. But Gilroy is already persuaded of the important shift away from production as the critical point for political development. Just as feminists from the early 1970s argued for the saliencey of the home and the private sphere as spaces for both political analysis and engagement, so also are the dynamics around community, which are formative of political mobilisations outside the remit of classical class analysis.

But how do the positions black people have found themselves occupying, how does the antagonism they experience, independent of their class position, tally with the explanation of social structures provided by Marxism? This is important insofar as it has been from within Marxism

that the most sustained and engaged thinking around race and its relation to class has taken place. Marxism offers an intellectual tradition of
radical thinking with a programme for political practice around which
it is possible to think about how racial disadvantage works and can be
overcome. It has provided the most pervasive analysis of capitalism.
The issue then is, what stake has the development of capitalism had in
the distinctive contours of racial oppression? Gilroy agrees with Miles
that race is an illusion, a fictive construct, but where Miles looks to the
end of race as a precursor to the achievement of unity of the working-
class (where black people surely belong) Gilroy reminds us of the
alliances bringing black professionals (teachers, social workers, lawyers,
health workers) together with poor and unemployed black people to
fight injustices (Miles, 1982). He refutes the idea of race as a kind of
false consciousness, an 'ideological effect' which undermines the political ambition for class unity. Not only does this perspective have a
narrowly labourist character, it also discounts the role of the black
middle classes, whose interests must then be entirely separate from the
black working-class. This disputes the legitimacy of racial experience.
Gilroy argues that sociologists like Miles have little understanding of the
political organisation which takes shape outside narrowly economic
concerns, which, as Gilroy puts it, have a utopian dynamic. The critique
of capitalism by black people has become, and he quotes Richard
Wright, 'a tradition, in fact a kind of culture'.

This comment provides the rationale for *There Ain't No Black in the
Union Jack*, both in the role of culture as historically carrying the potential for social criticism and political change, but also for its non-national
rhythms, its movements across the boundaries of the nation state. For
Gilroy the way in which issues around race will be understood requires
a historical analysis which emerges not just from the economics of racial
subordination. Thinking about race thus requires a conceptualisation
which connects with, but has a separate significance from, class. Gilroy
follows Hall's dictum that for black people 'race is the modality in which
class is lived' (Hall et al., 1978). One can see here a commitment to
retaining class analysis through the engagement of economics with history and political identity, but also a sharp determination to allow race
a specificity which is at no point collapsible into the notion that class
relations will at some point prevail and replace the local details of race
in the move towards unity and the bid for power. There is a double transition in Gilroy's analysis, from production and work as the nexus for

political consciousness, to community, urban environment, state, welfare system and home. There is also a shift from class as a category into which all other differences might eventually be collapsed, to race as an outward-looking category for independent struggles against injustice. But the category of race is simultaneously refused meaning which would tie it to some essential set of attributes. Instead, and again this is a crucial move, race is 'a political category that can accommodate various meanings, which are in turn defined by struggle'. Thus we find the clearest expression of Gilroy's thinking on race expressed in the first chapter of the book:

> race formation . . . refers both to the transformation of phenotypical variation into concrete systems of differentiation based on 'race' and colour and to the appeals to spurious biological theory which have been a feature of the history of 'races'. Race formation also includes the manner in which 'races' become organised in politics, particularly where racial differentiation has become a feature of institutional structures . . . as well as individual interaction. (Gilroy, 1987: 38)

But the greatest dangers that beset black political struggles are those of allowing such struggle to be enclosed by notions of either cultural difference or national belonging; these Gilroy labels 'ethnic absolutism'.

This is an easy trap to slide into, one which has also attracted figures from the British left, including Williams, Hobsbawm and E.P. Thompson; Gilroy argues that in each of these writers there remains a residual notion of the sanctity of nation and the integrity of Britishness. By connecting 'the whole way of life of the people' with certain traits of patriotism, and other distinguishing characteristics, it is possible to mobilise anew in a way which ignores the exclusionary impact of such rhetoric on the existence of black people living and settled in the UK. The left is no less guilty of this than the right. Indeed in an attempt to prise away from the right their populist hegemony many figures on the left sought to re-define a new kind of patriotism, a revived Englishness, but as Gilroy points out 'the suggestion that no one lives outside the national community is only plausible if the issue of racism is excluded'. Left nationalism even goes so far as espousing an admiration for the late Conservative minister Enoch Powell, whose 'rivers of blood' speech in 1968 ushered in an era of racial hostility on the part of indigenous whites to those they perceived as immigrants, strangers and people with different cultures. Gilroy is therefore charging the British left with conceding to Powellism.[3] In effect, what he is saying is that from the traditional centre left of the Labour Party (then and now) to the Eurocommunism of left intellectuals in the late 1970s and early 1980s there was a tendency to endorse the British way of life as an honourable and homogenous tradition, uninterrupted by the presence of peoples from diverse social backgrounds. Little attention was paid to the cruelties it inflicted on passport bearers from its former colonies.

This insularity was consequently blind if not hostile to the presence of others. For the Labour Party and those grouped around it, it meant and continues to mean an ambivalent if not hostile view of immigrants, newcomers, and those who need to be drawn into, and absorbed by, these venerable traditions. For the Euro-communists of the early 1980s, the 'national popular' was an attempt to plug into a vein of populist sentiment which so far only the right had succeeded in engaging with. This was a strategy of politicisation; it said that in order to get to the people and pull them more directly into supporting the left it was necessary to find and endorse their own popular traditions and festivals and, in effect, to be seen as a popular force in touch with ordinary sentiments, even when this involved love of royalty and monarchy and other national rituals (for example, the wedding of Charles and Diana). The left had no hope of coming to power unless it was able to understand the depth of such feelings. Both Euro-communist and Labour Party currents did indeed converge and helped to bring Labour back into power many years later, in 1997. Gilroy's point made some ten years earlier was that the exclusionary force of national popular rhetoric never looked to or invited response from British blacks or Asians. It imagined Britain as England and as homogenously white and unbifurcated by difference. New Labour today maintains this commitment to centre-left patriotism, with Home Secretary (1997–2001) Jack Straw angrily denouncing the left for its hostility to the sound principles of patriotism. New Labour now also gestures towards diversity, particularly in the aftermath of the race riots in the north of England, followed by the events of 9/11 in the USA.[4] Indeed there is coming into being a new modality of inclusive patriotism, the parameters and dynamics of which were rehearsed through both the death of the Queen Mother (April 2002) and the 50th Jubilee of the Queen (May–June 2002).[5]

Gilroy's advocacy of post-national politics found some resonance in radical politics in the late 1970s and early 1980s as he describes it through youth movements like Rock Against Racism and the Anti-Nazi League, and also through some of the activities of the left-wing Greater London Council, which was abolished by Mrs Thatcher in 1986. *There Ain't No Black in the Union Jack* was first published in 1987 and we might legitimately ask, have other such movements continued this momentum? Clearly the recent actions of the anti-capitalist protestors attempt to counter the further growth of corporate globalisation by mobilising on an international basis. But it is hard to find many intellectual voices arguing for a political analysis which is similarly beyond nation. African-American intellectuals recover the history of slavery and restore the experience, but without subjecting the USA to as ferocious a critique as Gilroy does to England and the defence of its 'white cliffs'. Somehow they remain remarkably American. Ulrich Beck argues forcefully for Europe to be understood as a space for cosmopolitan democracy. However such a perspective also needs to engage with Europe's own barriers, especially in regard to flows of labour from across the world (Beck, 2000). And Giddens himself (Britain's most prominent sociologist, also known and respected across the world), writes in the *Guardian* newspaper that in the light of the growing numbers of persons seeking asylum, the government needs to be 'tough on immigration and tough on hostility to immigrants' (Giddens, 2002). Thus, in the light of the decline of socialism and the non-existence of sustained opposition, Gilroy's voice is all the more singular, his allies increasingly can be found not in the academy, but as other dissenting voices.[6]

Outside Law, Inside Music

Where does this non-belonging come from, and how is it sustained? How are blacks and Asians in the UK actively stopped from being seen to belong? If national culture seeks to maintain some sense of homogeneity how is this achieved? One answer lies in, argues Gilroy, the criminalisation of black youth, which produces its own 'narrative of dispossession'. Here we see the next stage in Gilroy's analysis. Afro-Caribbean blacks come to be tarnished by the slur of crime, as though it is always a strong likelihood. As Hall showed it was instrumental from the mid-1970s onwards to portray 'mugging' as a sign of national decline (Hall et al., 1978). The Labour left at the time supported the idea that black crime was widespread in particular urban communities.

Gilroy considers the representations which assert crime as part of black culture, thus contributing directly to the idea of cultural difference in a recognisable and distinctive way. This suggests that there is an inherent disrespect for English law, and this is clearly expressed in Powell's speech. Blacks are disposed to being disorderly, putting law abiding citizens at risk. The centrality of police discourses in putting those law breaking images of black people and black youth into public circulation through the tabloid press is critically examined by Gilroy. From 1976 to 1985 there is a persistent concern with the management of the black community and the conveying of key meanings about this group to the white population. Gilroy describes the lack of police concern following the deaths of 13 young black people at a party in South London, legitimated through the already hostile connotations of the 'black party'. Thus cultural difference is established first at a political level through Powell, then at street level through policing practices from the mid-1970s onwards. This creates an ethos of national non-belonging in that crime is seen as 'an expression of black culture'. The symbolic value of this criminal culture is crucial to the effectivity of racial ideology. Race thus permits the policing of a 'law and order society' which is sustained through Thatcher, Major and beyond. To recap, we see a move in *There Ain't No Black in the Union Jack* from race and class, to nation and its limits, then, as though to explain how the limits of belonging are enforced, Gilroy traces images of black criminality which are constructed as signs of cultural difference and evidence of disrespect for the law. Black culture is thus criminalised and pathologised.[7]

This abject state is, however, radically contested by Gilroy. Black expressive culture with its redemptionist aesthetics provides a space for both politics and belonging. Black people are neither victims nor social problems, but agents able in conditions of historical adversity to give voice to collective experience in cultural form and, at the same time, rendering redundant the boundaries of the nation state formations which have been forces of exclusion. Thus, in the communicative forms of music a diasporic aesthetic capable of containing a profound critique of capitalism takes shape. Chapter 5 of *There Ain't No Black in the Union Jack* marks out a hugely important space in Gilroy's thinking. This is the space of music, of meta-communication which remains faithful to key elements of the slave experience (when literacy was forbidden on pain of death) while also appropriating the technologies made available by modernity to achieve a double effect. This is, first, to transcend the barriers of nation state and thus to create a global dialogue of affirmation and protestation. Second, there is neither the separation from science nor from philosophy which were the legacies of modernity and the Enlightenment to what came to be known as 'art'. Diaspora is the clear alternative to absolutism with its music connecting blacks in the USA with others in Jamaica and in the UK. Blacks here are thus bound to others elsewhere. Music helps to overcome the confines of nation, pre-figuring a non-racialised space and time. This has all been made possible by musicians' effective use of modern technologies.

Records become raw materials for creativity, 'dialogic rituals of cele-bratory consumption'. The routes these 'imported' objects pass through also give rise to further music-making which incorporates many ele-ments of what has been listened to from far away. Hence there come into being processes of cultural spread or 'syncretism' which obviates the commercial sphere through the setting up of pirate radio, sound sys-tems and other forms of musical self-organisation. The traditions which Gilroy describes are those associated with the music of Civil Rights in the USA. From tracks like 'People Get Ready' to the sounds of James Brown in the 1960s, for example, 'Say It Loud', to Fontella Bass singing 'Rescue Me', Gilroy sees music play a leading role in the consolidation of political consciousness. There are warnings from Sly Stone that 'There's a Riot Going On'. There are, of course, the pleas for 'Respect' from Aretha Franklin and then, into the 1970s, this current shifts direc-tion with a more satirical and carnivalesque dynamic from George Clinton's Funkadelic brigade, and also with the futurism of Earth, Wind and Fire. Gilroy shows how music acts as political critique and news reportage in, for example, Gil Scott Heron's precursors of full-blown rap in 1981. Rap is another reworking of antiphonal call and response tra-ditions, in 1982 a new era is ushered in with the classic commentary of Grandmaster Flash and the Sugar Hill Gang. If Melle Mel was indeed living 'close to the edge', this was a message which appealed to the dis-enfranchised black youth of the UK, whose response in the early 1980s was to riot in protest at aggressive policing, and to create their own reggae and 'two tone' black and white musical critique.

These rich musical forms find their way into the bedrooms of black British youths, conveying a sensibility of protest and the desire for change. The reggae sounds from Jamaica combine with black American music to create a profound critique of capitalism, with songs which challenge the kind of meaningless work it offers poor blacks, its policing and miscarriages of justice, its history of slavery and the miseries and sufferings of poverty. But from these accounts there also emerges within the musical forms, possibilities of escape. Sexual pleasure offers intimacies, the gratification of desires and moments of freedom. The music also permits a seeming escape from bodily realities including those of language. Gilroy suggests that the screams and wails, the shouts and cries of James Brown convey feelings so deep they cannot be spoken; this is the only means of their expression. This 'dramaturgy' of 'the ineffable' brings art and life together. There is nothing autonomous, distant or carefully bounded about this music. The direct address to the audience signals a more participatory relation. The black public sphere constructed through these incessant dialogues is continually being remade, worked on. It speaks to its audience through its own distinctive channels, in the playful shout outs of the DJs and MCs on pirate radio, in the inventive naming of performers on the illicit posters and billboards decorating the city streets. This is also a mode of black self-organisation, the dance halls, parties, clubs, record shops, sound systems, and small record companies are all carved out of a space which Gilroy claims eludes and transcends the processes of commercialisation. The achievement of a distinctive cultural space is tantamount to a small utopia in that it brings together art, everyday life, politics and history. Where European modernity has placed art in a special place, out of reach of the ordinary, this expressive culture is more democratic, more like how art ought to be.

Gilroy points out that this emphasis on music places him in a position quite removed from the 'productivist' and work-related concerns of classical Marxism. The way in which these cultural forms embody a political sensibility and are constitutive of black identities introduces a field of discussion which is also completely absent from what is usually called the sociology of race and ethnicity. This shows how innovative Gilroy's work is, combining history with sociological analysis of black youth cultures and with a reading of black musics as aesthetic forms. Recently Sharma et al. have looked to Gilroy's work on black music for a framework for understanding new Asian dance music (Sharma et al., 1996). In the US the interweaving of political critique with musicological analysis is also more familiar. But there is no doubt that the centrality of music to Gilroy's work challenges mainstream historians and sociologists for whom music exists either as part of the separate field of leisure or as a high art form. This raises a further question. How necessary is it to be familiar with music from Sly Stone to James Brown to fully engage with the argument of the book? The scale and ambition of Gilroy's work puts him alongside some of the most prominent historians in the world today; one wonders how many of the elder white Europeans among them would take the time to listen to even a handful of the tracks he mentions once they have finished reading.

How then to describe Gilroy's relation to the philosophers and social scientists whose concerns overlap with his own? Scholars who have considered the growth of the nation state and the transitions which are now confronting the new world order are by and large relatively inattentive to questions of culture, never mind music, even when espousing global cosmopolitanism. Those who consider global culture pay little attention to the complex meanings of dissident forms; instead their focus is on issues such as big brands and global markets. Others point to the continuing centrality of the nation state, despite globalisation, from the point of view of trade and economics. Few engage with these issues from the position of 'black and not black' as defined by Gilroy. Gilroy rehearses the transition from Marxism to a politics of the new social movements in the closing pages of *There Ain't No Black in the Union Jack*. He acknowledges the proliferation of political concerns from the body to the environment, from the city, and local community to the excesses of consumer culture. This is a recurrent strand in the later books where the impact of consumerism delivered through the medium of the visual image devastates the prized sphere of black communication, the musical tradition. And likewise in the most recent work there is a passage from what we might describe as 'movement to melancholia' as Gilroy's hope for an expanded post-Marxist politics fades in the light of resurgent global neo-nationalisms.

Take Me to the River

We have seen a triangle of black communication connecting Jamaica with England and the USA which functions as a public sphere for critical commentary on the lived experience of racialisation. The three key elements, music, history and trans-nationality, are, in *The Black Atlantic* (Gilroy, 1993) expanded into an argument about the post-slave world. This entails a more developed re-assessment of modernity and the way its freedoms were interpreted by black scholars whose experience was shaped by suffering and brutality, and whose bids for freedom necessitated travel and movement. *First,* there is the inscription inside modernity and Enlightenment of the people it enslaved; as Gilroy points out, their removal from historical and philosophical accounts does not mean their physical presence stopped them from being witness to, as well as part of, albeit in unfreedom, this great project. *Second,* there is a repositioning of the author himself, this time located within a European terrain, and taking up the identity of a black European. If the first book was largely dealing with the political and cultural landscape of the UK and the importance of challenging the many attempts to strengthen the boundaries of nation, in *The Black Atlantic* Gilroy traces the intellectual journeys of Martin Delany, Richard Wright, DuBois, Frederik Douglass and others through France, Germany, Britain and the USA. *Third,* there is a further attempt to subvert or rewrite the cultural studies tradition by subjecting to critique the authors whose work has fed into, and thus shaped, the existence of cultural studies. Gilroy remarks upon the literature which influenced Raymond Williams, from Burke to Ruskin and Carlyle, and reminds us of the racialising currents in their work. He also looks to the wider terrain of thought which has fed into and shaped the whole field of culture and cultural studies. The historians who considered themselves a good deal more radical than Williams also adhered nonetheless to the 'dream of socialism in one country'. In the USA Gilroy recognises the existence of a parallel current informing cultural studies, which veers to ethnic absolutism by endorsing an 'equally volkish popular cultural nationalism'.

Gilroy's main focus is on a different set of scholarly endeavours carried out in the most adverse of circumstances and barely recognised within even the recent history and sociology of modernity. Gilroy is thus drawn to the writings of travelling black scholars, scientists, explorers and novelists from the early 19th century onwards. His trope is that of travel and his favoured symbol is that of the ship. The forced movement of peoples during the slave period provides a shadow of memory for the generations which followed and whose life's work it was to document in writing and, in other often musical forms, the history of the world around them and their responses to it. The 'black Atlantic politics of location frames the doorway of double consciousness'. Martin Delany is an exemplary figure. A distinguished polymath, he published *The Condition, Elevation, Emigration and Destiny of the Colored People of the*

United States Politically Considered in 1852, he attempted to combine Christianity with a 'pan African flourish' and, an extensive traveller, he also spent seven months in England. Delany's work is informed by the dispersal of black people and this gives him cause to consider the idea of the 'black nation state'. Later, enlisted in the Union side, Delany endorsed an American patriotism and this, argues Gilroy, complements his earlier enthusiasm for a black state. But the more intractable question confronting Delany and others was how to envisage a means by which black people, despite their plurality and dispersal, could be brought together in struggles to overcome their subjugation? To imagine this entails understanding the workings of modernity, capitalism and the processes of democratisation. The difficulty is that the legacy of modernity is a concept of man with a stable identity and with a rooted location. This suggests an 'ethnic culture' inside a nation state. How to acquire full citizenship without advocating the nation state?

Among the writers Gilroy is discussing runs a strong thread of belief in the nation state as the means to overcome oppression. Thus modernity bequeaths to its racialised others the idea of nation. Many black writers do not consider these histories of music, so important to Gilroy, for the reason that they interrupt this narrative, they both transcend nation and ethnocentrism and they demonstrate inter-racial dispute and differenciation. Black music is a 'counter culture of modernity'. There is found in this music a morality encoded within a popular vernacular which is also able to look to a utopian future untroubled by racial oppression. Gilroy says music-making and performance is about finding strength to go on living. The 'slave sublime' is constitutive of a politics of transfiguration.

> Thus the vernacular arts of the children of slaves give rise to a verdict on the role of art . . . in harmony with Adorno's reflections . . . Art's utopia . . . is a freedom which did not pass under the spell of necessity and which may not well come to pass ever at all. (Gilroy, 1993: 38)

Art in the broadest sense is one critical means with which freedom can be envisaged. Hence Gilroy's focus on writing – fiction, autobiography – as well as music.

A fuller account of modernity requires a return to Hegel's understanding of the bond between master and slave as relational. This relation requires a slave's perspective which, though absent from subsequent accounts of modernity, does exist. In *The Black Atlantic* these accounts are central to his attempt to reformulate modernity on the basis that 'racial terror is not merely compatible with occidental rationality but cheerfully complicit with it' (ibid.: 56). One critical turning point in this experience, argues Gilroy, is when confronted with absolute brutality the slave defends himself physically against his master. Frederick Douglass's preference for death rather than submission becomes a structure of feeling where death is a 'release from terror'. Gilroy then shows how death as escape becomes a symbol of identity which appears and reappears through subsequent slave narratives and also in a wide range of black writing, from autobiography to fiction. This brings into being a 'conception of the slave subject as an agent' and a 'black spirituality which legitimises these moments of violence' . . . which also 'projects beyond the limits of the present'. Gilroy then locates his own endeavours within the framework established by DuBois and others. This is to offer a distinctive interpretation of modernity. In *The Black Atlantic* there is also a desire to complement the unfulfilled aspirations of the project of modernity as described by Marx with 'a redemptive critique of the present in the light of the vital memories of the slave past' (ibid.: 71).

Why does music possess such important status in Gilroy's work? Because it is able to carry within it the 'slaves' will'. With literacy forbidden there remained only a performance aesthetic; this 'grudging gift' is thus able to become an 'enhanced mode of communication'. To the present day this gift is also one which, because it has been largely ignored or overlooked by forces of domination, remains a point of access for expression among the black dispossessed. For those whose genius would otherwise have been quickly eliminated as marking an aspiration above their station in life, being able to make music from such profoundly disadvantaged circumstances as those of Bob Marley, Jimi Hendrix or Prince, is also a way of being indigenous intellectuals. This also subverts the various hierarchies of European aesthetics understood by authors from Foucault to Barthes as first the 'birth', and then the 'death' of the author. If, as Gilroy argues, the 'birth' inflated the role of the unique individual, taking art out of the hands of ordinary beings, the 'death' deflated the work to the status of text and removed from art its interactive and performative dynamics. However, this very capacity to create a special kind of aesthetics can give rise to dangerous authenticities of an 'untouched pristine Africanity' (ibid.: 101). At the same time there is also, in the permutations of new 12-inch versions of this 'changing same', other, unexpected, celebrations of inauthenticity as 'real', such as LL Cool J's 'Round the Way Girl' mix. Here the girl of his dreams has hair extensions and a Fendi bag. By suggesting the endlessly sampled artifice-aesthetic of hip hop to be a mark of true blackness there is a danger, suggests Gilroy, that the grand commercialisation of these forms on this basis, proceeds unhindered. As they reach wider audiences across the world, they are indeed marketed as 'black' possessing 'tidy patterns of secret, ethnically encoded dialogue' (ibid.: 110). This leads to a new essentialism (of anti-essentialism) based on artifice and inauthentic multi-sampled music as a commercial recipe for bringing 'black music' into the heart of the global cultural economy.

DuBois, witnessing lynchings outside in the streets while he was teaching indoors in the university, produces the most distinctively modern version of black political culture, argues Gilroy, one which recognises the role of education and also of non-linguistic forms to carry memories of slavery, and of 'aesthetic experience . . . as the favoured vehicle for communal self-development'. Most important is his concept of double consciousness which, as Gilroy describes, comprises the particularity of being black with the aspiration for a modern nation state, while at the same time being formed within the experience of a diaspora, with all its 'pleasures and dangers' (ibid.: 138). There is also a complex and ambivalent response by Richard Wright, who seeks out Europe and Paris in particular to live in and who is disparaged for leaving black American culture behind him. But this journey, claims Gilroy, allows him to describe the black experience of western modernity just at the point in which the post-war period was also becoming post-colonial. Gilroy's account of Wright's time in Paris suggests a new interpretation of his later work, one which sees the black male as pre-eminently modern. The scars impacted by racism are productive of a psyche more tormented than the archetypal figures of existential literature. In this context Wright ought to have been more fully present in the later commentaries on Sartre and de Beauvoir and also Jean Genet.

The Black Atlantic moves to its own momentous conclusion with Gilroy in the final chapter clarifying the argument and making even more emphatic his claims. Once again the terms and concepts which are deeply problematic are also required, but only after they have been tirelessly re-examined. Thus, tradition, when it is used as a means of providing a history for black people, typically means embracing the anti-modernity of Africanicity. This invoking of tradition means over-looking the terrors of slavery by going further back in search of a better beginning. In complete contrast to this back to Africa movement Gilroy proposes the unsettled, restless motions of diaspora. By showing how memory and narrativity are able to constitute 'black political counter-cultures', tradition can be re-instated in a 'non-traditional' mode. This mode is never linear or progressive; instead it is untidy, a 'living memory of the changing same'. Once again we see Gilroy return to the theme of death. Fear and danger, and thus the presence of death, are ever pres-ent and shape the distinctive aesthetics which have been so central to the book. In music and then in novels and in autobiography there is a des-peration, yearning and desire for redemption as well as mourning for loss, which produces the ineffable, the transcendent, the 'slave sublime'. Gilroy also asks, how can this be considered alongside memories of the Holocaust, how can the Jewish diaspora be understood in relation to this rewriting of modernity? Here, too, rationality is complicit with racial terror, here too is salvation sought through dreams of a nation state. It is this desire, however, which is in actuality a kind of death drive. Nothing is more iniquitous than a return to an imagined point of origin, the slaves' dreams of return to Africa in death . . . is 'their turn towards death'. If Zionism shares with black nationalisms all the dangers of ethnic absolutism, *The Black Atlantic* proposes a different way of remem-bering organised terror and suffering which looks outwards rather than inwards and which searches for viability through a politics of movement, mixture, impurity and hybridity.

Movement to Melancholia

There is a strong, unmistakable line of connection between the two earlier books and the more recent *Between Camps* (Gilroy, 2000), so much so that all three become part of a sustained enquiry into, on the one hand, the historical processes which, in moving from racialisation as slavery and as brutal practices of decisive non-belonging in relation to the categories of Modernity, leads then inexorably to a dangerous imag-ining of absolute difference, and thus separation by whatever means, which can be endorsed by racially subjugated persons themselves and which in turn gives rise to the spectre of global neo-nationalisms and militarisation. On the other hand there are transcultural possibilities for countering such 'camp mentalities'. These have been carried in and through black musics and the transcendent aesthetics afforded by their encoding of histories of suffering and hopes for 'freedom'; these musics have also connected with social movements which have sought to bring to an end differences brought about by racialising discourses and thus look towards a future of being 'black no more'.

The notion of black and not-black runs through Gilroy's work as a necessary paradox. Necessary because in the light of the resistance to opening out for critical examination the consequences of racial categorisations, which in turn would look to the dissolution of such categories, not only is the status quo upheld, but ethnic absolutism becomes all the more entrenched, with the effect that only by being 'strategically black', not as a mark of self but as an intellectual and political positioning, a mode of inter-disciplinary enquiry, does it seem possible to envisage the end of race. With this in mind, the concluding commentary on *Between Camps* traces those lines of thinking which, seemingly provocative, are also extraordinarily pertinent to an analysis of the world today and the possible catastrophes of neo-fascism (albeit in a very different mode from its 1930s predecessors), the acceleration of militarisation and its glamorisation in culture, and the 'new deal' which seeks to reconcile global capitalism with newly fortified 'united states'. Earlier in this chapter I suggested that Gilroy's assessment of the dangers of new forms of fascism espoused by black people themselves, particularly around grouping such as the Nation of Islam, were perhaps insufficiently grounded in detailed attention to the political culture of everyday life and the sensibilities and opinions by black people on both sides of the Atlantic (if these are the two main constituencies under discussion). It is only in the light of the successes of the right in a variety of forms that it becomes apparent that the regrouping of black people together with white under the banner of a post-racial socialism is so unlikely as to be almost unimaginable; more likely that black conservatism grows in strength following different modalities according to different social and cultural regimes, something Gilroy is well aware of in his analysis of hip hop (see Extended Notes at the end of the chapter).

Thus in *Between Camps* Gilroy poses the re-emergence of fascism against the desire for 'planetary humanism'. Indeed fascism not only has not really ever gone away, but many of its key elements find sustenance in the constellation of values currently configured around commercial imagery of blackness, in particular the prominence of the black body, the attribution to its codes of aesthetic meaning, including 'racialised glamour' and 'vital prestige'. Given the ease with which fascism can be forgotten by generations for whom education has become enmeshed with entertainment, there is all the more reason to uncover and discuss the experiences, for example, of black soldiers during the Nazi period, the experience of black people under the Nazis. Not only does this extended discussion develop further the earlier commentaries on the Jewish and black diasporas, it also seeks to lace them together by tracing the centrality of racial science to fascist thinking. Gilroy sees connections within the machinery of Nazi propaganda and the technologies of contemporary consumer culture, most notably the centrality of visual imagery as a way of 'giving life to the nation'. The body iconography perfected in Leni Riefenstahl's 1930s' film *Triumph of the Will*, a 'visual culture of race', finds itself uncritically replayed not only in the work of commercial fashion photographers like Bruce Weber, but also in that of the much praised gay photographer Robert Mapplethorpe. Being vigilant of these consequences of forgetfulness is as important as subjecting contemporary black commercial culture to scrutiny, particularly for its abandonment of communality, for forward thinking, for creating a 'wonderful culture of dissidence' in favour of 'conservatism, misogyny and sex'. These black arts no longer question the social; instead they seek intimate satisfactions in lifestyle and 'racial recreation', the 'bedroom' and the 'four wheel drive'.

There is a narrative line in *Between Camps* which sees the destruction of the dynamics of freedom and dissidence which were encapsulated in black expressive culture. Sex and the culture of the gym replace love and a politics and what Bhabha might call a political imaginary of 'the beyond'. Even death no longer resonates as a modality of political effectivity, something which historically registered in the memory of those who chose not to give in to death as a legitimate expression of black pain. Instead death in the ghetto, either through drugs, HIV or drive-by killings is almost unremarkable. The successes of neo-liberalism with the growth of its distinctive leisure culture make other forms of social organisation all the more difficult to envisage; thus there seems to be a more intense investment in the pleasures and thrills which capitalism has to offer. Black people are now permitted, through the license accorded to them by advertising imagery, to demonstrate what Gilroy calls 'corporeal vitality'. But while it is just this which Fanon beautifully described as exactly what was denied the black male ('I dream I am jumping, swimming, running, climbing', quoted in Gilroy, 2000: 255) it is now a mark of the limits of what can be achieved. No wonder, then, that Gilroy's voice becomes melancholic, but as it does so also is his writing more forceful, more emphatic in its expression of the existence of other possibilities of a 'resolutely nonracial humanism'.

Notes

1   The three books (Gilroy 1987, 1993 and 2000) could be seen as a trilogy, so coherent is the development of an argument about the dangers of ethnic absolutism, the proximity of fascistic sensibilities and the political desire for moving beyond race.
2   The precise contours of how ethnic absolutisms operate within racially subjugated communities requires more extensive analysis, in the UK as well as in the USA, for instance in the *Today* programme (BBC Radio 4, September 2001) it was reported that a handful of members of the Bradford Sikh community met with the neo-fascist British National Party on the basis of shared ideas about racial separation. However, this was immediately condemned by other members of the Asian community.
3   Tony Blair spoke in praise of Enoch Powell at his funeral on 18th February 2002.
4   In the aftermath of September 11th 2001 there have been a range of political interventions aimed at securing the inclusion of British Muslims; the emphasis has been overwhelmingly cultural or through religious or 'faith' initiatives.
5   Since the death of Princess Diana and the remarked upon visible presence of black and Asian people among the mourners at Kensington Palace, there have been attempts at subsequent state events, that is, the death of the Queen Mother (April 2002) and the Jubilee celebrations for the Queen (May–June 2002) to highlight as well as document similar modes of black participation.
6   Gary Younge, a *Guardian* writer, represents one of the few voices as forceful and attentive to the dynamics of racial politics as Gilroy.
7   The ease with which the current government, and especially Home Secretary (2001–2004) David Blunkett, picks up, once again, the rhetoric of black crime and the image of the 'mugger' preying on vulnerable citizens demonstrates something more than a re-working

of a law and order position; indeed it seems almost to suggest a direct challenge by New Labour to writers like Stuart Hall and Paul Gilroy. Gilroy rehearses some of these themes in the introduction to a new edition of *There Ain't No Black in the Union Jack* (see Gilroy, 2002).

Extended Notes

Snoop Doggy Dogg

Students will have noted that I have not so far engaged at great length with Gilroy in a more critical vein. Nor have I provided detailed accounts of those who have taken issue with his work. Gilroy is the most often cited black academic in the USA today. This omission on my part, is not because I consider Gilroy somehow beyond critique, nor is it the case that the work of his critics is not noteworthy; this is far from the case. What motivates the chapter above is a sense from students that Gilroy's work is both challenging and difficult, and what I have sought to do is to make some of the most important arguments more immediately graspable. One of the areas which students are drawn to in Gilroy's work is his writing on rap, but this is also where they claim to get very lost. Many cannot quite get what Gilroy is saying about contemporary hip hop music and in particular about Snoop Doggy Dogg. So in the notes that follow I take this as my task. I will try to take the reader through the chapter in *Between Camps* titled 'After the Love Has Gone: Biopolitics and Decay of the Black Public Sphere'. But before doing that, for the sake of a short debate, let me outline some of the criticisms levered at Gilroy by Laura Chrisman (Chrisman, 2000). Chrisman condemns Gilroy for offering a one-dimensional account of black neo-nationalist politics, which, she claims, are much more fluid and diverse than Gilroy allows. She also sees him as overlooking the possibilities for socialism in favour of a kind of cultural politics where aesthetics takes precedence over materiality; she charges him with imagining a politics based on 'a black utopian aesthetic premised on a death-drive' (Chrisman, 2000: 454). Let us look then a little bit more closely at Chrisman's critique. She argues that Gilroy overwhelmingly rejects the resources provided by the politics of both nationalist and socialist movements associated with black people in the first and third worlds and that he ends up, paradoxically, reifying a kind of 'pure' hybrid, an anti-essentialist but still black or ethnicist political paradigm. I think my own reading of Gilroy suggests something different, that the idea of 'black and not-black' permits the possibility of eventually moving beyond race. There is a resounding rejection, yes, of nationalism but a re-imagining and utopian extending of socialism to incorporate, but also go beyond, by means of the politics of new social movements, a concern only with economics. It is not the case that Gilroy suggests an anti-work ethic to be an unchanging characteristic of black culture, more that the politics of labourism have not historically embraced questions of race and ethnicity (neither at shop floor nor at official trades union level) and, in addition, 1970s neo-Marxism constructively demonstrated the importance of connections being made between work and home and community, for example, in domestic labour. Gilroy also refutes the idea that 'labour' can be the primary means of emancipation for black people, as was once envisaged by the Marxist left. Chrisman attacks what she sees as a one-sidedness in Gilroy's account of Afrocentric movements, which have gained ground, she claims, because of the worsening economic situation among black people in the USA. Gilroy's over-intellectualism divorces him, she suggests, from the reality of black people's lives. This leads her to challenge Gilroy's overblown aesthetics. Here she claims that he suggests that black art has more or less replaced black politics, and that with labouring gone as a source of possible emancipation, there is instead a kind of 'radical nihilism', that somehow death is preferable and this is coded into dynamics and currents in black expressive culture. Chrisman charges Gilroy with being too fatalistic in his account of the death-drive components in contemporary black culture, derivative of the legacy of slavery. His scepticism towards rationality and dialectics (part of his critique of Enlightenment thinking) leaves him with an account of black culture where even love is coded through the constant proximity of death and the endlessness of pain. Chrisman wants to remind readers of that other part of the slave legacy which sought emancipation through scientific rationality and labour power. For her that legacy is currently coded through contemporary black cultural practices like graffiti as 'industrial sabotage', and the humour of hip hop with its 'ironic and scatological aesthetics' is an important survival resource, in contrast to Gilroy's over-emphasis on death (Chrisman, 2000: 463).

This leads us conveniently to a brief discussion and clarification of Gilroy's writing on rap. It is the case that Gilroy makes the claim that there is a close historical relationship between the agency of the slaves and the contours and distinctiveness of contemporary black youth culture. However, where through the late 1960s and the 1970s this aesthetic yearned for freedom and justice, its trope in recent years is such that Gilroy envisages 'black conservatism'. This fact throws other black critics into disarray, leading some into defending questionable values. Gilroy acknowledges the difficulty, especially where there is some sort of ownership at stake, but he is also willing to confront the overt misogyny and the violence of much of hip hop culture. Of course it is marketed as such for white audiences and consumers across the world who also want to buy into transgression. Recognising that hip hop has replenished black music *per se*, and that it has given rise to many extraordinary new genres and sub-genres, his aim, however, is to ask, 'what's going on?'. Gilroy argues that the emancipatory politics previously encoded in a good deal of black expressive culture has been replaced by what he calls biopolitics of the black body. This emerges from a convergence of various strands, not least the growth of identity politics through the 1990s where the body is taken as a mark of self-identity and the body/mind duality is reinstated to the detriment of the mind which is now discounted. The earlier 'free your mind' sensibility of black music is disavowed and the very existence of a politics within this new realm of body perfection and wild sexual capacity is questionable and, claims Gilroy, for many other black critics, confusing and 'unspeakable'. Hip hop culture presents a massively redefined land-scape of black popular culture focusing on (heterosexual) sex, on the visual as much as the aural, on the interconnections not just with the sacred black church music of the past, but also with the very profane multimedia products made available by the global entertainment industry, in particu-lar violent video games and pornography. The glorification of guns and gangs is of course the hallmark of hip hop culture and it offers many pos-sibilities for moral panic (see Zylinska, 2005). Gilroy sidesteps this terrain and instead examines the depoliticising currents, for example, the way in which the street is no longer public space, only the space of drive-by vio-lence, and the family, once a metaphor for black solidarity, as in Sly Stone's 'It's a Family Affair', is now taken over by the rituals of sexual intimacy only, and there is also an insistent reconsolidation of gender norms (as Butler might put it). Even the death-drive, which in earlier musics (Al Green, for example) made manifest intense degrees of pain and suffering, has now given way to a normativity of death. Rap bespeaks a whole set of rituals whereby death is barely remarkable, where there is, as Gilroy hesi-tates to suggest, a kind of careless, indifferent 'postmodern' attitude to mortality. This can be seen in the endless invocation of motifs of mortality (Death Row records, lyrics which celebrate the rituals of the funeral and the whole iconography of death). This is largely a masculinist gangster par-adigm, where the female figure is the grieving mother or girlfriend, all of which reflects the decimation of the poor black community, in particular young males, thanks to AIDS, drugs, joblessness, imprisonment and gen-eral hopelessness. Gilroy's point is that these sounds and images are also subjectivising forces; they powerfully interpellate young audiences such that a whole chain of invidious values are constitutive of new codings of racial authenticity. How far is this from notions of 'racial uplift'? What has happened which has allowed the dream of a black public sphere for democracy and citizenship to be so brutally destroyed?

The music and the persona of Snoop Doggy Dogg allow Gilroy the opportunity to delve deeper into many of these themes. From the early and extraordinary track *187* (sound track for the film *Deep Cover*) to his best known album *Doggystyle*, Snoop exemplifies the distinctive combination of antiphonic song-style and the 'traditional chorus of sanctified voices' reminiscent of church, with transgressive desires, for money, for guns, status, for having sex 'doggystyle', for 'suicide, suicide, suicide' on the basis of not 'givin' a fuck'. The album is a cornucopia of stolen sounds and pop cultural references, including comic book obscenities, advertising jingles, gunshots, police car sirens, fighting blows, background party conversation, and everyday dialogue ('then she starts crying') which flows seamlessly into song, to produce something like a 'musical' or vernacular music theatre. But what about the dog? Is this 'virtue out of immiseration'? Gilroy is fascinated by the anthropomorphism; the dog persona permits a multiplicity of meanings. There is the bestial, transgressive, sex-obsessed 'snooping around' adolescent male dynamic, where 'radically alienated eroticism' has replaced the more spiritual and social 'sexual healing' of Marvyn Gaye. There is also a joky, celebratory self-debasement alongside cartoonish self-aggrandisement. If girls are all bitches, then Snoop is a big dog. But this becoming other-than-human leads Gilroy to reflect on other realms which are contrary to this inferno of boasting, bragging, badness. Nor just self-reflection on the low-down status of being-criminal, being in-jail, being poor, being addicted, being in-pain and so on, but also a radical attempt to be, if not quite dead, then at least out of the self, to be other than the racialised self, to being non-human, which in turn leads Gilroy via Levinas (with hints of Deleuze) to imagine the desire for a state of non-being, a subjectless space, where, prior to the self with all of its destructive needs and desires, there is a way of imagining being for the other, where goodness and sociality might prevail, where there is a glimmer of hope that 'lost humanity' might be 'restored' (Gilroy, 2000: 203). Gilroy goes so far as to quote Levinas' reference to the kind face of the dog in the context of the concentration camp, where, as an inmate, he had been stripped of his humanity. Gilroy is saying that this black pop cultural embracing of the dog deserves to be taken seriously philosophically rather than castigated and reviled or else merely defended as the voice of the black male underclass. The interesting thing, then, is that it is the music itself, its own autonomous force or power (in a Deleuzian sense) which offers some space of 'other than being'; it dissolves the self in the same way as drugs also do, and perhaps it is this which proposes, at a subliminal, Levinasian level, to the music makers, that is, Snoop, Dr Dre and the others, something of this possibility of goodness, salvation and solidarity (see also Venn, 2004). There is a de-subjectivising and 'co-emergent' capacity in music-making which numbs the pain and which is, as Gilroy earlier stated, 'a gift to the slaves'. This is, I think, what leads Gilroy to find an 'ethno-poetics' in Snoop Doggy Dogg. But at the same time this self-identification as dog also suggests that the neo-liberalised ghetto is a hell, a war zone, where all the things that money can (eventually) buy, are hardly compensations for the pain and misery of psychically impoverished black masculinity which has been tempted by, and then tainted by, the racialised biopolitics of neo-conservatism.

3

No Woman, No Cry? Judith Butler and the Politics of Post-feminist Cultural Studies

GUIDE TO THE CHAPTER

The effect of gender . . . must be understood as the mundane ways in which bodily gestures, movements, and styles of various kinds constitute the illusion of an abiding gendered self. (Butler, 1990: 179)

The production of texts can be one way of reconfiguring what will count as the world. (Butler, 1993: 19)

I never did think that gender was like clothes, or that clothes make the woman. (Butler, 1993: 231)

Mad about Boys?

This chapter will focus on three themes which can be traced right through the work of the American feminist philosopher Judith Butler, whose books *Gender Trouble* (1990) and *Bodies That Matter* (1993) are regularly cited as having had as big an impact on feminist thought as de Beauvoir's *The Second Sex* (Butler, 1990, 1993, 1999a; de Beauvoir, 1970). The *first* of these is the way in which Butler makes trouble for feminism, querying the existence of its foundations and interrogating its various claims. Her writing inaugurates and confirms a significant, indeed seismic shift, for feminism. There are other notable precursors of the move towards post-feminism, including those who like Butler query the self-evident quality of the category of woman (see Riley, 1988). But the appearance of *Gender Trouble* in 1990 nonetheless enacts – has the performative effect (to use Butler's own terms) – of bringing into being the disputatious troubling dynamic it announces by interrogating the stability and very existence of the category of woman which feminist politics has organised itself around. 'Who are "its" women'?, is the kind of question she asks. What kind of women does feminism have in mind, or institute for its politics to proceed?[1] And which women are in this process left out, excluded, or less immediately invoked by such a framing? Butler's work coincides (as she herself later describes) with a moment of breaking away from feminism by a younger generation of queer-oriented lesbians, for whom this sexual identity motivates a critique of the feminist politics of an older generation and also of existing lesbian and gay politics. But likewise, for younger feminist scholars, not necessarily lesbian, this work resonates because it offers a theoretical framework, influenced by Foucault, for reviewing the possibilities for political agency on the basis of an understanding of power as providing (and circumscribing) the terms for its own critique, and thus, for envisaging radical social change within these constraints. This too marks a shift from the previous generation for whom politics was directed towards a kind of grand revolutionary rupture, and, thus with a definitive move away from one power regime to another, though the consequences of taking power were rarely considered.[2]

For some critics, (for example McNay, 1999a) Butler's work suggests a narrower, perhaps individualistic politics. Others, including myself, have seen the politics of destabilising norms and deconstructing power by interrogating its foundations, more positively. This can be understood as a critical part of the process of extending radical democracy by continually examining the claims political groups, in this case feminism, make, in order to represent their subjects, in this case women. In addition this is a politics which is conceived of, in a post-structuralist move, as without either beginning or end, as dependent on no great truth narrative to drive it forward to some moment of grand finale, to the end-point of revolution, as though there was no politics beyond that magical point. The expansionist possibilities, wherein many different kinds of women can conceivably invent and revise different kinds of feminism and strive to maintain coalitional connections across their differences, suggests a means by which feminism continues to have an existence.

The *second* theme is the relation between Butler's writing on gender and the field of academic work described as 'feminist cultural studies'. If culture is relieved of those meanings which suggest a kind of delimited and recognisably unified set of practices (as in for example 'the culture of working-class girls'), and is instead understood as the sites of everyday life where power relations take normatively symbolic forms, then the practices which Butler describes as 're-signification', which for her mark the possibilities for radical critique, can be understood in these expansive terms, that is, as capable of operating and having effect right across the field of everyday life. Butler's post-structuralism propels her towards a range of discursive phenomena, the literary text, psychoanalytic texts, film, philosophical writing and, of course, feminist theory. This has been seen by her critics to indicate a turning away from what are understood to be larger political concerns, to those of language, images, even just words; in short, Butler has been accused of being at the forefront of the 'cultural turn'. While this criticism suggests a particular appropriation of 'the political' as always having primacy over the 'merely cultural', and being more closely connected with the various strong axes of power which in turn shape the kind of world we live in, and while this is surely a narrow and conventional account of the political, the question of how exactly re-signifying cultural practices work in a politically effective way must be continuously examined.

Thus my second theme is also that Butler's work is absolutely necessary to feminist media and cultural studies, that we cannot do without it. While this might seem unnecessary to state, given the extraordinary impact of Butler's work, there has actually been little sustained attempt to engage with this writing in relation to media or popular culture. Her work allows us to understand how, within popular culture, the 'heterosexual matrix' ('that grid of cultural intelligibility through which bodies, genders, and desires are naturalised' Butler 1999a: 194) retains its dominance. Butler's work allows us to navigate better the complex ways in which popular culture, in a post-feminist environment, where some degree of gender equality is nominally invoked and upheld, nonetheless works to reconsolidate gender norms. Whether in the context of successful television programmes like Channel Four's *Big Brother* (whose winner in the summer of 2004 was a transsexual called Nadia of Portugese origin), or in any number of other popular genres where the breaking of gender norms is a mark of the liberal underpinnings of the text, there are still invariably moves to differentiate between men and women in ultimately reassuring ways.[3] Indeed the complexity of the whole landscape of contemporary sexual popular culture where so many traditional assumptions are now routinely overturned, literally call out for an analysis informed by Butler's writing. It is far too easy to simply pin the label of postmodernism or post-feminism on the knowing, ironic style which characterises the now-mainstream iconography of popular pornography with its focus particularly on so-called 'girl on girl action', or on the inflated and 'hyperbolic femininity' of pin-up model Gisela Bunchen on the front cover of men's magazine *GQ* (August 2002). Therefore what motivates my own attention here in relation to this aspect of Butler's thinking is the extent to which popular culture continues to define and redefine the boundaries of gender, showing how much is still at stake in the marshalling of gender identities in terms of rigid difference even as those very differences are also being undermined so that the field of popular culture now comprises a to and fro movement between the doing and undoing of gender. This is also one of the key sources of fascination for, and hold over, the audience. Indeed the title of this section refers directly to a weekly magazine titled *Mad About Boys* which was launched for pre-pubescent girls in the UK in 2001. While a range of concerned commentators took issue with the encouragement of pre-adolescent sexual desire on the part of the target readers of the magazine (girls aged 7–10), no moral guardian or feminist contested the assumption of childhood heterosexuality. To the extent that this would be a much more shocking objection to make in the press or media, than to disapprove of precocious but reassuringly normal sexuality, justifies Butler's analysis of how exclusions are repeated across culture (in this case pre-teen popular culture) by announcement, in this case, that very young girls are to be understood as *Mad About Boys*.[4] My *third* theme in this chapter concerns Butler's engagement with psychoanalysis. This is so central to her work that any attempt to reconsider feminist media and cultural studies from the viewpoint of Butler's writing cannot avoid the distinctiveness and inventiveness of her reading of both Freud and Lacan.

Rewriting Feminism

The organisation of this chapter is as follows, first there is an account of Butler's remonstration with feminism, second there is an examination of her revision of psychoanalysis, and third I explore the theory of performativity in relation to popular culture. In a number of articles Butler challenges the claims about women which have been made by feminism including the means by which these are subsequently followed by demands or charters (Butler, 1990, 1992, 1993). On the basis of the assumption of shared oppression, there has been, over the years, for example, a call for unity, for women to come together, to forget their other differences and unite under a banner which allows feminism to represent them. (A current example of this might be the EU- and

UN-led programme for 'gender mainstreaming'). For feminism to claim
to represent women it has been necessary to bunch women together, to
identify them as sharing defining characteristics and in so doing to
ascribe to women such features in common. However, very often this
constitutive process is glossed over or concealed. Some feminists without
any hesitation claim to represent all women. This is apparent, for example, in the critique of pornography mounted by American feminist and
human rights scholar Catherine MacKinnon, when in fact she is positioning herself as self-appointed guardian of 'women' who are typecast
as victims unable to defend themselves against the violence of pornography. But as Butler (and also Brown, 1995) shows, not only is such
victimhood assumed, so also is the category of 'women' for whom
pornography is claimed to have this wholly aggressive function. There
are many women who feel no such unambivalent hostility to visual
imagery designed for sexual stimulation.

As a political movement and, thus, by virtue of being in some sense
in pursuit of the possession of representative power, feminism creates
its own subjects, it 'interpellates' (an Althusserian term) them into
being, hails them as 'women', when, for example, it makes claims on
the prevailing political system that 'women need free contraception
and abortion on demand'. And likewise, when feminism requests of its
subjects that they unite in the battle against universal patriarchy, then,
argues Butler, this category of universal patriarchy is mobilised as one
which can easily transcend cultural differences. In fact this is a particular strategy emanating from a specific political discourse seeking to
legitimate itself on a global basis (and seeking approval on the basis of
seeming to speak for dispossessed women across the world) without
necessarily considering the power relations (white western) which warrant its existence. Butler therefore posits feminism as a subjectivising
discourse, one which in repeating its claims is also able to bring into
being the women it seems merely to describe. But feminism also pri-
oritises certain claims and in so doing produces a ground or
foundation for itself. By this means feminism becomes identifiable,
and it marks out its own field of legitimate concerns. There is, for
example, an assumption of a stable category of women whose subordinate position within patriarchy will be attended to by feminism.
This gives rise to a hierarchy of demands (or charter) which as Butler
shows produce their own exclusions. Contraception, abortion and
easily available childcare are demands which assume a certain type of

female subject (heterosexual, a mother), but whose specific needs come to define what women *per se* need to achieve equality. Thus the woman who has no need of contraception or abortion by virtue of her lesbian desires finds herself not-quite-represented by such a charter. The same goes for the woman who is not a mother, or indeed the non-western (or non-white western) woman for whom contraception is a tool of the state which seeks to constrain her fertility on the basis of her ethnic status.

From the seemingly outside position from which such women speak, their disputatious claim to feminism, that it does not represent them despite its universalising statements, has an effect of breaking the foundations of feminism. But instead of seeing this as somehow the end of feminism, Butler argues it marks a point for opening up or renewing feminism so that it moves in another direction, so that having interrogated its grounding assumptions it becomes a non-foundational and endlessly revised political process. But what then of feminism's own exclusionary practice and the power it has to implement its own norms? For example, how central to feminism has the category of mother been? If it is agreed that a good deal of earlier feminist work was given over to the politics of mothering, to the point that being a mother can in some ways mark a shared set of interests which are closely connected with feminism, for example, maternity leave, childcare provision, the household labour of bringing up children, the transmission of feminist values to daughters and sons, economic dependence through marriage or economic hardship through single parenthood and so on, then the dominance of this aspect of feminism must surely be construed to non-mothers as in some way not 'meant for them' or worse, normative. That is, that the woman is not a real woman, as feminism would have it, until she is a mother; or that feminism does not apply to women without children. The impact of this expulsion from the ranks of the real women who are the true subject of feminism will vary, from those heterosexual feminists now in their forties or fifties who chose not to have children, to lesbian women who chose likewise, to the partners of lesbian women who have had children but who remain officially undesignated, and whose parental rights are minimal (does feminism legitimate their claims as lesbian non-birth mothers?), to the younger women now in their twenties and thirties who are not having children (Franks, 1999). Interviewed in 1994, Butler talked about the normative power invoked around the reproductive capacities of women in this age range, so that those who for whatever reason do not give birth carry an 'implicit sense of failure or inadequacy'; without the support of a 'pretty vigorous (and politically informed) community' there is a sense of 'failure, or loss, or impoverishment' (Butler, 1994: 34).

Feminism must therefore be more than just for mothers. Butler refers to the need for a 'community' of women (and community remains an anchor for politics in her otherwise disaggregating vocabulary) to dispute the centrality of motherhood in feminism's political agenda. Just as she wants to stretch the definitions of what it is to be a woman so that it embraces a much wider set of possibilities and potentialities than has hitherto been allowed, so also must feminism be opened up in this way. The implicit hierarchy of feminist political demands is in itself a strategy of power, a practice of representation of the few in the name of the many or indeed of all women in the name of universal womanhood. As Butler in *Gender Trouble* describes the power embedded in this process of constructing a feminist politics, so is it more possible to contest this feminist hegemony. Butler is in part undoing the imbalance which in the past disadvantaged lesbian feminist politics in favour of heterosexual issues (though this doesn't mean she leaves the category lesbian untouched, it too needs to be destabilised). To say this is to repeat Elizabeth Grosz's comment that within feminism, lesbian interests have been 'a local subcategory' (Grosz, 1997: 157).

But let me at this point raise a more sociological question. What happens if this normatively stabilised universe of heterosexual young women giving birth, leaving others languishing in the cloud of abjection which accrues from failure to respond to the dominant norm of reproduction, has quite quickly, in western countries (and also Japan), been transformed into a much less homogenous field through the refusal (itself a complex response to wider social factors and governmental pressures) to become a mother? (See Franks, 1999; McRobbie forthcoming.) What also happens when the conditions of heterosexuality for young women undergo some degree of transformation in that there is a loosening up in regard to the degree that it is still compulsory? That is, where (in western metropolitan culture) being lesbian no longer carries the same weight of social disapproval? Of course we would need to examine the processes of liberalisation within the still very dominant 'heterosexual matrix' as commented above in relation to the magazine *Mad About Boys*. We might even argue that through this liberalising process, through this sense of freedom now routinely made available to young women (with feminism duly taken into account as having played a role) so indeed are new modalities of constraint brought into being (McRobbie, 2004). The heterosexual matrix is loosened up, it loses its coercive, compulsory force, it allows degrees of choice, it permits experimentation, it encourages freedom, but perhaps all the more insidiously, to redraft the boundaries of power through a process of seeming matrix relaxation. There is also something of a reversal of hierarchies in feminism *after* Butler, with a good deal of energy and momentum emerging from a younger generation of lesbian feminists. There is a point at which queer politics gains high visibility around a specific set of demands pursued through sophisticated, spectacular, media-defined strategies. There is also a peculiar overlapping movement of repudiation of feminism in the broader culture, but there is less overt homophobia; indeed in the lifestyle supplements there is a celebration of gay and lesbian culture including marriage ceremonies. On television there are a range of new gay-oriented and highly successful programmes and there is also recognition of gay and lesbian rights at a political level (evident within New Labour). Yet at the very same time, there are still regular derogatory projections in regard to lesbian identity within the remit of the liberal media and often from the position of young heterosexual women whose statements of animosity betray heightened anxiety including fear and revulsion.[5] To sum up, the relations between heterosexual culture and gay and lesbian culture are subject to redefinition and redrafting within the terms of increasing liberalisation and recognition and also within the framework of highly sexualised consumer culture. The heterosexual matrix now exacts its dominance by more subtle means.

There is a sense in which, in and during the 1990s, Butler is writing along this axis of change. Her two books mark a moment of transformation, and for the left and for 1970s feminism, a sharp sense of loss and failure. If in the past feminism has had this special address to mothers, what role is left for it when so many younger women stop, or postpone until much later in the lifecycle, having children? If that whole lifetime of maternal work is omitted from the lifecycle of women, is feminism itself radically redefined, if indeed it survives as a political force? (There are of course the older feminists who argue that feminism is merely suspended until that point at which the younger women do have children, but this is often censorious, and it also presumes a claim to an essentialist feminism based on maternity.) Feminism is thus being radically reconfigured at that point at which Butler's writing, influenced as it is by Foucault, gains wide recognition. This marks Butler as a figure whose work can be drawn on by the earlier generation whose political thinking was heavily influenced by Marxism and psychoanalysis, and equally by the younger women, more interested in theory, more concerned with the micropolitics of power than with the monolithic struggles around class, race and gender which marked out the concerns of their predecessors, and much less constrained by the assumptions of heterosexual normativity. Butler's work provides a means of instituting a feminist politics which works in and through processes of splitting off, breaking up, dissolving and endlessly disputing. It provides a radical democratic template for feminism 'after the second wave', after Marxism and at what Butler calls the 'juncture of cultural politics, a period that some would call post-feminist' (Butler, 1990: 5). As Butler herself has emphasised, her critique of feminism does not invalidate the range of its claims, nor does it represent a kind of negation of its various efforts, instead she sees the interrogation of feminism as a means of retaining an openness, ensuring that feminism does not become fixed, closed or inattentive to its own regulative capacity.

Revising Psychoanalysis 1

Why psychoanalysis and feminism? Especially when psychoanalysis seems to belong historically to a generation of feminist scholars who were primarily concerned with the psychic processes which compelled women to take up positions within patriarchy, rather than within the assumption of heterosexuality? Psychoanalysis retains a constant place in Butler's thinking, she returns to it incessantly, partly because of course its focus is so directly on gender positions, on desire and the role of the unconscious. Juliet Mitchell read Freud for his account of male and female sexuality and consequently for his understanding of sexual difference, and Rose, in her feminist reading of Freud and Lacan, argued that the correct gender identity was not simply arrived at, but its instability and precariousness revealed itself in how it continually showed signs of failing (Mitchell, 1984; Rose, 1987). It is because of this threatened failure that in culture there are so many repeated, end-less invocations to the subject to take up the right gender identity. Butler revises psychoanalysis in its Freudian and Lacanian versions for its assumption of a primary taboo against homosexuality, so primary it remains virtually unacknowledged by all of those in this psychoanalytic tradition. There are two areas where Butler produces truly radical claims through her re-reading of psychoanalysis. First, as I show in this section, there is her critique of Freud's account of bisexuality and the dispositions which lead to the taking up of male and female identities, and second there is (as described in the section that follows) her challenge to Lacan for whom the entrance of the child into language and culture and hence into the sphere of intelligibility requires gender-specific positioning in regard to the Law, (or the Symbolic), which for him marks the threshold of the social. Failure to proceed in this way results in psychosis.

Underpinning both of these are the universal status and nature of the Oedipus complex and the incest taboo, and the way in which they provide a kind of portal into forms of life including kinship which are viable, which can somehow proceed, which carry juridical weight. Butler challenges Freud's account of gender identity by arguing that consolidated gender ideals carry within them (or rather inscribed on the body) 'the figure of the lost object of same-sex love whose preserved presence as such casts a melancholic shadow on its bearer'. Thus there is no more evocative heterosexual figure than the adamantly 'straight' man or woman whose carefully crafted, indeed impeccable masculin-ity or femininity, bespeaks the attachment which has been abandoned as impossible. Homosexuality is a taboo which precedes incest, its pri-mary repression ensures, however, that it retains a critical presence wherever heterosexuality is compelled. It calls into question the con-straints on desire required by the taking up of normative gender positions, and it thus reveals itself as a capacity for love which refutes the prescribed pathways. The radical claim is therefore to re-institute homosexuality, not as other than heterosexuality but as a capacity which is repressed for culture to proceed. This is a theme which con-tinues through Butler's writing, that is, the proximity of homosexuality to heterosexuality.

The second feature of Butler's critique is addressed to Lacan's notion of the phallus (the horizon of power) which male identified persons are understood as having and female as being. If the phallus is patriarchal power (or the Symbolic) and if having it is predicated on inevitable failure (in that the penis is inevitably a lesser thing than the phallus, just as the Law is beyond and more than those individuals who constitute its field of power), while being it fulfils merely the function of defining for men that which they are not, then Butler re-articulates the phallus, wrestles it away from the male subjects who have it, and as a signifier of power takes it up as the lesbian phallus, which, in possession of, in turn allows her to mount a challenge to the Symbolic for its injunctions which are such that sexual difference is a requirement for leading an intelligible life. The means by which Butler participates in this struggle is through her re-reading and revision of this particular and highly influential psychoanalytical paradigm. She argues that those who cannot be accounted for along the rigid lines of gender are rendered unintelligible, or abject, but given that this sorry state is exactly what needs to be so defined in order that normativity is achieved, these abject persons retain a haunting presence (or proximity) within the field of sexuality. Once again they are written into, through this disavowal, the language of normality. The term queer, which might be seen as such a designation, can as Butler shows, be made to re-articulate the conditions of abjection and challenge, as she herself does with great vigour, the processes of power which produce the heterosexual matrix.

But let me rewind for a moment and go back now to the taboo against homosexuality. A key part of *Gender Trouble* is the engagement with Freud's account of bisexuality. It is not surprising that this is of such interest as it is where Freud signals that heterosexuality is achieved, worked towards and then consolidated rather than simply being inherent. Following Levi Strauss it is assumed that the incest taboo and exogamous heterosexuality are cultural requirements; women are exchanged outside the family, homosocial bonds between men are built upon this structure and kinship becomes viable. Likewise the Oedipus complex ensures that under threat of castration the boy gives up his mother as an object of desire, while the girl resolves her penis envy and desire for the father by aspiring towards eventual femininity and maternity. But Freud's understanding of bisexuality, argues Butler, has already assumed the taboo against homosexuality, so that the dispositions which he describes are in fact two heterosexual dispositions within the one person. The masculine within the girl loves the mother, the feminine disposition, the father. Thus in Freud's account 'only opposites attract'. This is like saying that before the taboo there are many possibilities for love and desire which are then directed by prohibition towards certain zones of the body which are given legitimate sexual status to ensure heterosexual reproduction ('Pleasure is both determined and prohibited through the compulsory effects of the gender differenciated law' Butler, 1990: 87). This prohibition must also produce homosexual desire as a thing in order for it then to be repressed, thus 'the unthinkable is fully within culture but excluded from dominant culture'.

But if the prohibitions which repress homosexual desire also continually bring it into being or remind us of it, all the more they forbid it, then it has a twilight existence in and around the psyche; thus the law 'creates space for the preservation of the love'. The effect according to Butler is gender melancholia and the more full and proper masculinity or femininity is aspired to, the more apparent is the noted loss of the improper desire. The lost object then comes to be installed in or on the body. Thus fully endorsed femininity, of the sort found all the time on the pages of the glossy magazines, where models affect as a normative style, self absorption, aloof disdain, indeed a kind of turning away from the male gaze (camera/viewer) in preference for a seemingly fixated or fetishistic attachment to the repertoire of the wardrobe, demonstrates exactly an excessive, overriding and erotic attachment to the same-sex object which has been lost as a condition of being 'intelligible' within the culture. The lost object is thus preserved, incorporated and takes on an existence as heightened, or intensified fashion/femininity. 'The refusal of loss encrypts itself on the body' (Butler, 1999a: 87). The object of lost love retains a separate existence in the form of melancholia, internalisation and display. Fashion performs a double function: for the sake of gender normativity its official (and commercial) role is to propel girls and women in the direction of appropriate positions within the heterosexual matrix; at the same time, it is always an erotic reminder of the 'perfect woman'.

The film *Desperately Seeking Susan* (1984, dir. Susan Seidelman) provides a vivid portrayal of gender melancholia. Roberta (played by Rosanna Arquette) is a young suburban housewife whose husband has a sexual encounter with Susan (played by Madonna). Roberta's uptight, well-groomed and housewifely fashion image is in sharp contrast to Susan's makeshift, second hand, urban-bohemian style. Roberta is smitten by the image of Susan. Her own life suddenly seems dull, mundane and superficial. Her marriage is a sham, and her husband, whose infidelity initiates the narrative, is no longer important. It is not that she falls in love with Susan (this is not, after all, a lesbian film) but that the sense of 'loss' she feels can only be interpreted in terms of her becoming infatuated by the image of Susan. A good deal of the film comprises Roberta following Susan about Manhattan, sneaking glimpses of her, and spying on her lifestyle. Soon she is buying the same kind of vintage clothes, and by a certain point in the film her own style is totally transformed and she has become a Susan lookalike, in an acceptably subcultural, rather than a pathologically mimetic way. Thus Roberta has Susan's style encrypted on her own body, this makes her available for friendship with Susan, and the narrative eventually resolves with Roberta pairing up with Susan's boyfriend's best friend. Overshadowing the comic and mystery narrative elements of the film is a meta-narrative of female visual pleasure. This comprises a panorama of cityscape, fashion, the body and subculture. Subculture is both a repository for and a displacement of same-sex desire, while it also embodies a realm of bodily pleasures (clubbing, dance, music) which stand in sharp contrast with the tedium of heterosexual marriage. The film is full of such displacements, which are successfully narrativised as 'a comedy–mystery genre starring Madonna' and these in turn account for its great success especially among teenage girls. The film touches upon moments of sexual ambivalence in female adolescence which must then be transformed into recognisable heterosexual patterns so that normal life can proceed. The means by which this is realised, however, entails loss, melancholic attachment to particular fashion or subcultural items as well as excessive investment in female friendship (see Extended Notes at the end of the chapter).

To sum up, what Freud (albeit with some degree of hesitation, as Butler notes) assumes are primary dispositions, are, in fact, already the effects of a prior prohibition.[6] This is not the same as saying that homosexual love is itself foundational or primary, rather that the prohibition which compels heterosexuality for reproduction brings into being an organisation of sexuality which foregrounds and legitimates a range of pleasures and forbids others. But those forbidden others have an existence in order to confirm the legitimate desires and this creates a kind of troubling presence. This is where Butler's response to Freud echoes Foucault. Instead of there being distinct bodies and distinct sexes, there are practices and institutions and regulations which in speaking sex as this rather than that, bring into being what is to be deemed intelligible and what is not. Sex is thus an organisational category orchestrating the body along certain lines. 'If sexuality and power are coextensive, and if lesbian sexuality is no more and no less constructed than other modes of sexuality, then there is no promise of limitless pleasure after the shackles of the category of sex have been thrown off' (Butler, 1990: 124).

Revising Psychoanalysis 2

Utilising elements of Derrida's idea of the signifier always being haunted by other (in this case sexually transgressive) meanings, and also drawing on Foucault's notion of the productivity of power, Butler challenges Lacan's positing of the phallus as irrefutable, an origin which guards entrance to the properly marked body and sexual identity. If the phallus is also haunted by that which it seeks to exclude, if it is after all precarious too, then Butler boldly prises it away from the clutches of men, and uses it re-signify other possible meanings. Let me very briefly and at risk of generalisation recap on a theory which to those unfamiliar with Lacan can seem quite opaque. Lacan seems to be saying we are all subjectivised through language, only with this can a sense of an 'I' emerge (even though the fullness of the 'I' is an illusion). But the acquisition of this requires a passage through the Symbolic. This insists that we give up unruly or disorderly Oedipal desires, and as we do so we become subjects who are thus instituted through that very loss. We are always somehow lacking something and therefore seeking out or desiring that which we imagine will make us feel complete, whole. The Symbolic inaugurates culture and kinship, its power is irrefutable, and failure to proceed through this passage results only in psychosis; that is, we do not become properly human. The phallus is the mark of power and the site of law, its importance far outstrips that of the penis which men have, while what they aspire to is having the phallus. Women in turn with their phallic bodies, that is, the whole outline of the feminine physiology, and with their penis envy, are the phallus, they are what men want and they in turn must constantly make themselves into being what men want.

The phallus is, then, a symbol which guards the rules of kinship and heterosexuality, making sure these rules are adhered to. But it is also a 'transferable phantasm' and Butler seeks to lift this symbol-phallus away from its pre-eminent male domain. She 're-territorialises' it, and in so doing she blurs the boundaries between being and having it, and she in effect wields her own lesbian phallus by virtue of removing it from its elevated position at the very threshold of meaning and power. This energetic taking up is also one logic of the 'doing' of performative sex. If Lacan can only envisage the taking up of female power within the confines of the terrifying, devouring 'phallic mother', it is as though Butler is saying 'to hell with this, I shall take it up myself and challenge him at the very core of his thinking'. In this respect she goes where few feminist psychoanalytic scholars dare to tread, so respectful are they of the Lacanian Symbolic, and so fearful of psychosis. Osborne and Segal ask Butler, can the taking up of the phallus also be carried out by heterosexual non-mothers? (Butler, 1994) And could we not here add to this (and I am aware of the liberty I am taking), is it currently being taken up by 'devouring' young women of the sort seen swaggering on the streets of the UK, dressed according to the fashionable codes of a hardened, impermeable, tough 'hyperbolic femininity', drinking in excess, and leering at, as well as lusting after, men? Can there be 'phallic girls'? Butler's answer to her interviewers' question is, 'That's the question. What would it mean to separate the heterosexual woman who has the phallus from the phallic mother? It's an important thing to do' (Butler, 1994: 37). Perhaps an important thing to do at a sociological level might be to interrogate the complexities of aggressively confident young women and the anomalies of post-feminist identity (that is, in a context where some feminist gains have been achieved) and where young women are seen to be in possession of power. There is 'distance from feminism' as these young women prefer to emulate aspects of normative masculine behaviour while dressing themselves up in an exaggerated femininity which mockingly draws attention to its carefully crafted perfection, to the point that it too becomes a kind of drag.

The image of the 'ladette' is of a girl for whom gender equality with men is assumed, she literally takes or appropriates his public freedoms and thus partakes in bouts of heavy drinking, goes to lap dancing clubs, and pursues her sexual desires as she pleases. But this agency is not free-formed or voluntaristic, but is instead indirectly and with complexity and ambivalence a constituted and normative 'post-feminist subjectivity'. Insofar as some of feminism's claims for its women and

young women became entangled over the years with the routine practices of dominant culture (popular feminism), this then becomes also a
site for the assumption of gender equality recast to conform with the
requirements of a now increasingly neo-liberal popular culture. In such
an environment there is little if any need for a renewed feminist politics.
On the other hand these 'phallic girls' with their shiny, groomed, well-
toned, hard and muscular bodies, can be understood as 'having taken
hold of a symbol of male power'. This is close to Butler's idea that
power operates by also circumscribing the means by which it can be
countered. They have prised something of what has constrained them
and are able to act within the confines which this over-arching power
makes available for them. The phallic girl is also the ruthless television
blonde (as in the 1989 film *To Die For* directed by Gus Van Sant), she is
competitive, individualistic, and sexually devouring (like Samantha in
Sex and the City). Butler thus opens up the Symbolic to historicisation and
contingency; her own manoeuvring inside power, her willingness to take
up the phallus (thus undoing the very terms which compel appropriate
gender identity) provides exactly the kind of vocabulary needed for
understanding how changes, as reiterative practices, are so within power
and thus prey to further and immediate reconsolidation along normative
lines. The value of this is that it shows the complexity and trauma of
change in the field of sexual difference. Such anxiety around gender re-
signification and the extent to which it can possibly spiral out of control,
is what propels the proliferation and constant production of new forms
of popular culture where what is at stake is the need to pin down and
regain control of gender assignation and normative heterosexuality
even as it is now more visibly haunted by other possibilities.

Theory of Performativity

Performativity is Butler's best know concept, there are so many accounts
of her rendition of the performative that it has achieved great prominence inside and outside the academy. The great misperception is that
it suggests a kind of voluntarism and unconstrained agency, as though,
if gender is an enactment, a crafting on or stylisation of the body
according to certain conventions, then gender is also a kind of choice, so
that social transformation of gender relations would rest on a simple act
of self re-designation. As Campbell and Harbord point out, the note of

optimism at the end of *Gender Trouble* has given rise to simplistic and celebratory readings based on an understanding of Butler's theory as 'a
somewhat simple and willed act of cross dressing. If we don't like or
want to be one identity we can perform and act another' (Campbell and
Harbord, 1999: 231). Butler is dismayed that her complex arguments
have been reduced to this kind of banality. She makes strenuous efforts
to clarify that she is saying almost the complete opposite of this and that
the performativity of gender is a process of coercion, a forceful shaping
of the body along the narrow constraints of gender difference. What the
need for these subsequent clarifications reveals is the fine line in Butler's
work between the analysis of gender regulation and the possibilities for
change within and issuing from those regulative practices.

   Butler points to two main influences which helped her formulate the
theory of performativity. First Derrida's recounting of a story by Kafka
('Before the Law') where the power of authority somehow, on and
through the body of the person, precedes the force of authority, a situation which we might describe as 'outside the headmistress's office' or, as
Butler puts it, 'where the one who waits for the law, sits before the door
of the law, attributes a certain force to the law for which one waits'
(Butler, 1999a: xiv). And as she continues, 'the anticipation conjures its
object', and by this means power is 'installed' (ibid.: xiv). The second
source is the linguist Austin who described as illocutionary acts, those
announcements which performing what is being said, bring this new
state into being, for example, when the priest utters 'I baptise thee Marie
Louise . . . in the name of the father . . .'. There are others to whom
Butler also turns, particularly Althusser (himself influenced by Lacan's
critique of the subject as a fully formed 'I'), whose theory of ideology
rests on the process of interpellation, where the subject-space is produced as she or he is hailed as such. This theory was, of course,
enormously influential in cultural studies and it is in Butler's repeated
recourse to Althussser that her relation to cultural studies is most apparent. Interpellation was a key concept for a good deal of the early work
from the Birmingham Centre for Contemporary Cultural Studies.
There too was a critique of the pre-existing and fully formed 'I', and
there was a deep interest in how ideology was a subject-producing practice. Interpellation was used extensively in the analysis of media forms,
including women's and girls' magazines which were understood as
bringing their subjects or readers into being by hailing them through a
very direct mode of address. This was often manifest in the title of the

magazine – for example, *Jackie*, *19*, or *Just Seventeen* – as though to say 'hey you out there, in catching your attention by means of this name "Jackie", you are being instituted as a "Jackie girl", your identity is constituted by this weekly mode of address' (McRobbie, 2000a). However, it is a point worth making here that cultural studies (with the exception of Hall) subsequently failed to follow up the psychoanalytical underpinning of subject formation, nor did it fully engage with Foucault's notion of subjectivisation until a much later stage. That spectrum of interest in (feminist) cultural and media studies which runs from texts to youth culture and audiences has been lacking in sustained engagement with theories of the subject in favour of more sociological accounts of active audiences or subcultural resistance and this absence in turn accounts for a tendency to generalisation and lack of attention to the micrological interfaces between text and subject.

Performativity is utilised by Butler as a repetitive, processual, happening activity which brings into being that which it seems merely to describe. Thus, far from sex being a state of nature, an anatomical reality onto which gender is drafted (which was for a long time how feminist scholars influenced by de Beauvoir understood the taking up of masculine and feminine positions) sex is discursive, it too is cultural, it is brought into being by the convergence of any number of officiating discourses which pronounce on the birth of a child, as Butler reminds us, 'It's a girl', and in so doing the process of being 'girled' is initiated and will be continued in the passage of the person through any number of institutions throughout life. Thus the naturalisation of being and the designation of being male or female is in fact the result of a 'laborious process'. Butler's account of gender as a regulatory fiction is by now familiar, and has been thoroughly explicated by various writers. Salih for example reminds us that Butler argues that 'gender is not a noun (but it) proves to be performative, that is, constituting the identity it is purported to be. In this sense gender is always a doing, though not a doing by the subject who might be said to pre exist the deed' (Butler, 1990: 25, quoted by Salih, 2002: 50). Likewise there have been any number of discussions of Butler's account of drag. Her attention to drag is based on the way in which it dramatises the 'cultural mechanisms of fabricated unity', demonstrating 'gender's incredible'. As Lloyd explains, Butler's account of drag shows how 'there is no original from which gay, lesbian, transvestite subjects deviate; the original is itself a mythical figuration' (Lloyd, 1999: 198).

There is anxiety on Butler's part in case her work be wrongly associated with what she sees as the voluntarism or anti-theoreticism in cultural studies (though she exonerates Hall from this charge; Butler, 1999a). She is extremely wary of that work in cultural studies which is often seen as departing from a concern with constraint, and with regulation and with the perpetuation of injustices, on the basis that groups and individuals increasingly show a capacity to resist or subvert aspects of dominant culture. As any number of critics have pointed out this celebratory dynamic adumbrates the need for complex understanding of power by suggesting it can be too easily opposed, countered or thrown off by so-called active agents. This approach also often seems to see resistance everywhere, with the effect that the need for sustained oppositional politics recedes. (Included in this category would be the kind of work which, for example, romanticises youth subcultures.) I have caricatured, already and for the sake of brevity, this long and often not unreasonable series of accusations against strands in cultural studies. Indeed it is one thing to counter the pessimism and rigidity of Adorno's idea of the passive cultural dupes who are so easily manipulated by advertising and forms of mass culture, with an analysis of the active capacity to produce under circumstances of extreme hardship and constraint cultural forms (music, style, ritual) which embody dynamics of protest and affirmation, as Gilroy's 'black expressive culture' does. It is quite something else to posit a kind of free-floating freedom and agency on the part of consumers of mass culture to construct their own 'subversive readings' and thus undermine the power of the media. This kind of argument which sees cultural agency as evidence that power relations are less secure than might be imagined often coincides with a depoliticising current which refuses the effectivity of power and authority.

Butler insists on the absence of an 'I' who might 'do' or 'can do' gender in a subversive way. Any indicator of an 'active agent' is antipathetic to her entire analysis. She does argue however that the 'iterability' of performativity' is a 'theory of agency' but without, of course, an agent. There is no stable subject in this sense, nor can there be one. Butler must therefore draw a hard line between the dynamic in cultural studies which suggested a subversive capacity by agents on the basis of reworking or renegotiating received dominant meanings, and her own work. This allows for a very different, much more theorised, psychoanalytically informed, and also more narrow, 'entrapped' and more rigorously delineated possibility for re-signification, or re-articulation. The danger is in envisaging a too easy capacity to transform existing structures of meaning and signification, and given Butler's emphasis on pain and on the injuries routinely and repetitively dealt to those who remain outside of the grid of normative sexuality, there is indeed some degree of panic that she be understood as arguing that gender is a matter of choosing what to wear (or what not to wear). Butler adamantly wants to part company with those who endorse the exis-tence of individual agents, endowed with some capacity to bring about change in the gender system, as this is to ignore the way in which the effects of power define the contours of possibility for opposition or transgression. I would suggest that this anxiety on Butler's part, that she might be associated with a too easy model of radical change, is based on her understanding of how profound, embedded, entrenched, and absorbed through time are the normative dimensions of stable gender identities in the name of the reproduction of heterosexuality as a foun-dation of the social order. And so deep is the repudiation of gender instability as a possibility (as is apparent in 'throw away' and joky non-politically correct anti-lesbian comments by post-feminist journalists like that described in note 5), that momentary or fleeting transgressions or even organised social movements which seek to defy these regulative effects, must be understood also in terms of how the dominant order constrains such 'reiterations' and provides the conditions of existence for evasions or displacements so that hegemonic normativity is renewed, indeed revitalised, by such enactments. However, the glimmer of hope-fulness in the final pages of *Gender Trouble* ought not to be understood as retracted at a later stage, at the very least within certain historical con-texts, cultural and subcultural forms can be sites for the production of re-articulated meanings. More recently Butler revisits this terrain resist-ing once again any sense of ease with which style, ritual and subculture can be understood as mechanisms of subversion, while at the same time posing the question, '(H)ow do we read the agency of the subject when its demand for cultural and political and psychic survival makes itself known as style? What sorts of style signal the crisis of survival?' (Butler, 2000a: 36).[7]

Are we spoken into our gender and our bodies? In *Bodies That Matter* Butler confronts her feminist critics who insist on the substance of the body, on the indisputable reality of menstruation, menopause, child-birth, on the intransigent lumpiness which reminds us of our sex. She says being so reminded is a linguistic event, 'one might say that going to the gynaecologist is the very production of sex' (Butler, 1994: 33). The performativity introduced in *Gender Trouble*, takes on, in *Bodies That Matter*, a much more coercive function, 'Sex is the regulatory ideal whose materialisation is compelled' (Butler, 1993: 9). The term reiteration is used to describe the repetitive dynamic which ensures the correct designation in the production of bodies. Thus performativity becomes the reiterative power of discourse to bring into being what it names, granting sexed bodies a kind of license to live, so that to be an 'I' is to have a sex. Only by recognising oneself as a girl and taking up the space of designation as girl, can a culturally intelligible speaking subject emerge. 'The matrix of gender relations is prior to the emergence of the human' (Butler, 1993: 7). But power is not a single mechanism, rather it is 'reiterated acting' which proceeds with 'persistence and instability'.

Thus we see the revision of performativity so that it becomes a series of practices which mark bodies according to a grid of intelligibility in such a way that the body itself becomes a familiar fiction; it becomes known, a formal entity on the basis that other characteristics and possibilities are negated. But these other characteristics cannot be definitively eradicated, precisely because they both produce and replenish what is to be legitimated and what gains social recognition and approval. The abject is critical to these defining practices and is also forever being pushed away, out of sight. 'To identify with a sex is to stand in some relation to an imaginary threat' (Butler, 1993: 100). Thus gayness is all around straightness, which forces the Law to produce as spectres of horror the 'phallic dyke' or the 'feminised fag'. Performativity in this context comprises the continuous ongoing processes of boundary marking and rigid demarcation which because of this proximity, because heterosexuality and homosexuality are forever in bed with each other, intertwined, makes the task for the Law all the more daunting. To bring this lengthy discussion of gender normativity to a conclusion, I would like to suggest that, among the many aspects of Butler's work, there is one dynamic which points to the need for a revision of the study of gender and sexuality in feminist media and cultural studies. This would require a more robust theorisation in regard to subjectivity, and also better use of psychoanalysis. Butler's psychoanalytic writing, and her account of the injuries wrought by the heterosexual matrix, also have a particular and still under-developed address to young women, since the process of being girled remains at the core of her concerns. 'Being called a "girl" from the inception of existence is a way in which the girl becomes transitively "girled" over time' (Butler, 1999b: 120).

Notes

1   Feminist scholars indeed might be seen as bringing into being the categories of 'women' needed to sustain the emergent field, for example, 'ordinary women' or 'the housewife'.

2   Laclau and Mouffe (1985) and Laclau (1990) offer the most developed post-structuralist critique of Marxist teleology in relation to 'revolution' which they re-define as a 'transcendental signifier'.

3   Programmes like *Big Brother* fixated as they are on bodies, gender, and sexuality under surveillance of the cameras, positively call out for the attention of young scholars. The most recent (and again hugely successful in terms of ratings) series, incorporated the fact that Nadia's transsexual status remained unknown to the inmates, while of course the audience was fully aware of this fact. The dynamics of knowing and not-knowing provide a useful axis for revisiting the terrain of 'passing'.

4   *Mad About Boys* in fact only lasted for a few months. However, the idea of persuading pre-pubescent girls as young as 7–10 in the direction of boys, in particular boy bands, gives other magazines new opportunities. A similar process of aggressively marketing childhood heterosexualisation can also be seen in the marketing, by fashion retailers Next, of a T-shirt for girl toddlers, aged two to three, carrying the words 'So Many Boys . . . So Little Time'. This shows the percolation of currently high fashion sexually bold and ironic T-shirt logos for young women, for example, 'Fuck Me I'm Famous', or 'Porn Queen', down to the level of baby girls still in nappies, and not surprisingly gives rise to condemnation by various moral guardians as well as complaints from parents.

5   A clear example of the abject status of the lesbian and the liberal repudiation of gay sexuality is by post-feminist *Guardian* columnist Shane Watson who, writing about the success of the cheap fashion store Topshop comments quite gratuitously, 'crediting the under-19s with the Topshop explosion is a bit like believing all lesbians look like the (beautiful) ones they assembled for Channel Four's The Truth About Lesbian Sex' (Watson, 2002 *Guardian* G2: 5).

6   As Butler says of Freud on his uncertainty about bisexuality 'At least he throws up his hands in the air' (Butler, 1994: 11).

7   This quotation comes from an article written by Butler in a volume dedicated to the work of Stuart Hall and the article itself draws on the subcultural analysis of Hall (and Hebdige) to reconsider style and ritual within what is pejoratively described by Zizek as a 'homosexual . . . universe' (Butler, 2000; Hall et al., 1976b; Hebdige, 1978).

Extended Notes

THIRTEEN . . . A Precarious State of Becoming

The final sentences of the chapter above on the work of Judith Butler suggest a theme running right through her work, which is that of being 'girled'. In fact it has a shadow existence in her three main books on gender, sexuality, and power: *Gender Trouble* (1990, 1999a), *Bodies That Matter* (1993), and *Antigone's Claim* (2000c). For example, in *Gender Trouble* she revisits the narrative of Herculin Barbin the so-called hermaphrodite whose life was protected and safe as long as she remained within an all-female school environment, but was cruelly exposed once she came to the attention of doctors, lawyers and experts. And in *Antigone's Claim* Butler re-examines Antigone's courageous act and the cost she must pay for her defiance (see Further Materials I). One senses that there is a good deal more work to be done on 'girling' practices in the light of, and in response to, Butler. What follows is a review of the recent film *Thirteen* (2003) where this kind of convergence of Butler's academic interests with my own, is, I think, very apparent. *Thirteen* is a film made in a very short time (26 days shooting in and around Los Angeles), on a small budget, by a first-time director (former set designer Christine Hardwicke). The sheer intensity of the narrative and the visceral portrayal of emotional chaos on the part of the 13-year-old girl at its centre (played by Evan Rachel Wood), mark it out as exceptional. *Thirteen* is an achievement which far surpasses films trading on rawness and edginess and claiming to have special insight into contemporary teenage malaise. Larry Clark's infamous *Kids* (1993) is the obvious comparison in that like Hardwicke, Clark has gained the trust of the young people he films and he too constructs his scripts from their everyday talk and adopts a naturalistic film style to gain a seemingly insider view. But what is quite different in *Thirteen* is the determinedly non-voyeuristic 'adult gaze' on the part of the director. Instead there is a much stronger, indeed frantic and compassionate identification with both the teenage Tracey and with what she is going through, and also with her hard-working mother (played by Holly Hunter) who sees how, for her daughter, the processes of growing up push her to the brink, towards a familiar but nonetheless terrifying kind of madness.

This film is able to move beyond the more usual cinematic explorations of adolescent identity and crisis through making brilliantly good use of two quite simple devices. First there is the style of film-making which is frenetic, breathtaking, compressed and with sometimes collage-effect scenes, rapid shots (many of which were apparently filmed in one go), and shaky hand-held camera angles. This fast cutting is combined with a fragmented soundtrack, which jolts and jars and makes absolutely no concession to the more standard device of pop music evoking in a direct way the emotional landscape of being a teenager. The high-volume noises are interspersed with fragments of language, shrieks of still-childish exuberance conjoined with expletives and dark mutterings. These formal elements produce a narrative which just hangs together and no more, and this in turn conveys the borderline between life and death, the thin margin between reckless fearlessness and sublime hopefulness which mark out the terrain of being female, 13-years-old and growing up in America. Hardwicke also manages to bring the bewilderment, fear and panic of the mother into the centre of the narrative by extending the same breathless camera work to her movements. Formally, then, the film enacts the falling apart of the mother and daughter relation through the event of the dangerous interloper (a new best friend), and without even a hint of heavy-handed psychoanalysis it also manages to play out the intense and mutual pain of separation.

The second dynamic which shapes the film hinges round the script itself and the way it was written. The collaboration between the director and Nikki Reed, 15 by the time the script was completed but based on her account of her daily life aged 13, was an adventurous undertaking. Hardwicke had been the girlfriend of Reed's father during this time. She must have witnessed many of the angry scenes, and the film was made possible by her being able to encourage Nikki Reed, who like the character Tracey in the film was losing track of all other interests, to enter into a co-writing project in a way that did not feel intrusive, judgemental or exploitative. (She also plays the part of Evie in the film.) This is an ethnographic danger zone, and it is Hardwicke's achievement with Reed that the narrative avoids many obvious pitfalls, while at the same time recognising that between them there is a shared shock and fascination in regard to what it means to be in this precarious state of 'becoming'. What guides the camera is, then, a sense of sheer uncertainty and of unknowing as to the reasons for much of Tracey's rage, but also an unsentimental and deep sense of regard for the teenage 'other', a kind of protectiveness and embrace. In this context the film could so easily have fallen prey to moralism or didacticism, but these are amazingly absent.

The film narrative covers a period of months, during which time 13-year-

old Tracey, who has been a good poetry-writing student, becomes enamoured by the glamour of a more sophisticated girl known as the 'hottest
chick' in school. Her desire to become Evie's friend pushes Tracey to transform herself; she must dispense with the trappings of childhood and create
a very different body image based on low-rider jeans (of course) midriff-
skimming tops, jewelry and vast quantities of make-up. But saying goodbye
to childhood also requires distancing herself from more comforting relations, from her brother, less grown up friends and of course her mother. Evie
swaggers about high school, successfully pulls as many boys as she likes,
experiments with drugs and enjoys the excitement of shop-lifting in bou-
tique shops crammed with 'girlie' objects: thongs, more make-up and bright
baubles of necklaces and bracelets and other decorations. Tracey wins
approval by exploiting a theft opportunity and from then on gains access to
a different universe of danger. Her schoolwork rapidly deteriorates, her
mother moves from mild alarm to panic, as her daughter's aggressive often
drug-fuelled anger sees her lashing out at those who love her most. She also
provokes her mother's good looking but ex-coke addict boyfriend by calling
him a loser, she hits out at her mother's attempts to earn a living at home
through hairdressing by stealing from the purse of one of her clients, she
subjects everyone around her to torrents of verbal abuse and she also cuts
herself in the family bathroom. One drug experience leads to another, the
dangers of which far outweigh the sexual rituals of learning how to make
out with boys. The close friendship with Evie who has been partly abandoned by parents and guardian results in Evie moving in, and Tracey's
mother Mel taking on some of that responsibility too. But this passionate
attachment is bound to explode; Tracey's anger pushes her to cut herself
more aggressively, and when she looks in the mirror what she now sees is
a girl who has been taking drugs and who is pallid, over made up and
almost ravaged. Eventually the girls separate, and without any recrimina-
tion on the part of Tracey's mother a degree of calm and exhaustion prevails.

This film comprises, within its own modest cinematic economy, a wonderful sociological commentary on the scale of changes for very young
girls in recent years. There are also a number of themes which have rarely
if ever been dealt with in such a rich and thoughtful way, so what follows
extrapolates from the combination of that which seems to be new and relevant to the moment, and that which is more generally pertinent to the
acquisition of gender. Most noticeably, the latter entails in the film the
crafting of an appropriate female self which is also a coercion, a normative
requirement. But this brings with it incalculable and ungrievable injuries

and losses. The power of having to become a 'real girl' gives rise to rage, but this seems inexplicable only because it is assumed that becoming a real girl is uncomplicated and desirable. This anger is more acute when the girl in question freely pursues her wayward desires and succeeds in forming a passionate attachment in the form of a new and very glamorous best friend.

What the film establishes is that the intensity of love is by no means directed in a straightforward way towards the heterosexual object of desire, that is, the boy. There is a good deal of girl/boy sex as a technique and accomplishment. And there are various attempts at more sophisticated sexual encounters including the two best-friends setting themselves up as teenage temptresses in the style of porn queens with a dance routine and an attempt to snare an older neighbour into something more dangerous. But all the passion is actually between the girls; they are each other's love object not by declaring themselves as lesbian (although they try out kissing technique on each other) but by finding themselves within an undemarcated zone of intimacy, attraction, proximity and exclusiveness. Indeed one of the best moments in the film occurs when the still unsophisticated Tracey first catches sight in a desiring manner of the in-crowd girls led by the glamorous Evie as they parade catwalk-style through the schoolyard. When she has transformed herself so that she has the right kind of look she lands her date with Evie by means of a mobile phone number and is triumphant. And once she has proved her metal by stealing cash from a woman's purse they become inseparable. What is the nature of their love for each other? Absolute proximity? Being together all the time, being like each other, having the same amount of good looks? Moving in with each other, even sharing a mother as Mel steps in to look after the precocious Evie who also seems to unconsciously understand the psychoanalytic dynamics which are at work by fulsomely kissing Mel in appreciation of her generosity and liberality? All of these create the dramatic tension throughout the film. So what is achieved in *Thirteen* is a much closer examination of those friendships, frightening because they are so passionate, which take place in the interstices of sexuality, in a realm where nothing is settled, where heterosexuality has not fully been established as a requirement, but beckons as what is to be assumed. And of course where there is such ambivalence, uncertainty and danger, desire and enjoyment are all the more heightened. The two girls in the film flaunt their sexual confidence with the boys, but back at home they also become children again, playing with each other, and jumping up and down on the bed with a child who has come to stay, shrieking on finding the family dog asleep in the teenage bedroom. The question the film asks is, then, what is the source of the pain and anguish of departing from childhood, what is it that must be relinquished, and what makes a girl like this so angry with life and with herself?

Thirteen also shows is what is new and unprecedented in relation to the lives of young girls in the post-feminist affluent West. These are girls who are the subjects of a new kind of freedom. They are quite unmarked by those forces which even at such a young age literally hung over the energies of previous girls reminding them that their time of enjoyment would soon be over, and that at some point, in the not too distant future, they would be, could only be, wives and mothers. Nothing of this sort hinders the frenetic activities of Tracey and Evie. There are no different expectations between sisters and brothers, both Tracey and her brother experiment with drugs, and look for sexual opportunities. It is Tracey who pushes past even the peer-imposed barriers in relation to danger and excess and it is her brother who eventually confronts her, telling her she needs help. The film carefully avoids simplistic suggestions about consumer culture exploiting young girls' anxieties, as well as their new freedoms to adorn themselves as they please without the risk of being condemned for looking 'tarty'. Nor is it the case that they are preyed upon by sinister drug dealers. There is no hint that they are the vulnerable victims of feminist successes, or indeed that after this string of dangerous encounters they will each learn their lessons and return to some zone of safety. The film's intelligence rests on precisely these refusals. The world into which young girls can now move more freely and can have high expectations of themselves is one that is also full of difficulties. To go hurtling into such a world through a drug induced 'purple haze' is in itself indicative of the need for something chemical which dulls the pain.

If there are no easy resolutions, the film's understated sense of hopefulness emerges from its careful observations. The ex-coke addict boyfriend scorned by Tracey is decent and respectful of her suffering. In an America where teen films still skirt anxiously around mixed-race relationships, mixed-race intimacy is an unremarkable norm. And in a low-income household a mother can not only make ends meet and look after her children, but can also look attractive, and maintain a warm circle of friends and neighbours. So much for the dysfunctional poor looking 'single mom'. So much for the end of community. The film also holds out for sustaining an intergenerational bond between young and older women. When motherhood, in relation to such young girls as these, will veer towards over-protective-ness, at just that point where daughters urgently need to safeguard their own intimacies, the drama of repudiation sets in. Thus the film records a kind of departure in conditions very different from that of an older generation.

4

Look Back in Anger: Homi Bhabha's Resistant Subject of Colonial Agency

GUIDE TO THE CHAPTER

Introduction

I propose here that the work of Homi Bhabha contributes to cultural studies a new understanding of resistance re-cast as a politics of meaning and translation. This insight is derived from the perspective of the colonial subject, within a post-colonial frame, by means of the Foucauldian model of power as productivity. Although influenced by post-structuralism and thus concerned with subjectivising practices, such as those enacted by colonisers that aim to create docile peoples, Bhabha is most critically absorbed with theorising colonial subjectivity and agency. His interest is in the inter-subjective moment, the point of 'cultural openness' (Kim, 2001) at which the meaning of the address (or enunciation) by the coloniser is taken on board by the subject. This is a crucial space because the process of translation allows the possibility of subversion, of the twisting of meaning away from and out of the hands of the coloniser. Following Benjamin in his well-known essay on translation, there is always within the culture of the colonised an untranslateable residue (Benjamin, 1973). This, Bhabha argues, need not be conceived as inevitably that which embodies tradition. Rather it can be, and is mobilised and put to work in terms of contestation and opposition. This is a productive resistance which is concurrent with a notion of performative agency, in this case within a space shared by post-colonial peoples, in particular the low-paid migrants who now live in the cities of the West and the artists and writers whose subject matter (their agency) refers also to that experience. That said, one of the recurring difficulties with Bhabha's work is that his actual engagement with the realm of the inter-subjective, or indeed with colonial practices, is fleeting and observational, even instinctual rather than analytical and sustained.

But let me lead the reader through the labyrinthine passages of Bhabha's thinking, bearing in mind that as a literary critic his primary points of reference are the fields of world literature and the arts, including cinema. Bhabha has made a number of theoretical breakthroughs in the field of post-colonial thought by moving out of or beyond the fixity of categories normally used to understand relations of power and knowledge across and within the boundaries of nations or cultures previously conceived of as discrete. He offers a different account to Said in that his concern is with the disruptive currents which make the practice of orientalism less unimpeded than Said suggests (Said, 1978). Bhabha pays attention to the micrological or phenomenological level. He draws on the kind of small details, affects, feelings and observations which are the subject matter of novelists or poets or, in the case of Fanon, reflected through the specific experience of being a black psychiatrist from Martinique working in French Algeria. Bhabha is acutely interested in internal processes, on the psyche and on the impact of colonial power on subjectivity. I would suggest he casts a novelist's eye on the world, looking up from the inter-subjective, the encounter of peoples, to the fields of history and nation. This is the movement of his writing but it does not mean he is anything like an ethnographer; he does not produce his own accounts of some verifiable social reality.

Thus when critics like Robert Young and Bart Moore-Gilbert bring to bear in their most helpful and sympathetic readings of Bhabha's work, his inattention to uprisings and resistances that took place throughout the colonial period, in favour of the resistance modality implied in for example 'mimicry', it needs to be said that the liberties and waywardnesses of the artist or novelist are also his (Young, 1990; Moore-Gilbert, 1997). There is a formalism in Bhabha's work which comprises a *movement beyond*. That is, if we approach his work as though it was a series of poems or short stories or novelettes, we would surely come to the conclusion that his concepts are also what shape and give distinctive form to his work. *Hybridity* and the *third space*, the *time-lag*, the *in-between* and the *beyond* are the key to his writing in the sense that they are implemented and implicated throughout. He uses them to develop his argument. Their sometimes jarring, seemingly awkward and rarely actually defined presence nonetheless provides the momentum to push the argument forwards, into the realm of *the beyond*. The work continually challenges the reader who is looking to be able to 'translate' Bhabha's concepts into a 'social reality'. But we cannot expect the 'real historical event' or 'uprising' to appear in a conventional academic mode in Bhabha's work any more than we could expect Salman Rushdie to write a realist account of the history of partition. And if, in turn, we replace the word theory with that of writing, reminding ourselves of the Barthesian legacy which Bhabha also inhabits, where the 'death of the author' gives way to modes of writing which have challenged the centrality of great authors and their historical canons, then we are also closer to where Bhabha might also be seen to fit in (Barthes, 1977). We need to bear in mind the critique of literary greatness in the figure of the uniquely talented artist (as a central dynamic of the European Enlightenment), and the imperative role of literature in nation building, with at the same time the deconstruction of the category of theory as something which is carried out in a certain way within self-contained academic disciplines with the effect that social theory firmly belongs in the field of social sciences, literary theory in literature and so on. Theory for Bhabha is also a hybrid of psychoanalysis, Marxism, Derridean philosophy, post-structuralism and phenomenology and consequently what is produced is not a single identifiable entity 'post-colonial theory'.

Thus we have two ways of seeing Bhabha. First, we see him with a novelist's imaginative vision which moves disruptively from the everyday, the banal, the local, to the bigger and re-imagined realm of social and political history, re-imagined because its temporality and seeming linearity has been decisively broken through Bhabha's notion of the *time-lag*. Second, we see him as the theorist who is also concerned with concepts and processes and imaginative application rather than system building (in the style of Bourdieu), and who then puts his concepts to work in the service of his arguments, which are often prompted by perceived weaknesses or failings in the work of figures like Said, Jameson, Foucault. If we describe Bhabha's work as antithetical to fixity and to the rigidities of normative categorisations, then it is inevitable that he, like Stuart Hall, considers identity as being simultaneously defined in terms of unfulfilment and lack (following Lacan) and also of 'more than' in the sense of more than the sociological and empirical realities of sex, class and ethnicity. There is always 'more to' and 'less than' personal identity, for example, than the categorisation according to class or sex or ethnicity. Bhabha defines this 'more to' or 'more than' space as that of the 'beyond', and it is this term which also allows him to think into the future, and at the same time to find a way as a cultural theorist of understanding social change from the viewpoint of the postcolonial. What do I mean by this? Bhabha explains in his introduction to *The Location of Culture* that the 'demography of the new internationalism' requires a shift in perspective so that it is the voice of the exile, or the refugee or of the displaced which establishes a frame of understanding (Bhabha, 1994). The boundary becomes then a starting point. Is his then the voice of the exile, the displaced or the marginal? Yes and no. He is schooled in the European canon, he is hardly an impoverished asylum seeker, but his is also a voice which partakes in the resistance of mimicry, the waywardness of translation, the ambivalent playfulness of writing from another, non-European, perspective.

Across the arts and in literature there is a prevailing sense of movement and fluidity, '"National" cultures are being produced from the perspectives of disenfranchised minorities' as Bhabha puts it (ibid.: 6). In addition, in current literary criticism scholars are returning to Dickens or Jane Austen and re-reading them from the viewpoint of their account of empire. It is now commonplace to point out how so much recent writing published in the UK is by authors who might be seen as coming from the margins: Salman Rushdie, Hanif Kureishi, Zadie Smith, even the Scottish writer James Kelman. Such work breaks with the notion of a homogenous national community, just as it disputes the march of history, modernity and progress. They are 'otherwise than modernity' (ibid.: 6). Innovation increasingly comes from artists whose work is transnational and translational. Histories are re-visited in a multi-mediated way. Bhabha's writing helps us to understand more fully a series of interconnecting movements where post-colonial literary critics and historians re-read texts and documents. Artists and writers use the freedom of their own practices to begin from the unruly or hitherto marginalised locations, previously overlooked because they belonged, or referred, to seemingly unimportant spatial regions. A formal quality of much of this work is then the deliberate obliqueness of vision.

Bhabha's own writing both explicates and is a crucial part of this movement; he writes from the everyday, the lived reality of colonial and post-colonial authority where experiences are necessarily constrained by dominating institutions and their discourses and where within this space of permitted agency meaning can be recast or turned around in the manner Butler terms re-signification. This produces distortion when subordinated peoples are expected to copy the manners, behaviour and education of the coloniser. Their mimicry unsettles the ruler, precisely because the space of translating from one culture to the other also provides a space for insubordination, or antagonism. In this sense Bhabha's 'translation' comes close to Butler's 're-signification'; indeed in a recent exchange Butler draws on Bhabha's notion of cultural translation (see Butler, 2000b). There is the refusal, for example, of the servant to carry out his or her duties in exactly the specified way, and there is also the refusal to 'return the gaze' in recognition of deference.

These acts wound the narcissism of the colonial, resisting the demand for knowable subjects. When recognition is refused the coloniser recoils in paranoia and disbelief, 'Why do they hate us?' (a refrain repeated so often in the aftermath of the attacks of 9/11). The politics of translation is Bhabha's own reworking of Derrida's argument that meaning is never firmly tied down and fixed, but is instead forever haunted by the traces of other meanings. This in turn opens up a space not just for ambivalence but for the politics of re-articulation. It is in this in-between space that the subversive possibilities of translation emerge. These can be registered through body and affect. This arena of insubordination warranted through the imperfect translation is a constant motif for Bhabha; to some extent it is exactly where his argument is directed and manifest, in a space or terrain where things that do not translate and yet which are not simply signs of tradition, are to be found. In some ways this is also the ambivalent space of critical artistic practice. As other critics have pointed out this particular 'location of culture' casts the potential for art alongside the potential for oppositional practice on the part of poor and disenfranchised peoples.

But is this not, asks Young, a sleight of hand inattentive to the disparities of power between the cosmopolitan artist and the impoverished migrant? (Young, 1990) And I would add, is this the logic of the politics of meaning, that when politics is re-defined as re-articulation then its micrological existence can be found in associational if not organisational ways, and perhaps more worryingly wherever the theorist cares to look? Further, if Bhabha's theoretical writing is also a form of re-articulation and thus of politics and agency, is it the case that its social effects are such that there is a (limited) constituency through its audiences or readers or students? Textual activism partakes through the movement of meaning from Bhabha's writing outwards to the scenes and scenarios, the conferences and events where it is further translated. By this means, it could be argued, Bhabha participates in the politics of post-structuralism as well as post-coloniality through constituting a 'community' on the basis of a shared sense of always-uncertain meaning. To understand Bhabha in this sense avoids the trap of consigning theoretical work in the post-Marxist era as a retreat from engagement with what is normatively understood as the world of real politics. But this does not solve the outstanding difficulty of translating Bhabha's writing into a body of thinking which registers ambivalence and the complexity of psychic responses, while also being accessible to politics in a more expanded sense (though of course what expanded politics is, in contrast to micro-logical or textual politics, is also contentious; perhaps the very act of writing a 'textbook' account of Bhabha is constitutive of expanded politics).

From Bhabha's perspective art and theory are subjectivising practices which can create politicised cultures, this is their distinct productivity. This is the 'agency of the author' (Kim, 2001). But what of the everyday actions and ways of living of peoples who have migrated and find themselves carving out a living in the cities of the West? Here is found the 'insurgent art of cultural translation'; here also is found a newness which is again 'otherwise than modernity'. Moving between art and the experience of migrant peoples, Bhabha points his readers to the domestic and affective realm which literature is able to conjure, 'unhomeliness' for example, or from Henry James the 'incredulous terror' of experiencing displacement, of not being at home. From Nadine Gordimer he remarks on how everyday domesticity and the environment of 'the home' became the very ground where the challenge to apartheid took place. Art and literature are capable of bringing into being intrinsically ordinary intensities. The intimacy of experience where ruled and rulers co-exist reminds us of Gilroy making a similar point. Black people were close to and part of European modernity – in its bedrooms and kitchens – the backdrop to its conversations. It 'happened' in their presence.

So there is no question of black people or migrants coming 'belatedly' to modernity. Indeed Bhabha argues that the 'time-lag' by which modernity sought to distance itself from the perceived slowness of its others, is actually critical to modernity. It needed this temporality to achieve domination. By writing (or bringing) this exclusion back into modernity as its condition of existence, or its constitutive outside, a different kind of modernity can be arrived at, one which is not so unlike Gilroy's 'counter culture of Modernity'. This is, according to Bhabha, a way of speaking back from these necessary margins, or 'original spaces', a 'post-colonial translation of Modernity', which disputes the pastness or slowness typically assigned to others. These voices in turn make modernity non-linear, combatively present and defiantly vibrant. In art and in writing, through this disputing of modernity's temporality, there is also performative agency, in that to write in this way and with memory as a forceful presence is to 'move beyond' to create a space for those who might share such 'historical trauma'. Such work is therefore associational, as is black popular music with its participative and performative dynamics as Gilroy so persuasively argues. Bhabha's claim is that the subjectivising practices of these kinds of art coincide with those pursued in less exceptional realms, in the everyday lives of migrant and subjected peoples whose capacity for cultural translation produces a chain of associational possibilities. The bonds between art and experience are actualised by Bhabha as the promise of politics.

From Class to Community

So far I have tried to show how the 'time-lag' is not just proposed as a provocative counter to the temporalities of modernity and postmodernity as they are typically imposed, but as a means of redefining these entities from within their own spaces. Modernity (and indeed postmodernity) are being proclaimed by western critics as having certain spatial and temporal consequences while other non-western locations are nonetheless described as 'timeless' or 'in the past' and thus not part of these consequences. Bhabha brings these other spaces powerfully back into the picture, their alleged state of being 'in the past' is indeed a critical part of the present just as their distance is integral. Hence Bhabha's notion of 'time-lag' which throws into disarray the march of time as it is described by even the most sophisticated critics, and offers consequently an expanded and discordant vision of time, space and experience. The Harlem Renaissance, for example, gloriously re-mixes modernity just as *The Satanic Verses* reveals the limits of Jameson's postmodernity (see Chapter 6). Bhabha is, then, writing a post-colonial theory, which, influenced by Foucault, Said, Fanon, Lacan and others, proceeds by introducing a range of tools and concepts which challenge current understanding by virtue of their seeming to come from the space of 'the other'. While attempting to break down binaries (the West/the rest, Occident/Orient, powerful/powerless) as themselves strategies for regulation, the question remains of the 'colonial subject' and his/her agency in colonial governance.

What Bhabha opens out for examination is the response, the agency of colonial subjects. Indeed his own agency as a critic is mobilised to effect a new critical language for understanding; this is his agency through writing-into-being new positions, new points for enunciation. Bhabha also wants to transcend the rigidity of opposites, the way in which key thinkers have relied on binaries of black/white, West/rest. He considers that Foucault is limited in his attention to European discourses, while Said's analysis of orientalism as a strategy of knowledge and power is inattentive to response, to the reception of orientalism. Bhabha also looks to Fanon and indeed is possibly most indebted to him for his deep insight into the psyche of the oppressed other. But he also draws on both Freud and Lacan and the way they have been used in current post-structuralist thinking to understand difference, repetition, and most importantly the 'split' subject and the illusion of wholeness or full subjectivity, also the non-coincidence of the conscious with the unconsciousness, the construction of the subject in language.

With all of this in mind we might ask what exactly is Bhabha's contribution to cultural studies? And how does the concept of resistance figure in this work? I would suggest this is best explored by considering two themes: first, the displacement of class by community most clearly developed in his essay 'How Newness Enters the World', and second, Bhabha's reconceptualisation of the stereotype as described in 'The Other Question' (Bhabha, 1994). But framing these two concerns is a fundamental question, which shapes the way in which Bhabha writes. How is new knowledge produced out of existing canons which have only served the interests of the socially dominant and for the purposes of ensuring subjugation and subservience? When the European Enlightenment world of discourse, statements, reports, diaries, fictions, images, facts and figures has been interrogated and understood as knowledge about the world in its entirety while in effect being from a small corner of the world, how do other knowledges come into being? These are questions which have been primary for post-colonial scholars, from Gilroy, who follows the movement of the journeys of black populations historically and contemporaneously, back and forwards across the Black Atlantic, to Spivak who queries the voices of representation but finds herself one among these voices. Gilroy looks to how earlier generations of black intellectuals and artists and writers have understood the world of modernity which they have found themselves inhabiting while Spivak asks, 'what is it to speak?' 'On whose behalf is representation conducted?' (Gilroy, 1993; Spivak, 1988).

If texts and representations are constitutive of that which they describe, then texts are also actions, hence writing brings into being new ways of thinking about colonial domination, produces a new horizon of language which in turn leads readers into new possibilities:

writing as event, writing as new reality. This is a key to understanding Bhabha's work, his work moves us *beyond*, by interweaving critical inter-rogation of existing cultural theory (for example, Jameson) with literary readings of writers and poets such as Rushdie, Morrison and Walcott, and then by drawing on the work of other cultural theorists to arrive at a point at which the agency of the colonised can be articulated. Thus Bhabha's own work opens out new possibilities for social understand-ing. Both Bhabha and Butler are engaged in a protracted argument with the Marxist tradition which remains committed to notions of the centrality of class as the nodal point to which other political categories such as race or sex must converge and be subsumed by, in order to see through political transformation. Both repudiate this demand while respectful and indebted to Marxist thought. Both legitimate a textual politics of transformation in language and writing; both resist a kind of easy politics which is referred to as somehow outside the text, 'in the real world'; both inevitably resist calls to action as though in preference to the act of doing theoretical work. Despite the difficulty of their work, each is faithful to a political ambition, there is no total retreat into theory; this trying to hold both dynamics together while also forging a new kind of politics in many ways accounts for the unruliness and truculence of their texts.

In the essay 'How Newness Enters The World', Bhabha counters Jameson's attempt to grasp the new conditions of global capitalism within a Marxist framework which now needs to be modified. In Jameson, as Bhabha reminds us, there is a shift from state to culture and cityscape, there is an emphasis on the spatialised and decentred subject bewildered and disoriented by change and there are also the difficulties faced by the critical theorist to interpret the world. But the idea of 'cog-nitive mapping' falls short according to Bhabha because it is posed as a strategy for overcoming the difficulties of not knowing, which comes about through the bewilderment of strangeness in the community, the appearance of discordant social identities which are resistant to merging with or into the more reliable signs of class. Bhabha recognises that for Jameson 'the demographic and phenomenological impact of minorities and migrants within the West may be crucial in conceiving of the transnational character of contemporary culture' (Bhabha, 1994: 214), but he cannot let go of a particular temporality as the 'developmental narrative of late capitalism encounters its fragmented postmodern per-sona' (ibid.: 216). Jameson is deeply troubled by 'this encounter with the global dialectic of the unrepresentable'. Thus the differences between the two, and Jameson's problems involved in cognitively mapping the 'new international space' have got to do with Bhabha acknowledging fully the 'conditions of communal emergence' which come from the displaced peoples who in their cultural activity point to the 'possibilities of other times', while Jameson remains committed to class as the key determinant for social understanding. Bhabha accuses him (while also acknowledging the 'complexity of Jameson's ambivalence') of 'wounded' narcissism in this respect. This lies in Jameson's insistence that class can provide a kind of glass or mirror for seeing the real conditions (at the bottom of the stream) of how the world works, as other politicised social movements (who are caught up in, as Bhabha quotes Jameson, 'libidinal investments of a narrative kind') fail to provide a way of ensuring the conditions for social transformation. Indeed if only class can provide 'race and gender with its interpellative structure', then the 'sovereignty' of class is 'an act of surveillance'. In short, Bhabha's reply to Jameson is to argue that class cannot have the injunction to speak on behalf of other categories, the decline of classical Marxism rests on the loss of the 'ontological priority' of class but from this there emerges 'the possibility of a politics of social difference' which is 'genuinely articulatory' in its understanding that 'to achieve an effective political identity or image' it must be prepared to work at the 'borderline negotiations of cultural translation'.

The reference to articulation reminds us of the connections between Bhabha's thinking and that of Stuart Hall, and this suggestiveness about negotiation and the possibilities of cultural translation also gives rise to a wide range of questions. How does minority discourse function in Jameson's postmodern city? To answer this Bhabha turns to Salman Rushdie's *The Satanic Verses* for its account of the 'liminality of migrant experience' (Rushdie, 1988). Bhabha explains, 'The migrant culture of the 'in between', the minority position, dramatizes the activity of culture's untranslateability: and in so doing moves the question of culture's appropriation beyond the assimilationists dream' (Bhabha, 1994: 224). If translation is a staging of cultural difference, then, claims Bhabha, it is the foreignness which is the 'unstable element of linkage', the 'indeterminate temporality of the in-between'. Thus 'translation is the performative nature of cultural communication' embodied, for example, in Rushdie's 'migrant hybrid'. But, he continues, can discourses such as this become representative? How can groups who do not have

class to give them an 'organicist history' produce 'interpellative structures'? There is the 'affiliative solidarity' of artistic practice (not unlike
Gilroy's position). There is also a definition of community which
Bhabha borrows from Chatterjee, who sees community as something
that 'haunts' civil society by acting as its double, as a 'subterranean
potentially subversive life within it because it refuses to go away'. The
colonised turn away from civil society and in so doing produce a different space 'marked by the distinctions of the material and the spiritual,
the outer and the inner' (Chatterjee quoted by Bhabha, 1994: 231).

Community is therefore a discourse marking the process of 'becoming minor', just as it is also a space of resistance in that it eludes civil
society. In the urban environment community is the 'territory of the
minority'. But how does the community speak? 'How does it name
itself, author its agency?' Bhabha again turns to art, in this case diasporic
poetry, to see how this happens. In Derek Walcott's work there is a suggestion that ordinary language of migrant or diasporic peoples
'prefigures a kind of solidarity between ethnicities'. And so, community
can function to provide associational possibilities among different
groups. The artist or writer who expresses such potentialities through
the 'productivity of cultural openness' (Kim, 2001) plays a key role in
producing change in the community and also introducing newness as he
or she works through these interstitial spaces. As Kim suggests 'eventually the diasporic Other enunciates' (ibid.). Rushdie dramatises conflict
and antagonism through blasphemy, Walcott 'provides an agency of
initiation that enables one to possess, again and anew, the signs of survival, the terrain of other histories' (Bhabha, 1994: 232). These forms
produce a different and alternative post-colonial history which in turn
create possibilities for the diasporic subject to emerge.

The Other Question

One of the most significant essays by Bhabha particularly for students of
media and cultural studies is 'The Other Question', which first appeared
in 1983 but was subsequently revised and reprinted in *The Location of
Culture* (Bhabha, 1994). Bhabha challenges work on sexual and racial difference in Hollywood cinema which understands the stereotype as a
point of fixity and security of meaning. By showing how ambivalence
pervades the relationship which motivates the construction of the

stereotype, Bhabha destabilises the power the coloniser anxiously asserts. In many ways this essay demonstrates the full range of Bhabha's thinking. And even though it was written at an earlier point in Bhabha's career it stands as a useful way of concluding this discussion for the very reason that it returns us to popular culture. Because it refutes the assumption that the stereotype is a simplification, and argues for its complexity and its centrality to the practices of colonial governmentality, and because it also asserts the centrality of the 'visual and auditory imaginary for the histories of society' (ibid.: 76), 'The Other Question' offers a brilliant post-colonial perspective on media, culture, and the politics of the image. Bhabha argues that the stereotype is a form of knowledge about 'the other', but far from securing certainty it in fact betrays the instability and uncertainty of relations between the powerful coloniser and the powerless colonised. Following Foucault's claim that power is inevitably countered by contestation, the stereotype is an attempt to fix the colonial subject so as to thoroughly and emphatically know him or her. But Bhabha points to the paradox that the stereotype appears to embody the fullness of knowledge yet it is so anxiously repeated that there is a sense in which it cannot guarantee certainty. Ambivalence pervades a much more fragile relationship than the coloniser wants to admit. Thus what is known about the Irish, the Asian, the African needs to be anxiously and endlessly repeated; it must forever circulate in culture. Hence the repetition across time and space of the jokes about the 'stupid Irish', the 'duplicitous Asian', the sexuality of the black male. Power and control are wrestled from the coloniser because the relationship with the other is also based on desire. This so disturbs the psychic balance of the coloniser that the stereotype takes on an excessive overblown character. It is both repeated and also enlarged, it is *more than* in order to be *less than*. Hence the physical prowess of the black athlete, hence the excessively aggressive drunken Scots. The desire emerges from the recognition of lack; to paraphrase Lacan, this is something I am not, therefore I am not whole, therefore because this other promises wholeness, I desire him or her.

It is the fear and the fascination of the coloniser which compels the construction of the racial stereotype. This makes the stereotype a 'complex, ambivalent, contradictory mode of representation'. But this is also a means of seeking legitimation. If the stereotype shows the other to be degenerate then it can be claimed that others are incapable of self-rule (the feckless Irish, the drunken Scots). The stereotype is then a critical instrument of government, it renders others knowable in such a way as to justify the superiority of the coloniser. This degeneracy is also to be feared, hence the anxious attempts to pin him or her down, in order to fully know the other. She or he can never be anything other than what the stereotype permits, he or she will always resort to type. 'They are all the same'. The point will always come when she or he is nothing more than what is expected. The fear and fascination or the economies of power and pleasure have the effect of making the stereotype also a kind of fetish. This reduces the fear on the part of the coloniser by giving to the other some more familiar object-like quality. The fetish dimension represents a tussle to take away some of the qualities that make him or her so very different. As Bhabha says, 'for fetishism is always a "play" or vacillation between the archaic affirmation of wholeness/similarity . . . and the anxiety associated with lack and difference' (Bhabha, 1994: 74). The stereotype produces on the part of the coloniser both power and pleasure and also anxiety and defensiveness; it is then 'the primary point of subjectification in colonial discourse'.

It is of course Fanon who understood the impact on the psyche of being seen and pointed out as black, and thus a person to be feared. The white child who is frightened by Fanon's blackness recognises his difference and turns back to her mother disavowing his humanity. This in a sense seals Fanon's fate as a split subject, just as it confirms the power of the look. This emphasis on looking points Bhabha to Foucault's account of surveillance as a means of regulation, but again this is disrupted by the fantasy and ambivalence, love and hate which are then forced to find some resolution in the field of seemingly paradoxical stereotypical attributes, both loyal and sly, both obedient and cunning, both gentle and aggressive. 'Colonial fantasy plays a crucial part in those everyday scenes of subjectification in a colonial society which Fanon refers to repeatedly' (ibid.: 81). However, what remains is the return of the oppressed, the traumatic agency of the colonised who is subjected to stereotypical practices. There is space inside the stereotype precisely because it is not the straitjacket it seems, which allows the colonised a degree of space to twist around and project back some of those fearful properties. He or she can look back in anger.

There are unresolved strands in this essay; various critics have pointed to Bhabha's inattention to the more problematic aspect of Freud's account of the fetish as a 'primitive' device for containing fears. In feminist theory fetishism has been used to explain how the sexual or pornographic image of a woman (with her demanding and threatening 'other' sexuality) is often accompanied by an object close at hand, something she is playing with, for example a whip, a pair of high stiletto heels, or a beach ball if she is in a swimsuit, and these objects assuage the ancient fear of castration. But how exactly this works in the racial stereotype remains unclear in Bhabha's account. Also perhaps because it was written early on in Bhabha's work the focus in this essay is more on the destabilisation of textual meaning than on the actual agency this permits the colonised. This remains a potential rather than a specified practice. There is a mere hint that the stereotype can be made to re-signify and can thus be played back as oppositional practice. Judith Butler provides a more thorough means for showing how this happens, as the subject twists the interpellative structures of being designated 'queer' into a subversive performance, a form of agency. However the importance of Bhabha's essay is that he provides a framework for understanding as an active and productive relation both the power of such designations and the instabilities which in turn permit the possibility for turning those meanings around for a subversive effect. There is of course also the injury enacted on the body of the colonised, as Bhabha reminds us of Fanon turning away, reeling at being seen in this way (that is, where the young white girl recoils in fear at the sight of the black man). But it is this kind of scene, and crucially the recognition that it suggests a common condition that that of 'being black', that affords Fanon the occasion to decipher its traumatic significance for racial experience. By utilising this in his own work he in effect turns it around, he uses it to produce an account of fractured and split black subjectivity. He also uses it to analyse the force of being seen in a particular way, as though to indicate, 'this is all you can ever be', that is 'you can never be anything more than just black'. In short you can never be a normal man, you can never be 'not black'.

Father Ted

Bhabha therefore relies and expands on Fanon's account of being understood as a distinct 'type' of racialised being. The injurious designation is (as Butler has also argued) a point for possible re-signification. Bhabha's analysis stops short here, but we might consider the extent to which within the field of everyday culture, and especially in music and media, the stereotype has become an instrument for new modes of self representation which 'talk back' against those forces which are perceived as having previously utilised this device as a strategy for knowledge and control. As minorities slowly gain space in the field of representation and particularly in mass mediated forms, colonial agency takes on a diversity of possibilities. As Gilroy has shown African-American popular culture, in particular hip hop music draws decisively on the derogatory imagery (dog, sexually licentious male or female, criminal) of the racial imagination to construct a fearful vocabulary of cultural response through the visual and auditory range of hip hop music. Gilroy's recent argument does not, however, confirm such articulations as necessarily oppositional. The overblown and exaggerated invocations of prowess of Puff Daddy and others merely stage a 'bad' presence within an otherwise unrearranged social structure dominated by money, masculinity, and the pleasures of the consumer culture. This is not to deny what Bhabha elsewhere calls the 'uncontrollable innovations of youth', but it is to recognise that cultural reiterations along these lines are simultaneously inscribed within other narratives of belonging rather than unbelonging, in this case under the dollar sign. Thus the reworking of the stereotype also intersects with the socio-cultural environment, which in the case of 1990s American hip hop, comprises a depoliticised neo-liberal climate based on global entertainment, individualism and success.

This 'problematically oppositional' re-articulation of the stereotype could, however, be countered by other examples, also from the popular media, where there is a distinctive playfulness (within the frame of comedy), which more clearly fulfil the ambition which Bhabha's work leads us towards. The Channel 4 television comedy series *Father Ted* (scripted by two Irish writers) provides a wildly exaggerated version of the *more than* 'stupid' Irish. Absurd stupidity provides narrative coherence between the four main characters, from the psychotic drunk and retired priest Father Jack, to Father Ted himself, affable and innocent, to the sublimely dimwitted young curate Father Dougal played by Ardal O'Hanlon and the priest-loving and grotesquely deferential housekeeper Mrs Doyle. But since the series is also a satire on the Irish priesthood, stupidity comes to stand for the inflated status of Catholicism in an increasingly secular Ireland. The stereotypes are 'returned' to the cultural location where historically they emerged from within the colonial regime (in this case rural Ireland), but from this point they re-emerge hilariously overblown, not just as a mark of new found cultural confidence (to be able to laugh at ourselves), but to playfully interrogate and thus inaugurate questions of cultural identity. *Father Ted* deftly refutes the archaic location (time-lag) of religion by employing anti-realist devices throughout the programmes. By pushing tradition (deference to the dog collar), modernity (the priesthood forced to modernise) and post-modernity (scandalously playful references to priestly homosexuality) alongside each other so that they collide, *Father Ted* shows what post-colonial popular culture can achieve. The stereotypes carry the excessive, enlarged characteristics described by Bhabha, but rather than being *more so* in order to be *less than*, their comic productivity creates *cultural openness*, so that sex and religion, alcoholism and domestic violence find a new way of being engaged with. The angry response by the Catholic church to the programme and the palpable relief when its leading actor died of a heart attack, thus bringing the series to a premature end, demonstrated its political effect. Similar kinds of arguments could be made about the Scottish *Rab C. Nesbitt* character (drunk, dishevelled, wearing a string vest) and also the BBC television comedy series *Goodness Gracious Me*. The title for this highly successful series is taken from a pop record/film track of the early 1960s featuring Peter Sellars 'blacked up' and playing the part of the stereotypical Asian doctor whose imperfect mimicry of the English phrase 'Goodness Gracious Me' makes him a figure of fun.

The passage of these counter-stereotypes into the wide field of popular culture demonstrates also the capacity for domestication and degrees of liberal self-congratulation; this is certainly true of *Goodness Gracious Me* and subsequent programmes, including *The Kumars At No 42*, whose recognition across the national media as well as places for its cast members on the stage at the Jubilee celebration in June 2002 suggest achieved multi-culturalism as a kind of comfort and closure. But must the stereotype only look back in anger, what are the social and political effects of comedy? Despite the inevitable management of such endeavours so that they become less critical, more warm and engaging, it is nonetheless my contention here that the writing and production of these programmes comprise in Bhabha's terms, popular post-colonial agency. They use as their raw material understanding of how the stereotype has worked in the past as an attempt at fixity, how it has circulated and found a certain familiarity among the colonisers as well as the colonised. Made to re-signify and talk back, these counter-stereotypes are played back to a mixed audience of viewers, British and Irish, British Asian and white British. Both *Father Ted* and *Goodness Gracious Me* have the capacity for producing new and expanded meanings in relation to national and transcultural identity. Their writers are producing popular texts which articulate with many of the dynamics of cultural theory thus showing also the potential for widening the sphere of critical engagement from a position of marginality or obliqueness.

Extended Notes

Readers at this point might understandably query the function of the extended notes attached to each chapter. So far these have ranged from additional commentary and update (Hall), to further clarification (Gilroy), and in the case of Butler to a reprint of a review of a film, the narrative of which enacts both the pain and injury of adolescent gender acquisition, and the intensity of passionate attachments within the frame of same-sex friendship. However, I am aware that there is a danger that where films, television programmes or art works are the focus of attention in this condensed and abbreviated way, it might seem that they suggest an unspecified relation to, or indeed an application of, the cultural theory which precedes them. Or that one might somehow now be expected to read these texts in a particular way, armed with the vocabulary gleaned from the cultural theorist in the preceding chapter. This idea of application is to be avoided, in so far as it suggests two quite separate systems, one of which has the ability to unlock the key to understanding the other. Let me suggest instead two things, the first of which is an interlocking, intersecting series of flows, overlaps and cross-fertilisations which envelop both the theoretical works which are the subject of this book, and the various cultural practices which I also refer to. The cultural theorist encounters films, books, pieces of music and these, according to the use made of them and the degree of attention given to them, extend his or her existing understanding, so that without these forms theory would not exist in quite the way it does. But these do not exhaust or delimit the capacity of theory, instead they enlarge its orbit, expand its field of influence and thus underpin the wider potentiality of the work. Thus the Orson Welles film *Touch of Evil* helps Bhabha to begin his formulations of the racial stereotype, and it also contributes to its further development, but after a point film might itself be superseded, or even discarded, as it is no longer the point of attention. But then, and this is the second point, cultural theory, in this case post-colonial theory, thanks to that film, helps us to understand aspects of the world more profoundly. Bhabha brings to the film a critical vocabulary which allows us to see the film differently. If we understand Bhabha's work as itself a kind of subjectivising practice, those who are its subjects might also be post-colonial film-makers who then bring to bear on their own film work elements of this subjectivisation. Cultural theory, as part of the academic canon, flows through many classrooms and institutional spaces, it also moves out into the world of galleries and into the field of public comment, for example, into arts and cultural journalism. It can also be drawn on by political activists and by grass roots groups. As this happens the writing is also retranslated in the process, as Butler's (perhaps dismayed) comments in relation to the dissemination of her theory of performativity indicate. Exactly how this happens would require detailed sociological attention, but let us acknowledge that there are pathways through which theory moves. Sometimes the line of flight is quite visible, but often this is not the case. Thus with the film *Thirteen*, discussed in the previous chapter, the point of my analysis is to highlight how Butler's work enhances our under-standing of its power and intensity. In this way I am positioned as mediator, cultural intermediary, or pedagogue. This input is something then of a sup-plement to the film text. While we might surmise (or glean from the director's notes) that the writer and director were familiar with feminist social psychology, Butler's writing brings out what is already there but remains liminal, mysterious and opaque (the sources of anger and pain) which are illuminated by her account of 'gender trouble'.

Yinka Shonibare: African Dandy

Okwui Enwezor writing about the work of the British and Nigerian artist Yinka Shonibare argues that ' Shonibare's work is about the ironies and alle-gories of authenticity and the myths of race, and the complex language of distancing that is often loaded into the wobbly vessel of ethnic stereotype and colonial mimicry' (Enwezor, 1997: 96). Shonibare's art exists therefore, in a relationship of close proximity to cultural theory. The circuits which connect Shonibare with Bhabha are discernible, although neither refers directly to the other. We can pick up traces of the writing of Gilroy, Hall and Bhabha in Shonibare's interviews and comments, but not in a way which suggests a mechanical application or simply pedagogic influence. Shonibare emerged as part of a generation of so-called 'young British artists' which has tended to repudiate the Marxist, feminist and anti-racist writing which influenced many artists who came to prominence from the mid-1980s onwards, including the film-maker Isaac Julien, the artist Sonia Boyce and photographer David A. Bailey. Shonibare took part in the con-troversial Sensation exhibition in 1997-8 alongside Damien Hirst whose antipathy to the political values of the previous generation is well docu-mented. Like his counterparts Steve McQueen and Chris Ofili, Shonibare resists the box of having to be 'too black' but, more so than both of these

other black British artists, Shonibare enters into an elaborate playful dialogue with the pressures on someone like him to engage directly with
ethnicity. His playfulness, however, is not embraced at the cost of politics;
he maintains both simultaneously, with work which is seductive, humorous
and politically challenging. He engages with male sexual pleasure and
licentiousness. He plugs into aspects of popular culture (his African Dandy
work owes something to the black dandyism of Prince), he is constantly
interrogating the racial stereotype, and by tactics of displacement and
replacement he subverts it with enjoyment (as in the Dandy series of photographs). Shonibare is best known for his prolific use of a kind of cotton wax
print (found by him in Brixton Market South London) usually assumed to
be African in origin but in fact the product of a complex production history
which incorporates Indonesian techniques of wax printing taken up by
Dutch companies in the late 18th century which in turn was copied by
manufacturers in the north of England and subsequently modified for large
African markets. Shonibare then dresses his work in this fabric and in so
doing moves easily between sculpture, painting, fashion, 'tailoring', instal-
lation work and 'tableaux vivant' photography. The work as a whole is
possessed of incredible energy and exuberance. Shonibare leaps about with
obvious enjoyment from one project to the next. One piece of earlier work
titled *Double Dutch* (see the cover of this book) played back the tropes of
modernism, inflected as it has been with so-called primitivism, by means of
a series of 50 or so abstract blocks or squares set on a candy pink wall; the
squares were, however, dressed in the Dutch wax print, which were in turn
painted over by Shonibare. Following this there has been a prolific output,
the best known of which include sculptural headless mannequins (or shop
window dummies) dressed in Victorian styles, but constructed and presented in a riot, or cacophony of Dutch wax cotton. Sometimes the prints
themselves incorporate images taken from contemporary popular culture or
else they refer to current political issues. Shonibare clearly loves history, is
immensely influenced by post-colonial writing and has a fascination with
the Victorians. But he is also intensely curious about contemporary British
popular obsessions with costume drama and 'restoration'. He has produced
a reduced scale Victorian-style house mise-en-scène interior (*The Victorian
Philanthropist's Parlour*, 1996) with every surface covered in fabric, and he
has also (re-)dressed figures from the world of British art, in particular the
painting by Gainsborough titled *Mr and Mrs Andrews*, now turned into
headless sculptural bodies dressed once again in the bright coloured print
fabric. This is a semi-grotesque (*Mr and Mrs Andrews Without Their Heads*,

1998), humorous mimicry of an art work considered to be central to the construction of Englishness and the imagined community and debated within the field of art history and cultural studies on the basis of the famous essay by John Berger. In this respect Shonibare is revisiting those debates and adding something new to them. His is also (echoing Bhabha) an oblique vision, achieved through the use of print and textile. This interrupts and makes everything in Shonibare's work vibrantly patterned which in turn debunks the time-honoured materials and techniques of high art. Throughout the work there is an engagement with movement and with what I have called in relation to Bhabha 'movement beyond'. Here movement refers to the violent historical relations between empire and colony, the exchanges and appropriations of commodities, and the flows of persons and ideas back and forth, from so-called centre to so-called periphery. Shonibare's transcultural postmodern work mixes and re-mixes, and by bringing his own specific Lagos-based cosmopolitan cultural references back to the London Brit-art world, makes it seem (or at least the world of Hirst, Emin and others) barren and parochial, self-aggrandising and complacent, intellectually closed rather than open. Without abandoning politics, indeed quite the opposite, he refutes any notion of black victimhood, and instead produces an energetic 'live' art.

I want to focus on one particular piece of work produced in 1998, which comprised a set of large-scale photographs (one of which appeared as a 'public art' poster on the London Underground). The series is titled *Diary of A Victorian Dandy* and it draws loosely on *A Rake's Progress* by the famous British artist of the 18th century, Hogarth. The *Diary* is a kind of post-colonial fantasy work comprising five large photographic prints, each of which charts a moment in the day of a black dandy. Shonibare gives himself this role, and also uses actors to play the parts of maids and butler, fellow pool players and aristocratic friends and acquaintances. The transgressive fantasy elements are visible in the degree of fascination and attention given to the black dandy figure. At every point in the day he is centre-stage, he is tended to and he is able to do what he pleases, that is, he is a subject of pleasure and whim. Whatever he wants he only has to ask for. Is he subverting the master–slave relation? The maids and the valet gather round his bed as he awakens, to take his orders for the day. In the early hours the same maids become sexual 'playmates', for himself and three men friends, in a Victorian orgy-type scene. During the day he finds himself at the pool table in the company of men and once again he is the subject of rapt attention and admiration. Everyone seems to love him. He also delivers a lecture in the library of a grand stately home where his audience is a group of gentlemen who are clearly impressed while the maids gather shyly at the door, as though trying to catch a glimpse of the great man. Later in the evening before the night descends into debauchery there is a social occasion in another great house. Here the black dandy finds himself the focus of everyone's attention: one woman is singing, others seem infatuated, while the men also look on in envy and approval. In each of the prints there is a great detail of period detail, and rich colour (the Dutch wax print is dispensed with for this work). And, as with all of his work, there is a multimediated quality as though we are looking at the images through many lenses each one superimposed on the other. First, there is the inversion of the Hogarth-type prints. The humble black servant figure usually hidden away in the corner is now himself the master tended to by maids and a valet. Then there are the historical references to black travellers and intellectuals who did indeed achieve prominence in British learned circles through the 18th and 19th centuries, but on top of the inversion and the historicisation, there is also the stage-set, costume drama feel to the photographs; the viewer cannot but make connections with popular British television drama where literary narratives are often excuses for one erotic scene after the other, with the sexual tension heightened through attention to items of clothing, for example, petticoats, bodices, tight breeches and so on. This last element introduces humour into the art work. There is a sense of pastiche, the viewer feels as though in contemporary multi-cultural Britain, such a series with a black character at its centre, is just about to go into production for scheduling on a Sunday evening, the usual slot for such drama. This introduces light-heartedness into the work. At the same time the dandy theme holds the series together, the literary figure who is inevitably an outsider, making every attempt to find a place in high society and succeeding, but only up to a point. His immaculate clothing and his fashionable look make him a spectacular and attractive figure, he is playing a role in order to gain social acceptance and thus his identity is of course a sham. But is this not what identity inevitably is, asks Shonibare? If exclusion is constitutive of what inclusion requires in order to consolidate its always shaky sense of identity, then Shonibare imagines himself inside the door, at the table, alongside the ladies of the house and in bed with the maids. At points one is reminded of Prince's highly charged super-erotic pop videos. The fantasy is of being inside and getting hold of what has been forbidden. I would suggest there are multiple references here to black masculinity and success in popular culture and to those aspects in Bhabha's work on the racial stereotype where the black male finds himself normatively expected to be 'more than', in order that he also shows himself to be 'less than'. This is not, then, a series of images which 'look back in anger', nor does it repeat Fanon's wound on being looked at in fear and hatred, but it does somehow incorporate these other looks in the play of looks exchanged between the characters in each of the photographs. Who is looking at whom and on what basis? This is the question Shonibare seems to be asking. What underlies admiration, fascination, even love in racialised encounters? What social and psychic relations are inscribed within the process of black people gaining 'notional' acceptance into the ranks of class stratified and now seemingly multi-cultural English society?

5

'Needs and Norms': Bourdieu and Cultural Studies

I wanted, so to speak, to reintroduce agents that Levi-Strauss and the structuralists, among others Althusser, tended to abolish, making them simple epiphenomena of structure. And I mean agents not subjects. Action is not mere carrying out of a rule . . . they (that is, agents) put into action the incorporated principles of a generative habitus. (Bourdieu, 1990: 9)

Bourdieu offers a specific account of how the social field works. It is a competition, not just for life and security as in Hobbes, but for advantage, and not just material advantage as in Marx, but more general symbolic advantage. (Dreyfus and Rabinow, 1993: 40)

Clearly informed by a Marxian conception of class, although reformulated in less substantialising terms, Bourdieu's work offers a reading of social practice that re-introduces the market as the context of social power, and argues that social power is not fully reducible to the social practices they condition and inform. (Butler, 1999b: 113)

Bourdieu against Cultural Studies

Why is Bourdieu, somebody who, in recent years, has been hostile to cultural studies, going as far as to describe it as a 'mongrel domain born in England in the 1970s . . . a "discipline" which "does not exist in the French university"' (Bourdieu and Wacquant, 1999: 47), nonetheless a figure with whom so many working in cultural studies so regularly engage? There is, to be sure, a consistent concern with the perpetuation of social inequities by what we might call cultural means. There is also a preference for trying out theoretical concepts through empirical investigation, rather than by working at a high level of abstraction only. And there is also a deep and relentless concern with what is required to bring about radical social change, and how this is constantly thwarted. More specifically, this interest in Bourdieu from within cultural studies might also rest on the fact that, as early as the 1970s, Bourdieu saw quite clearly the way in which the economy of western societies was being increasingly drawn by a cultural agenda. As heavy industry was being dismantled, and as the old consolidated social classes were also breaking up, there was a shift towards the provision of services and the creation of the need for these services. As he points out in his magisterial volume

Distinction (published in English in 1984, in French in 1976) many of these activities were of a social or cultural nature, from the availability of psychotherapy and yoga classes, to the huge growth of the consumer culture of lifestyle. Bourdieu anticipated sociologically what later became known as the cultural turn, laying out its constitutive features by examining the cultural producers and their class location, and also the cultural consumers and their various class locations. He argued that 'imposing needs rather than inculcating norms' marked a decisive moment of domination. This was also a way of negating older forms of collectivities and solidarities among the dominated (working) classes by creating, through new means of persuasion and seduction, the illusion (or misrecognition) of identification by means of consumption (Bourdieu, 1984: 154).

Bourdieu has therefore been, since the start, a sociologist concerned with the complexity of post-industrial society (even though he often draws on his earlier studies of Kabylia in Algeria to elucidate the work on contemporary urban society). He develops an analysis which in some respects is complementary to the many neo-Marxist acccounts of the relations between culture, society and economy including the work of the Birmingham Centre for Contemporary Cultural Studies. But there is also, running through a good deal of his work, a sustained argument with cultural studies, particularly, as he sees it, for its inflated romanticisation of resistance. And, also concerned to re-introduce agency, as the quotations above suggest, Bourdieu goes to great lengths to differentiate his model of social action (practical sense), from those cultural studies models of active, expressive, 'working-class' culture (Willis, 1978). Bourdieu's work can be characterised as theorising action more expansively, so as to all the better understand its limits, its re-inscription within the forces or fields of constraint. This is an immensely rich account of action in that it encompasses 'unthought' action, mental structures, ritualistic bodily practices which are also historically deposited in the habitus and absorbed in persons as a kind of unconscious 'feel for the game', a feel which, for dominated people, so frequently as to be predictable, veers towards submission, to knowing one's place in the hierarchy and bowing to social authority.

Bourdieu also replaces the concept of class (which was key for the early Birmingham Centre for Contemporary Cultural Studies work) with that of social space, where classes are the result of the power of fields to institute specific social groups as classes. The concept of field allows

Bourdieu to conceptualise power as dispersed and also autonomously located in and operating through the complex array of institutions and social bodies of modern society. Thus, to an extent, field replaces capitalism in the Marxist sense. While the changes wrought upon the working classes by the power of advertising and consumer culture are well-rehearsed, Bourdieu brings something very specific to the debate; not just the mass of empirical and statistical detail which informs *Distinction*, but rather an account of cultural differenciation as a powerful means of actively proliferating divisions and inequities through modalities of symbolic violence. Access to the field of culture (and to its modes of classification and judgement) marks out a point of intense power struggles, its processes play a key role in reproducing structural divisions.

Though overwhelmingly concerned with the structures which underpin (objective determinations) cultural practice or lifestyle, Bourdieu's approach is also counter-posed to structuralism and post-structuralism. At points in *Distinction* and on many other occasions Bourdieu clarifies his objections to semiology and structuralism, and spells out his reasons for preferring a mode of cultural analysis based on social rather than on textual relations (Bourdieu and Wacquant, 1992; see also Butler, 1999b). He is not concerned with the production of dominant meanings within or internal to a given system of signification, let us say a television programme or an advertisement. Rather he is concerned with how and where cultural forms or objects (which could include television genres) fit within a wider grid of classifications, which in turn secure relations of symbolic power. However, he shares with Levi-Strauss, and Althusser, a commitment to structuralism as providing a tool for dismantling common sense perceptions of the social world as a kind of transparency. His concern is to examine social relations and positions within the field of power and the regularities which can be shown and which in turn demonstrate constraints on the possibilities of action for subordinate groups. As many commentators show, Bourdieu's work is shaped by strands in philosophy and in the social sciences, in particular the writing of Husserl, Wittgenstein, Merleau-Ponty, and Durkheim.[1] From these diverse writers and from the phenomenological tradition, he develops an understanding of perception, embodiment, practical sense and habitus. But to make a claim for Bourdieu's work in regard to cultural studies, it is important to remember that he was also a participant in those debates which were central to the 'new left' in the 1960s and 1970s. Yet there is a marked distance from the neo-Marxism of the time. With Althusser there is a shared sense of topography, a spatial model of separating culture from economy, a way of marking a move away from traditional Marxist economism (Althusser, 1971). But where Althusser develops the concepts of ideology (material practice) and interpellation (subject producing practice) as the means by which domination is naturalised for social reproduction to take place, Bourdieu recasts the socio-political terrain in terms of field, and expands the sphere of economy outwards rather than upwards to encompass additional forms of capital, notably social capital, cultural capital and symbolic capital. Bourdieu also 'fleshes out' Althusser's relatively empty category of the subject, not by reinstating some fully conscious self-directing concept of man, and certainly not by endorsing the understanding of the subject capable of rational choice extolled by contemporary liberal economists, Bourdieu instead posits an embodied subject heavily inculcated by a habitus which acts invariably to produce dispositions and inclinations which tend towards compliancy.

The reader might for a moment reflect on how close Bourdieu is to Butler in this respect. For Butler, Bourdieu provides a 'theorisation of social practice' (Butler, 1999b: 113). I shall return to her debate with him in the final section of this chapter, but we might take note of Bourdieu's attempt to overcome the dualities which cast the explanatory force of objective, determinate structures on the one side (that is, structure), and on the other, the realm of experience, practice, and subjective relations (that is, action). While like Butler the balance in his writing is towards constraint, he endeavours to embrace and account for the embodied rituals and the bodily dispositions of the habitus (with examples) as inseparable from the field. They both must be thought together, because they are so deeply entangled. As Butler shows, Bourdieu envisages this entanglement as a kind of staging or encounter so that the habitus can confront the field, without necessarily succumbing to it, however Butler is not wholly convinced by this separation of habitus and field; she declares such an encounter as 'disingenuous' since the 'habitus is from the start implicated in the field' (Butler, 1993: 118).

Now let me move to another site of debate altogether, the more grounded, less abstract, empirically oriented field of media and cultural studies. There have been intermittent exchanges between Bourdieu and a handful of figures in this UK-dominated cultural terrain, but mostly Bourdieu refers to these in passing.[2] Garnham offers a critical account of Bourdieu's work on the basis that it almost precludes the possibility of a radical 'political project' emerging because 'agents internalise social structures in the habitus as cognitive structures or classificatory schema that operate below the level of consciousness and discourse' (Garnham, 1993: 179). Garnham explains that these classificatory schema are also in the Durkheimian sense 'arbitrary', they are there and held in place as common values for the sake of social cohesion. Bourdieu adopts this 'cultural arbitrary' from Durkheim. The point of the cultural arbitrary is that the actual symbolic configuration or specific set of signs are not important, they are arbitrary; what is important is that they perform a specific function, they do the work which is required of them. For example, the fact that a certain way of speaking or accent, let us say the braying tones of a 'hooray Henry', is indelibly associated with the assumed superiority and rightful self-importance of the English upper classes, is itself arbitrary. It could just as easily be another way of speaking that has played that same role, the 'Sloane Ranger' (so named by Peter York) could, for example, speak in an entirely different accent; what is important is that this 'voice' has come to play this role in maintaining authority and in commanding respect (York, 1984). In Bourdieu's account this enables social reproduction to take place. The cultural arbitrary encourages the inclination of the habitus to the field, ensuring that social legitimation is more easily secured. This voice and the bodily gestures and styles with which it is associated (the Barbour jacket, the string of pearls), create a sense of social authority so as to be indistinguishable from it. Bourdieu presents a model of social space which is less determined by conflict than the Marxist dialectical account, and without the pervasive 'trouble' that in Butler's writing always haunts the bid to ensure the power of enduring social relations. Garnham is also the more conventional Marxist here, he is (as Butler is in her engagement with Bourdieu) interested in how the classificatory schema can ever be dislodged, how these schemas which are constitutive of mental structures, ways of perceiving and ways of acting which are also 'unthought', can actually be changed. He rightly points to Bourdieu's attention to the education system where a radical disjuncture between the needs of the labour market and the expectations of those now in possession of qualifications (degrees) can produce something of a break in the value system. Garnham argues that this does suggest the possibility of breaking with, or seeing through, the illusion, suggesting in turn that the habitus might not be so overwhelmingly binding. But for Bourdieu instead it only means that new forms of system maintenance have to be found, as the habitus and the field seek to find a new stability or fit.

In *Distinction* Bourdieu argues that an example of this can be found in the emergent forms of the cultural economy. Two distinct class fractions converge on this site in pursuit of employment. But, where a Marxist sociology might envisage such a situation as one where social contradiction leads to possible politicisation, this is not how Bourdieu understands it. For him anxieties around education and qualifications (the result of change in the field of labour market and economy), are orchestrated so as to avoid disruption and discourage critical awareness. There are the declassé middle classes who do not possess the top professional qualifications of their peers who go on to medicine or law, and who therefore gravitate downwards towards lifestyle careers, such as top chef, landscape gardener or fashion designer. (Bourdieu points to the new preponderance of women in this group.) But they are joined by the new, upwardly mobile, lower middle class who now do have some certificates but not of the sort that would secure entrance into the over-crowded professions; they too then veer towards this semi-legitimate area of cultural economy where they can invent jobs with grand sounding titles, for example, lifestyle consultant. This group is enchanted by the 'dream of social flying' and overall it demonstrates 'cultural goodwill' to its social superiors. While there are invariably proliferations of new categorisations and symbolically violent modes of differentiation, the cultural intermediaries are inclined to social conformity. In his account of this group as collective bearers of dominant ideology whose job it is to spread its values to the population in the form of consumer culture, with all the various products, tastes, and preferences that entails, Bourdieu comes close to agreeing with Althusser's theory of ideology, but once again he fills the spaces of subjecthood out by giving to them the embodied presence of (gendered) actors who come from specific class fractions and whose new habitus of work produces dispositions such that there is endorsement of the dominant cultural field. Bourdieu theorises social practice, then, within a framework of enduring social stability, and his understanding of the classificatory schema as arbitrary is what precludes his emphasis on meaning or content. That he or she is, let us say, an 'arts advisor/administrator', is only of significance as a position which invariably perpetuates dominant cultural values. This in turn disallows any concern for that role as also being one of ambivalence or of the possibility of other meanings (which may haunt the schema) being possibly taken up by groups of 'arts advisors/administrators' who can appropriate or twist around meanings for their own alternative or oppositional purposes. In contrast to Bourdieu's focus only on embodied position, Garnham mentions the radical journalists (as a group of cultural intermediaries) who are able to use the idea of 'freedom of the press' so as to 'utilise the very legitimacy of the concept as the basis for a critique of current press practice and the realisation of a more extended concept of press freedom' (Garnham, 1993: 186).

In my own research on another type of cultural intermediary, small-scale UK fashion designers, I likewise have suggested (drawing on interviews and observation) that the value of cultural entrepreneurialism, as pronounced by government as a new normative mode of economic self-actualisation without support of state, welfare and employment regimes, can conceivably be re-deflected so as to be productive of new cultural and artistic communities embedded in urban economies and partaking in a chain of critical, micro-political activities, including an attempt to blur the distinctions between work and leisure (McRobbie, 1994 [1989], 1998). Alternatively the strictly entrepreneurial aspects of this kind of working practice can also be sidelined if not ignored. This element becomes a strategic hat to be put on for those occasions that some kind of government subsidy or funding arrangement needs to be attended to. Bourdieu, in contrast, would surely see these groups as struggling for position in a cultural field where the odds are against them and where they actively endorse a value system which is that of the dominant group (that is, the values of entrepreneurial capitalism). That these local subcultures seem also to invert the values of financial security would be to him merely a mark of the distinctiveness of their claim to the cultural field (Bourdieu, 1993). In sharp contrast to this, I extend the politics of subculture developed by Hebdige into the field of labour and everyday life, that is, into cultural work, suggesting that there is no definitive break between the symbolic re-articulation analysed by Hall et al. and by Hebdige and manifest in style, and cultural practices pursued as a way of making a living (Hall and Jefferson (eds), 1976; Hebdige, 1978). What from a cultural studies perspective might be seen thus as a site of struggle, a point where there is great investment of concern on the part of government (restless young people in a post-industrialising economy), precisely because it also marks out a possibility of discontinuity and contestation, for Bourdieu would be instead part of the means by which the new surplus of cultural producers struggle to assert themselves as unique or differentiated providers of services for the expansion of lifestyle and cultures of consumption.

How then might we summarise the relation between Bourdieu and cultural studies? These are different, but also convergent, pathways. The shared interest in dominated culture and in the means by which symbolic violence is enacted upon the man or woman of poor taste marks an area of overlap. Several passages in *Distinction* where there is very rich description of the sense and feel of poverty and then of affluence and comfort are sharply reminiscent of Hoggart's literary ethnography of working-class life *The Uses of Literacy* (Hoggart, 1957).

> If a group's whole lifestyle can be read off from the style it adopts in furnishing or clothing, this is not only because these properties are the object of the economic and cultural necessity which determines their selection, but also because the social relations objectified in familiar objects in their luxury or poverty, their 'distinction' or vulgarity, their 'beauty' or their 'ugliness' impress themselves through bodily experiences which may be as profoundly unconscious as the quiet caress of beige carpets or the thin clamminess of tattered garish linoleum, the harsh smell of bleach . . . Every interior expresses in its own language the present and even the past state of its occupants, bespeaking the elegant self assurance of inherited wealth, the flaunting arrogance of the nouveaux riches, the . . . shabbinesss of the poor and the gilded shabbiness of 'poor relations' striving to live beyond their means . . . (Bourdieu, 1984: 77)

There is, then, a connection with strands of writing from early cultural studies, although Stuart Hall's work is much more influenced by Althusser and Gramsci and with the reworking of the relations between culture and economy in a non-reductionist way. But as Garnham points out, Bourdieu draws from Marx as much as he does from Durkheim; the economic field is a base line of social organisation and other fields refer back to it through their own dynamics of struggle for capital. And in so far as the classificatory schema sets itself up as universal, where in fact it operates to the advantage of the dominant social classes, it is not so unlike the dominant ideology thesis of Althusser. It too relies on naturalisation and on misrecognition for its effectivity, although of course Althusser's concern with the materiality of ideology proposes close attention to the politics of meaning and thus to textuality. But one key difference lies in the way early cultural studies work looked specifically to different social groups and subgroups and their distinctive cultural practices in an attempt to understand not only the forces which secured consent and stability, but also which produced rupture and 'crisis of hegemony'. In varying degrees these diverse constituencies, for example, black youth, white working-class youth ('the lads'), then also punks, and other subcultural groupings, found some kind of capacity for political expression. These took shape within available cultural forms (such as popular music) but through rearrangement of these codes they unsettled the assumed social relations of consent by disrupting the dominant interpretation of reality, or adding to those pre-existing accounts others which were more disputatious. Bourdieu's rather dismissive response to this kind of work is tempered only by his agreement with Willis, that 'the lads' have in fact only a small degree of room to disturb dominant social relations in schooling, and that this very counter-cultural practice itself is one of the means by which their long-term adjustment to sub-ordination is secured.

Field and Habitus

I have already introduced at least two of Bourdieu's key concepts: field and habitus. But more needs to be said about them if we are to be able to decide on their value for cultural studies. The field provides Bourdieu with an 'open and closed' spatial model for understanding social struc-ture. It encompasses the infinity of layers of organisations, institutions and practices which are characteristic of advanced societies. Bourdieu takes the economy and market as his two primary concepts upon which he then builds up his theory of fields. These proliferate but follow the principles of the capitalist market economy. The field constrains, man-ages and orchestrates the kinds of practices which can take place within its frame. Social groups are organised within these fields. Subgroups also seek a place and gain recognition as they compete for a higher position within the field. Within capitalist society the economic field is dominant. The artistic or cultural fields are part of those fields in dominance in modern capitalist society but in relation to economy they are domi-nated. We might then imagine Bourdieu's fields like a series of Microsoft's windows: endlessly superimposed as they are 'opened', but dependent on the original software windows system, which in this sense is that of market economy and capital. Newness or innovation within this field system comes about as subgroups push themselves forward and struggle for position. Because fields also accommodate such subgroups and adjust to take them into account, they are flexible while also 'container' entities. McNay explains the field as:

> a network or configuration of objective relations between positions. The distribution of certain types of capital – economic, social, cultural and symbolic – denotes the different goods, resources and values around which power relations in a particular field crystallise. Any field is marked by a tension or conflict between the interests of different groups who struggle to gain control over a field's capital. In the final instance, all fields are determined by the demands of the capitalist system of accumulation, however, each field is autonomous in that it has a specific internal logic which establishes non-synchronous, uneven relations with other fields and which renders it irreducible to any overarching dynamic. (McNay, 1999b: 106)

McNay also points out that like Foucault, Bourdieu works with a diffuse and spreading, expansive understanding of power. The concept of field allows him to develop a model of social organisation which can account for change while also showing how the field is able to constrain such forces to produce regularities. The field is, however, also the means by which power and capital are managed and conserved. What is at stake in the field is access to power, and thus the struggles that go on inside it would be the equivalent of the conflicts and crises which Stuart Hall or Paul Gilroy might also examine, but in a less bounded, circumscribed and demarcated way. Where Bourdieu would insist on a field-based approach to issues of youth crime, race and media, Gilroy and Hall would recognise the degrees of 'relative autonomy' which the media have in dealing with these phenomena, and they would then pursue an analysis, immediately concrete and historically specific, which dissects and analyses the relations between media, state and politics (Hall et al., 1978; Gilroy, 1987). In both *Policing the Crisis* and in *There Ain't No Black in the Union Jack*, Hall and Gilroy did not need anything as abstract as the field of government, or the field of media, to be in place before embarking on the work. Their methodology might then be seen to be more improvised, more driven by the urgency suggested by the observations and available material and events around them. In contrast and despite Bourdieu's repeated emphasis on the value of empirical work, much of his writing on field and habitus is much more abstract and removed from the urgency of the politically focused analysis which drives much of the cultural studies work of the 1970s and 1980s. (For a recent and extended account of Bourdieu's engagement with the field of media see Couldry, 2004.)

There are real difficulties with the concept of field in the context of contemporary globalisation. There is a sense in which both these concepts (field and habitus) work more successfully in a bounded, 'nation state' to 'nation state', kind of way. It is indeed possible to talk about the journalistic field or the cultural field or artistic field in this kind of way, but if we start from the premise of the fast flows of global media and interconnective and intersecting journalistic fields, or what Appadurai calls mediascapes, plus the concomitant flows of peoples, as producers and consumers, then the idea of a field of global media is surely too large and unwieldy to produce the nuanced understanding which Bourdieu's model suggests (Appadurai, 1990). Yes, of course, the field of global media comprises of many struggling subfields, and is also characterised by competition for access, and by obstacles for dominated groups without access (as a political economy of global media would also show). But would the idea of the global media field be able to account for the seemingly endless capacity for rapid intersection and cross-fertilisation of so many transnational media and cultural forms? These global communications networks require a flexible workforce where it is also difficult to draw 'field-specific' lines of competence and activity. For example, high-skill work need not be associated with cosmopolitan elites (through processes of off-shoring) and global cities like London and New York are home also to very low-paid media producers and exhausted multi-taskers barely scraping a living in these 'long hours', de-regulated, 'new sweat shop' areas of work (Sassen, 1991; Ross, 2003; McRobbie, 2004). While we might talk about the field of employment, or the field of global cultural labour, giving rise to a proliferation of subfields including that of freelance self-employment (where in Bourdieu's terms there would be various struggles for position), the requirement from Bourdieu's perspective that we understand this within the frame of field theory is not necessarily more productive than, for example, the frameworks of new micro-/macro-political or cultural economy developed by, for example, Sassen (2000), Du Gay and Pryke (eds) (2002), and Scott and Power (eds) (2004). Flows, networks, movements and processes of individualisation do not sit comfortably with the terms of the field. Perhaps indeed power works most productively now by superseding and making superfluous categories of spatial fixity like the field. The question is, can the field, a concept which relies on, and requires, a notion of (albeit permeable/fluid) boundary, engage with the dynamics of change in a 'speeded up' world? What if one of the means by which contemporary power works most effectively is to refuse the boundary form of the field. If power is now liquid, and if, as Lash argues, structures appear to be in meltdown and if this has become the most effective means by which power is able to operate with the help of new technology and instant communications, then can it be said that the field still is able to act as the generator and custodian of structure? In this context where is the field and what does it look like (Lash, 2002)? Of course the question of where fields start and end was regularly put to Bourdieu in interview and his answer was that 'the boundaries of the field can only be determined by empirical investigation' (Bourdieu and Wacquant, 1992: 100).

If the field is a structured social space within which relations of power are pursued through struggle for position, it is Bourdieu's notion of habitus which provides the flesh and bones to his model of social organisation. It is the most interesting of Bourdieu's concepts and the one upon which his theory of social practice rests. The habitus refers to the sphere of active, lively, social life, and to the ways in which we live our daily lives. It precedes the individual, giving to him or her a sense of the past, a memory of the distinctiveness of that specific milieu which is particular to that habitus. As Butler puts it, this is how the body (in the habitus) becomes a 'site of incorporated history'. The habitus marks the space which gives to the individual what I would describe as his or her fullness of social being (bearing in mind the problems of using a word like fullness). As Bourdieu says 'To speak of the habitus is to assert that the individual and even the subjective is social, collective. Habitus is a socialised subjectivity' (Bourdieu and Wacquant, 1992: 126). This is the terrain into which individuals are born and through which they acquire, at a pre-conscious level, a whole set of dispositions. Bourdieu sometimes calls this a 'feel for the game' to emphasise that it comprises actions which to an outsider might appear utterly calculated and reasonable, but which are carried out in an automatic 'unthought' way. But this is also the basis for 'regular modes of behaviour, and thus for the regularity of modes of practices, and if practices can be predicted this is because the effect of the habitus is that agents who are equipped with it will behave in a certain way' (Bourdieu, 1990: 77). This is then a 'practical sense', 'the directedness of comportment' (Dreyfus and Rabinow, 1993: 38). Most significant is the way in which the habitus appears to orient itself towards the field so as to accommodate to its 'wishes'. Underlying this aspect of the habitus is Bourdieu's more political question, why do people whose subordination depends on their seeming consent to the dominant social order, which in turn invariably acts against them, acts to confirm them in their place of domination, still however acquiesce? The habitus allows him to try to answer this question through a generalised idea of mental structures, or cognitive patterns, which are inseparable from bodily or corporeal responses. As he puts it, at one point with bluntness 'the dominated are dominated in their brains' (Bourdieu, 1993: 41).

The habitus accommodates group 'customs' and habituated actions comprising gestures, inclinations, dispositions which are so routine, so 'unthought', that they perform social positionality in their fields almost as an instinct. The habitus comprises skills, information, and these are the basis for action, they both permit it and curtail it. Lipuma relates the concept of habitus to class suggesting that 'the distribution of probabilities of lifechances for a given class is internalised via the habitus' (Lipuma, 1993: 24). Garnham explicates how the habitus delimits what is 'thinkable', it is 'the key structuring mechanism between the real world and the thought world' (Garnham, 1993: 183). That is, this is also where the classificatory schemata mentioned earlier are actually internalised, the 'mental and corporeal schemata of perception' (Bourdieu and Wacquant, 1992: 16). Bourdieu also suggests that social power depends on an inclination on the part of social groups to require stability, regularity and predictability, the relation between habitus and field is such that this can be produced and reproduced as 'social order' with the habitus flexible enough to manage change, unforeseen events and even upheavals. That it can embrace change, and be generative of newness and also appear to operate on a spontaneous unthought basis, is what gives to the habitus its tremendous force. It is this which prompts questions to Bourdieu like 'does the habitus reinforce determinism under the appearance of relaxing it'? Is it the site where, as he puts it, the 'somatisation of social relations of dominance' is secured, so that people are lulled into trust in the structures? But then he pulls back saying 'people are not fools' (Bourdieu and Wacquant, 1992: 130).

The many articles and chapters given over to engaging with this concept of habitus, including all the interviews with Bourdieu himself where he explicates at length on this concept, are a mark of its centrality to his thinking and also a sign of the clear importance of the idea, particularly for its ability to fill out the missing spaces in Althusser's 'empty' subject of ideology. Bourdieu has also made great attempts with this concept to overcome traditional dualities of body and mind, and likewise in sociological terms he has sought to transcend the impasse which is often reached between those who argue for objective determinations of structure, as against those who focus on subjective aspects of action. There is no other sociologist of his generation so persuasive in the account of social practice. And because Bourdieu is also a political thinker, the concept of habitus lies at the centre of his account of the enduring features of social stability. For McNay the habitus goes some way in explaining how even for feminists the norms and instincts and habitual practices around motherhood can 'kick in' in surprising and unexpected ways, maternity can override the most well-considered arguments about shared parenting and this is suggestive of the historical residues and stored memories in the feminine habitus which are activated in motherhood (McNay, 1999b). And likewise for Butler the effectivity of the habitus might be that at an unthought and corporeal level, it is able to shape that which is thinkable and unthinkable in relation to sexuality. The habitus then of the heterosexual matrix would refer to the lived spaces of gender normativity and family life ('the embodied rituals of everydayness' as Butler puts it) which are so inclined to shoring up the requirements of the field that the pursuit of wayward desires is virtually unimaginable (Butler, 1999b: 113). But herein lies the difference between both thinkers because Butler argues that what is unthinkable is also based on that which is thinkable but repressed; it comes back to haunt the margins of habitus and is then lived out in terms of loss or lack. What could have been otherwise, is therefore always close to what is. And this opens a margin of hope, where the possibility for political and social change can be envisioned. If the habitus was as successful as Bourdieu would have it, there would hardly be a gay or lesbian movement. Now while we could go on here, indefinitely pondering what Bourdieu's response might be to the fact that these political movements do indeed come into being, his response presumably would be to focus on how normativity is still achieved. Yes, he would suggest that, as Calhoun puts it, 'contrary action' of this type within the sexual habitus, is not 'foreclosed', but it would still find itself leant upon (perhaps by the fields of politics and the law) to fit with requirements and to act in a particular way, for example, to seek certain forms of state recognition and to embrace the terms and conditions for wider acceptability within the social field, for example, through legally sanctioned partnership and involvement in consumer culture (Calhoun, 1993: 75).

Cultural Capital and Distinction

Distinction draws on research data (in the form of graphs, diagrams, interview material and statistics) which allows the analysis to proceed. Bourdieu also intersperses his text with lengthy footnotes so that the reader can only barely discern the differences between the two. In an interview Bourdieu commented that he did indeed attempt a 'discursive montage' effect in the book (Bourdieu and Wacquant, 1992: 66). The study seeks to present a materialist analysis of taste and of the consumption of culture and art, as a counter to Kantian aesthetics, which poses the merely pleasing perception of art as delight, with the more gratifying response which instead relies on the 'disinterestedness' of contemplation. In this attempt to refute Kant, by means of sociological analysis, Bourdieu considers how there are embedded in such perceptions on the one hand a connection between popular (and working-class) taste as that which offers pleasures of a merely sensual and even base type, and the colder, more formal gratifications which are 'independent of the charming of the senses' and which are in turn the means by which dominant social classes preserve their privilege (Bourdieu, 1984: 42). Focusing on patterns of cultural consumption, Bourdieu shows how social inequalities are actively generated through the classifying power of taste as it operates according to this Kantian schema. Class divisions in complex modern society are produced and reproduced in the realm of taste, and what appears to be generic to the works themselves and the capacity of persons to differentiate, is in fact a non-innocent process by which class-divided society perpetuates itself. In this section I will restrict my concern to two aspects of *Distinction*, each of which has proved of great relevance to work in contemporary cultural studies. These are, first, cultural capital and, second, Bourdieu's distinction between 'scholars and gentlemen'. Traversing each of these concerns is an understanding of how symbolic power works to reduce the emancipatory possibilities of critical understanding as a pre-condition of radical social change.

Cultural capital is an expanded form of capital, (Bourdieu also talks of social capital as an asset of contacts and connections). It is based on the possession of specific competences, like economic capital it can be usefully traded, and it is a kind of personal asset; however, it is not reducible to economic capital, and not all who possess material assets of wealth or property are in possession of cultural capital. The possession of cultural capital provides its owner with a key instrument for maintaining social dominance over those who are not in possession of these competences. Largely owned by those with high educational qualifications and also with particular familial backgrounds where cultural knowledge of the fine arts and classical music is taken for granted, these social groups are able to ridicule or abuse those without such expertise thus ensuring their crippling sense of social inferiority, indeed shame, by means of this symbolic violence. If it is the case that on questions of taste, there are routinely expressed, strong degrees of disgust or revulsion, if the idea of being associated with people 'like that' who consume the wrong kind of food, or who wear the wrong kind of clothes, produces 'violent repudiations' as Butler might put it, then surely 'class struggle' is thus pursued through processes of culture and consumption. Indeed the concept of cultural capital allows Bourdieu to show how fierce and pervasive class antagonisms are within specific class fractions (for example, upper middle class in relation to middle middle class, and lower middle class in relation to upper working class). Bourdieu in a sense 'comes upon' the concept of cultural capital as he investigates the responses of people from different class positions (through occupation) in regard to their perceptions or knowledge of culture. He does this by tracking both knowledge and means of perception and expression to particular works or artists, musicians, composers and other similarly cultural persons and works, as against social background, education and occupation. The correlations show how cultural capital has tradeable value, it can be used in a number of labour markets where it is useful over and above the set requirements of a particular job. Indeed the most valued aspects of cultural capital are those most difficult to acquire, since these are not normally part of the educational curriculum but are instead associated with the advantages of a certain type of familial environmment, one where, for example, a mother who does not work and who herself embodies high cultural capital in her 'exquisite taste', is able to pass this on to her children in a leisurely and unhasty way. Simply by providing a specific kind of home where classical music is ever present, where piano lessons are a routine part of growing up, where paintings and precious objects are not so much commented upon and dwelt upon but are simply there, 'as though by an immemorial gift' (Bourdieu, 1984: 35), indeed maybe even disregarded because they are so very ordinary and unremarkable in such a cultivated home, this mother is able to ensure her children acquire, in the right kind of way, this 'disinterested' capacity.

Bourdieu's wonderful phrase for this kind of comfort and aptitude is that it suggests 'distance from necessity'. The mother has all the time in the world to ensure her children simply absorb as a kind of 'second nature' a feel for beautiful things and objects. And this ease with which they later enter the world in turn has a value, it marks them out as endowed with unique and advanced ability to discern the quality of fine things. It also marks them out immediately from those who have acquired similar knowledge but in a much less rarefied way. Indeed the manners of the 'gentleman' (or his female counterpart) are able to 'show up' the too keen or indeed too 'scholastic' manners of his or her middle-class and university-educated counterpart, with whom such a high-ranking person, to her or his horror, might be in competition for a job. Thus we move onto Bourdieu's marvellously rich distinction between gentlemen and scholars. This latter type of person betrays his or her lowly origins through over enthusiasm for the kinds of things or topics which are so normal and unremarkable to the gentlemen that he can be utterly relaxed about them. Enthusiam suggests that these fine things are out of the ordinary, quite special and of specific value, when to the 'aristocrat' they are simply there and connected with him or her so naturally as to suggest that he or she is indeed a superior species of person whom God himself might have appointed to occupy such rank and status. If not God, then at least the duration of time, since these are things, after all, that are handed down within an aristocratic family over the centuries. More importantly the hint (or maybe the shudder) of disapproval for knowledge based on study and on the acquisition of academic qualifications is also a reflex which protects the 'natural status' of those who have such talents independent of the vulgarity of actual learning; hence, Bourdieu argues, their preference for a non-scholastic language, one based on 'spiritual' or non-linguistic responses invoking for example the 'timeless', the 'magical' or the 'ineffable' as though true appreciation of these things is actually outside of the possibilities of the learned response (as though to say, 'actually it cannot be taught') but is still within the special capacity of the favoured few. By this means again minute but pervasive class distinctions are both preserved and (re)-produced anew. The scholar is not only too enthusiastic, but is also frequently in danger of giving himself away. There is always the possibility of being shown up for having learnt these 'airs and graces', particularly when so many of these are not part of any academic curriculum. For example, there is the danger of not being able to strike up just the right kind of rapport with a waiter. As Bourdieu explains this is about 'knowing how to be served'.

The point of this almost supernatural grace on the part of those class fractions for whom culture provides such supreme added value, is that if it is the case that it were to become apparent that all of these competences could indeed be learnt, then, in a sense, their 'game is up', their 'cover is foiled'. This could even mean that their privileges might have to be shared with those upstarts from within the ranks of the educated middle classes who could conceivably teach themselves what otherwise appears to be a unique and special set of attributes. This would then give way to social mobility and perhaps even to some loss of status. Hence the repeated attempts to preserve distinction; hence the vigilance on the part of the cultured upper classes to find ways of further differentiating themselves. Where Bourdieu more or less leaves off in this debate, is also a point at which we might want to press ahead. At the heart of his analysis of the range of perceptions of legitimate works of art is the suggestion that art works and musical forms which are considered of high value require specific kinds of knowledge for them to become meaningful. Without this it is not surprising that uneducated working-class people look at, for example, a 'pile of bricks' in an art gallery with, as Bourdieu puts it, 'panic mingled with revolt' (Bourdieu, 1984: 33). If, however, the fact that what is required is detailed internal knowledge of form, and if, for example, debates being conducted inside art worlds by artists and others, were to become more widely understood, then the sharp sense of pain or injury at what seems instead mere ignorance or stupidity would be lifted.

This is what education offers. It is only when it is explained that abstract expressionism in fact directly refers to previous dialogues within groups of artists and critics, and that it is also concerned with the whole idea of painting and paint itself, and with questions of form, that it becomes comprehensible. And if, likewise, the difficulty of certain forms of poetic language are explained so that the reader can understand that poetry is also about form, that the shape of the poem itself, the relation of its parts to the whole, its organisational form, is actually critical to the meaning it produces, then the fear and the confusion and the anxiety can be lifted.

Much of art is then about form, and is about the internal codes which happen, at any one time, to be dominant within such a field. By this 'breaking of the spell', argues Bourdieu, the world of high culture can in fact be demystified. Indeed if Bourdieu's own sociology was to be widely distributed, perhaps even popularised inside and outside the academy, then all of these strategies and devices for preserving privilege and wealth and status in the hands of the very few would be revealed for what they are – instruments of class power devised so as to bruise, humiliate and intimidate all but the most powerful groups and social classes. However, there is another scenario. There is the way in which demystification can be utilised primarily as a means of gaining position as a newcomer within the field. The primary means of gaining status is by trying to play the game. This means attempting to learn the manners of the gentleman and as long as this strenuous effort is made then those in power need not have too many fears that they will find themselves imperilled in their position and authority, if, for example, the middle-class aspirants are overwhelmingly concerned to emulate their social betters. They can learn all the codes they are able to, but if this knowledge and these competences stop short at revealing how overall these continue to be used to repel outsiders, and to humiliate those for whom such things must remain out of reach, then we are talking about how subgroups within a field struggle for their own recognition and in addition with how emergent fields and their corresponding habituses incline towards legitimation of the dominant field. The only fear the upper classes might have is that of being crowded out with those who aspire to join their ranks. In short de-mystification need not inevitably lead to democratisation of culture. (However I would argue that there is still the potential for critical understanding by these means. Cultural studies itself is a strategic intervention in the academy emerging out of a range of pedagogic practices which sought to achieve this kind of demystification effect. This can be seen in the work of a range of figures whose writing shaped, or even invented earlier cultural studies, from Brecht and Benjamin to Hoggart and Williams, even John Berger, and then directly to Stuart Hall. In all of these writers the disenchantment dynamic of critical pedagogy is of key importance.)

Breaking the Spell

The great disappointment underpinning Bourdieu's writing is that there is so little possibility of radical social change, that everything is always already inclined towards conformity to the social order. As Butler puts it, 'this achieved congruence between field and habitus establishes the ideal of adaptation as the presiding norm of his theory of sociality' (Butler, 1999: 118). In short it would be possible to conclude that for Bourdieu the field (let us say the field of 'capitalism') is an 'unalterable positivity' (or as Mrs Thatcher famously said, 'there is no alternative'). Again, following Butler, the habitus does indeed suggest a 'virtue of necessity' where 'submission to an order is to become savvy to its ways (Butler, 1999b: 118). With his model of what might be described as 'almost sheer domination', Bourdieu shows himself to be a social theorist of constraint. Butler upbraids him for failing to see the way in which ambivalence is inherent in these habitual processes of inclination to conform to the objective demands of the field. After all, subjects are formed, claims Bourdieu, through processes of mimeticism, but this requirement, according to Butler, always carries some necessary realm of failure. Butler might suppose, then, that 'being savvy in (the) ways (of domination)' does not preclude ambivalence wherein lies a margin of possibility for the 're-appropriation of discursive power'. That is, just as her ideas of subjecthood involve being 'interpellated by prevailing forms of social power', these regularised practices of authority can allow for the 'improper use of the performative' so as to even be able to 'expose the prevailing forms of authority and its exclusion' (Butler, 1999b: 123). Butler, then, is more able than Bourdieu to gesture to such practices of radical resignification as can be seen to work within feminism, gay and lesbian politics and anti-racist movements whereby terms of authority (for example, freedom, democracy) can be 're-territorialised'. Bourdieu in turn cannot quite run with the notion that radical social change might take these forms, and in his later more polemical work he is scornful of such efforts. What, then, is needed to 'break the spell'? In a magnificent and maybe desperate gesture Bourdieu holds out for the ability of the kind of reflexive sociology he professes to provide the possibilities for this kind of critical capacity. But then modesty perhaps kicks in, or else his own inclination to anticipate the forcefulness of incorporation to the demands of the (educational) field. These, then, seem to stop him from imagining that his sociology in conjunction with other forms of critique (the work of the theorists in this book, for example) might accrue sufficient symbolic power to disseminate more widely, through the educational system, the political possibilities that become available with scholarly 'disenchantment'. This makes him a relatively lonely thinker, where in fact the symbolic violence of everyday life which he analyses in such detail has been the trigger for radicalisation for many in the field of cultural studies, as well as in sociology. Bourdieu is not so alone. These endeavours have in turn produced vast libraries of works which provide the instruments for further disenchantment. Moreover, such works also leave the library and enter other circuits and in these multifarious ways they are and can also be constitutive of radicalised communities in the field of education and beyond.[3] Bourdieu attributes too much to the field of sociology, weighing it down with the burden of critique, under which it buckles, and perhaps too little to neighbouring modes of scholarly activity such as cultural studies. He is, in this respect, constrained by the disciplinary boundaries which are also, magnificently, of his own making.

Notes

1   The four volumes which provide the best introduction to these debates are Bourdieu, 1990; Bourdieu and Wacquant, 1992; Calhoun et al. (eds) 1993; and Shusterman (ed.) 1999.

2   For Bourdieu's footnotes and short comments on Birmingham Centre for Contemporary Cultural Studies see Bourdieu and Wacquant, 1992: 80–1.

3   The literary theorist Terry Eagleton in his recent memoir describes the ritualistic humiliation on the part of the working-class boy who found his way into Cambridge in the 1960s and who was

radicalised in the process. The writing also (unconsciously?) displays psychic ambivalences of the sort Butler would emphasise, alongside something like Bourdieusian subservience and deference (Eagleton, 2001).

Extended Notes

What Not To Wear

Drawing on Bourdieu, here I examine forms of female symbolic violence found in mid-evening television programmes given over to the so-called 'make-over' that is, the transformation of self with the help of experts in the hope or expectation of improvement of status and life chances through the acquisition of forms of cultural capital. The public denigration by women of recognised taste (the experts and presenters) of women of little or no taste, brings a new (and apparently humorous) dimension to this kind of prime-time television. These reprimands span the spectrum from the schoolmarmish ticking off for poor grooming, bad posture and unattractive mannerisms, to the outright sneer, or classroom snigger directed towards the unkempt young, single mother wearing stained trousers as she drops off her child at school. Over the last few years this genre of popular television has achieved huge ratings and has attracted a great deal of publicity on the basis of a format which brings experts in taste together with willing victim in need of improvement. (My interest here is primarily in two BBC television pro-grammes, *What Not To Wear* (WNTW) and *Would Like to Meet* (WLTM). For full details see the BBC website (www.bbc.co.uk). There are also many new, hybrid genres, in one series both gardener and interior designer team up to make over house and garden, in another two women cleaners shame a victim in the hope of encouraging him or her to become more clean and tidy, and in a recent and kinder US programme, five gay men help a straight man each week to improve his home, self-image and fashion sense.)

These programmes actively generate and legitimate forms of class antag-onism, particularly between women, in a way which would have been socially unacceptable until recently. That is, the rules of television were such that public humiliation of people for their failure to adhere to middle-class standards in speech or appearance would have been considered offensive, discriminatory or prejudicial. However, now denigration is done with a degree of self-conscious irony, both the presenters and the audiences are assumed to know that no harm is intended, and that this is just good fun. It is now possible, thank goodness, to laugh at less fortunate people once again. And the message is that the poor woman would do well to emulate her social superiors. While men are involved, as both experts and victims, this is largely a female genre of television and the overall address is to women (see Brunsdon, 2003). And this female address corresponds to the changing identity of women in contemporary Britain. No longer primarily defined in terms of husbands, fathers or boyfriends, girls have been set free to compete with each other, sometimes mercilessly. Public enactments of hatred and animosity are refracted at a bodily or corporeal level. But is this just girl against girl or are there specifically class dynamics? I would argue that there are clear class elements, redrafted along the lines of the merito-cratic model promoted by the Blair government. People are increasingly individualised, they are required to invent themselves, they are called upon to shape themselves so as to be flexible, to fit with the new circumstances where they cannot be passively part of the workforce, but must instead keep themselves employable, and adapt themselves and their skills for the rapidly changing demands of the labour market.

Thus, class makes a decisive reappearance in and through the vectors of transformed gendered individualisation. Walby has suggested that with full participation in the workforce, class differences between women (in terms of income) are becoming more marked than ever (Walby, 1998). She has also described the enormous disparity of income between younger and older women (with the latter much worse off). And although racial disadvantage weighs more heavily against black males than females, there remain marked inequalities of access in relation to education and careers between white and black women. Overall, this scenario would suggest gender transforma-tion including widespread fragmentation and dispersal, but with younger, well-qualified, white women moving towards a more secure middle-class position. Change and movement are a feature of women's experience in recent years. How do these changes connect with the sharpness of the class antagonisms in these programmes? Of course as Bourdieu and many others have shown women have by no means been immune to the articulation of sharp and often cruel class distinctions. Working-class women have been very aware of the denigratory judgements made against them by their middle-class counterparts particularly in regard to their appearance and non-respectability (Skeggs, 1997). Indeed middle-class women have played a key role in the reproduction of class society not just through their exem-plary role as wives and mothers, but also as standard bearers for middle-class family values, for certain norms of citzenship and also for safeguarding the valuable cultural capital accruing to them and their fami-lies through access to education, refinement and other privileges. The question is, when women become more detached from traditional family roles as a result of movement into the labour market over a lifetime, how does this effect class society? What are the cultural forms and the wider repertoire of meanings which seek to give shape to, and retain control over, new gendered hierarchies? Is it the case that through the prism of individualisation, class differences are reinvented, largely within the cultural and media field, so as to produce and reproduce social divisions now more autonomously feminised? Does the move into the workplace displace the masculine inflection of class values with a wide range of more feminised meanings? Perhaps it was an easy mistake for feminists to make, to assume that the gains of feminist success in terms of the winning of certain freedoms (to earn your own living, to be entitled to equal pay and so on) would bring with it, for women, an extension and enlargement of feminist values of collectivity and equality. Female individualisation is, then, a social process bringing into being new social divisions through the denigration of low class or poor and disadvantaged women by means of symbolic violence.

Let me consider two illuminating journalistic moments, each of which is indicative of a social dynamic which reiterates these specifically feminine modalities of symbolic violence, as processes of class differentiation now thoroughly projected onto, and inseparable from, the female body. From now on the single mother will be understood to be an abject person, a social category, a certain type of girl whose bodily features and disposition betray her lowly status. This too marks a reversal of the language of liberal welfare values for whom the teenage mother was someone to be provided with support. A new virulent form of class antagonism finds expression through the public denigration of the bodily failings of the girl who at a too-young age embraces motherhood. Thus Christina Odone (Deputy Editor of *The New Statesman*) provides a more serious-minded (if inevitably laced with some irony) version of this recent form of boundary marking practice by writing that 'top range women . . . prefer to leave reproduction to the second eleven . . . a bump risks becoming as clear proof of a working-class background as the fag hanging from someone's lips'. She goes on to say that a teenage mother produces a 'socially autistic child with little expectation and even less talent' (Odone, 2000). In the same vein, but this time emerging from within the heartland of tabloid pop culture, one of the girl singers formerly from the pop band Atomic Kitten (Kerry Catona) finds herself widely referred to on the Popbitch website (www.popbitch.com) as 'pramface', that is, she is deemed to look like the kind of poor, low-class girl with a baby in a pushchair. Other derogatory forms of female social classification include 'minger' (or 'pig' as the *Sun* labelled runner up for 2002's *Big Brother* television contest, Jade Goody).

What does pramface mean? A kind of girl. What kind of girl? Not dressed for work, therefore not earning an honest living. But not a student. With a baby, but looks single, that is, not sufficiently attractive and presentable to attract a long-term partner. She must be unmarried and dependent on benefits. As a seemingly recognisable social type, it is assumed there must be many like her. The insult is thus indicative of a renewed practice of social re-ordering. The bodies of young women are to be understood according to a scale running from impoverished single maternity marking failure, to well-groomed slim, sophistication marking success. The pramface girl who is poor-looking and with a child in a buggy, is in sharp contrast to the 'A1' girls who can spend a disposable income on themselves and aspire to full participation in consumer culture, and through this differentiation class distinctions are now more autonomously (that is, these are all single girls) generated, within what Bourdieu might call the media or journalistic field and refracted through the youthful female body. This is a relatively recent phenomenon. Denigratory speech unashamedly, indeed spitefully, directed towards girls by other girls is associated with pre-feminist old-fashioned 'bitchiness', that is, it belongs to a time when girls were encouraged to see each other as enemies in the competition for men. Hurtful comments about body image, shape, style or poor taste would be considered as belonging to the school playground, and vociferously condemned by liberal-minded adults and teachers as a form of bullying. Likewise sniggers about living in a council estate or having a mother who does not look well off, might be expected to be met with a sharp reprimand.

Bourdieu's writing allows us to re-examine symbolic violence as a vehicle for social reproduction, this time through a particular (post-feminist) temporal nexus of female individualisation, the body and the world of cultural objects. The victim of the make-over television programme presents his or her class habitus for analysis and critique by the experts. The programmes comprise a series of encounters where cultural intermediaries impart guidance and advice to individuals ostensibly as a means of self-improvement. The experts guide the victims through a series of activities, from shopping, cooking and interacting with people, to flirting and going on dates. A key (entertainment) feature of the programmes (and one which most invites a Foucauldian analysis) involves spying on the victims by means of hidden video cameras, as a way of seeing them ethnographically (that is, *au naturel*); the victims also have a chance to report back on their progress with video diaries. Bourdieu is so useful here because he theorises taste, while also understanding the body to be at the centre of what McNay calls 'modern strategies of social control' (McNay, 1999b). McNay also reminds us that Bourdieu considers how social inequalities are perpetuated as power relations directed towards bodies and the 'dispositions of individuals'. Bourdieu focuses on constraint and injury, on practices of symbolic violence and their effectivity. The 'corporeal inculcation' of symbolic violence is, McNay argues, 'exercised with the complicity' of the individual. These programmes would not work if the victim did not come forward and offer herself as someone in need of expert help. On the basis of her own subordinate class habitus, the individual will have a 'feel for the game', a 'practical sense for social reality' which means that in the context of the programmes, she will instinctively, and unconsciously, know her place in regard to the experts, hence the tears, the gratitude and the deference to those who know so much better than she does, and who are willing to share in this knowledge and expertise. In the two programmes *WNTW* and *WLTM* the habitual knowingness of the body is confronted with the demand of the dominant field that the victim/participant copies or partake in a kind of mimesis, so that the habitus might be modified to conform with the requirement of good taste. If, as Butler suggests, the habitus is the space for the generation of social belief in the obviousness of dominant social reality, then the cajoling, reprimanding and encouragement of the presenters and make-over experts provides clear insight into the operations of the field as it attempts to alter the habitus, while also inculcating the realism of the unachievable. As Butler again suggests, the habitus and the field move towards congruence with each other through processes of practical mimesis (Butler, 1999b). But in these programmes the class field and habitus of the cultural intermediaries must also remain separate (hence unachievable) from that of the victims. There is no suggestion that the victims will ever truly belong to the same social group as their improvers. This is made clear by the consoling words and concluding comments on the part of the experts who retain an ever critical and sceptical eye. Among themselves they imagine that, once they have departed, the victim is bound to return to her bad old ways. Thus we might say that what is happening in the programmes is that there is an attempt to transform the female working-class habitus by means of shaming, instruction and the momentary celebrity glamour of being on television. The habitus is to be brought into line so as to conform with the 'needs and norms' of the emergent consumer-dominated cultural field, and by these means women are both individualised and rendered respectable. Now that women have decisively entered the labour force, female consumer culture has, in Blair's Britain, come to occupy a key site in regard to the possibilities for female upward mobility and by this means the map of social class is redrafted in gender terms. With the eradication of the old, traditional working-class, these programmes and their equivalents across popular culture and in the tabloid press, construct a new feminised social space which is defined in terms of status, affluence and body image. More generally, by these means women are subjected to more subtle practices of power directed to winning their consent to, and approval of, a more competitive, modernised, neo-liberal, social order.

Bourdieu's concepts of cultural capital and cultural intermediaries provide fine tools for understanding these programmes as a genre. It is only possible here, however, to provide a hasty sketch of how this might be done. On the television programmes the cultural intermediaries, for example, usually refer to, or unambiguously enact, their own class backgrounds by bringing this to bear in the way in which they present the programmes. Often the women are upper middle-class in voice and appearance and impart aspects of the cultural capital which they have accrued effortlessly. Their knowledge about good taste comes naturally because it is simply part of how they have been brought up. There is 'distance from necessity', there is nothing too urgent, too over enthusiastic, too *arriviste* about their expertise. They have had all the time in the world to learn about the kinds of things not taught at school and not on the academic curriculum. They simply know this stuff, they know how to put together an outfit without even thinking about it, they know which colours work, they know how to throw a wonderful dinner party and make it look as though there was no labour and no anxiety and no planning involved. They also know what 'not to wear'. They signal various degrees of disgust or repulsion, or bodily displeasure at those who do not possess such good taste as themselves. The two young women who present *WNTW* are well-connected young women of upper-middle-class background (boarding school, mix with royalty and so on). Their body language in the programmes indicates a leisurely approach to life and work, the sprawl over the sofa as they watch the video clips of the victims anxiously trying to choose an outfit, and they laugh and giggle at their mistakes. Of course as Brunsdon has pointed out, it is not without irony that we now see so many upper-class girls try to earn their own living successfully by drawing from, and popularising, their own store of cultural capital (Brunsdon, 2003). (It is surely a bit like selling off the family silver.) Taking Bourdieu's analysis into account and adding my own comments above about gender changes, we could conclude that figures like the two presenters, Trinny and Susannah, now find themselves in the workplace, since they too no longer expect to rely on a male partner to look after them financially over a lifetime. What it is to be an upper-class woman now means something rather different: it means competing against well qualified middle-class counterparts in the labour market. There we have it, no longer 'gentlemen and scholars' as Bourdieu describes, but 'upper middle-class girls and educated girls'. Through this new matrix of gender and class, articulated most clearly in and through the fields of culture and media, new forms of class differentiation are being produced through processes of symbolic violence. It would be an important sociological exercise to track and analyse the role of insult and wounding comments or looks in these programmes. My own notes reveal comments such as 'look at how she walks', 'she looks like a mousy librarian', 'ughh she has yellow stained teeth', and 'she looks like a German lesbian' (*WNTW* and *WLTM*).

In conclusion, there is cruelty and viciousness often reminiscent of 1950s boarding school stories where the nasty snobbish girls ridicule the poor scholarship girl for her appearance, manners, upbringing, accent and shabbily dressed parents (however, virtue usually wins out and these nasty girls come to grief). Programmes like *WLTM* and *WNTW* are self-vindicating on the basis that the victims are adults, they are willing participants and submit themselves to being made over with great enthusiasm. This is popular entertainment which uses irony to suggest that it is not meant to be taken literally, it does not necessarily mean what a literal reading would suggest. Moreover, populist television values and audience approval might suggest interpretations other than those based on my account of symbolic violence. This again would require a good deal more work, but let me put it this way, it would be possible to analyse these programmes as rather more open-ended in relation to taste and self-identity than a Bourdieusian analysis allows. Sometimes the ordinariness and the unkempt image of the victim retains a resilience and obstinacy, despite and against the efforts of the experts. In short, textual- and audience-based research on these programmes might suggest tension, uncertainty and deep anxiety in regard to class, status and identity, as women find themselves now prominent as subjects of social change. But the overall value of Bourdieu's writing is that it shows more forcefully how social rearrangement along gender lines takes shape within media and popular culture by means of habitus adjustment to ensure conformity with the requirements of the fields of employment and of consumer culture.

6

Jameson's Postmodernity:
The Politics of Cultural Capitalism

Too Cultural?

One of the most prominent features of Jameson's writing is his unswerving, sustained and endlessly revitalised commitment to Marxism and, with this, an envisaged transformation from a capitalist to a socialist society. There are a greater number of references to Marxist terms like classes, proletariat, mode of production, ideology and consciousness than in any of the other cultural theorists in this volume. The paradox is that, at a time when a Marxist revolution couldn't be further from becoming a reality – indeed becomes almost unimaginable, such is the grip of capitalism as a world system – Jameson's critique of this system, almost as soon as it was published in 1984, instantly became a classic piece of writing, read by scholars across the world. The world of the arts, culture and higher education (in particular the Anglo-American axis) seemed to need this magisterial article, to provide a sweeping and magnificent explanation of the new centrality of culture as a full-scale 'mode of production'. At the time, in the dark days of Thatcherism in the UK, exuberant cultural politics (in music, film, fashion and subcultures) conveyed a sense of popular opposition to the successes of British conservatism. Theorising the significance of culture in these terms provided a renewed justification for cultural forms of intervention and indeed for cultural studies itself. Jameson was able to show, after all, just how important culture was.

The fate of Jameson's paper was, first, to achieve incredible prominence, then, somehow stripped of its Marxism by its wider, more popular audience, to be understood by critics as providing an analysis which was 'too cultural', at the expense of the whole range of socio-economic and political forces. The work, then, finds itself accused of enjoying what it attempts to understand. But this is a misreading. Jameson is first and foremost a Marxist literary critic not a social scientist, his field of expertise is textual analysis not the analysis of patterns of media or cultural ownership and control. He also occupies a position within the tradition of Marxist literary theory. His antecedents are Lukacs and Goldman, Brecht and Benjamin, Adorno and Horkheimer. Consequently many of the questions which have been put to Jameson informed by the intellectual agenda of cultural studies (for example, reception, audiences, youth subcultures) overlook the singularity and coherence of his political and aesthetic project (McRobbie, 1994 [1985]). These more sociological issues (emanating from a British cultural studies perspective) which might conceivably point the way to dynamics of resistance or cultural critique not addressed in the original article, are answered and more or less repudiated by Jameson in the 1991 book, as associated with social groups or movements rather than with the imperatives of class struggle, and are thus a diversion (Jameson, 1991). The very questions which might be seen as opening up the cultural forms for wider social or political usage, Jameson discounts as either personal matters of taste (and he itemises his own preferences) or as belonging to the 'libidinal' and pluralistic politics of identity. In his subsequent clarifications, he more fully addresses the possibilities of a contemporary Marxism. The importance of pedagogy is key to this, it is flagged at the end of the 1984 article and developed as a means of maintaining the politics of class struggle in both the 1991 book, and then more recently in his work on Brecht (Jameson, 1998). The dilemma for Jameson is how to reconcile cultural politics in the age of late capitalism with the current non-centrality of social classes whose substitutes (new social movements, groups) for Jameson only hinder the proper formation of classes. The value of political art and the method of Brecht provides him with some possibilities for this task (Jameson, 1998).

It is unusual for a single article like 'Postmodernism or the Cultural Logic of Late Capitalism' (Jameson, 1984) to make such an enormous impact that it becomes a common reference point, an article which journalists and other commentators outside the academy seek out to reassure themselves that they know what they are talking about when discussing postmodernism. Indeed in the 10 years following publication of this seminal work (which, as Spivak argues, actually carries out the performative task of bringing the postmodern into being; as she puts it 'to say everything is cultural is to make everything *merely* cultural' see Spivak, 1999: 334), the ideas in it so thoroughly entered the vocabularies of cultural commentators and their readers that the concept of postmodernism eventually became exhausted, through over-use. The essay also served a valuable commercial purpose in print media spaces fighting for survival and doing so by target marketing younger readers with an interest in accruing further cultural capital through the fine arts of 'cool' taste. The *Guardian* newspaper (in the UK) was particularly enamoured by these ideas for the reason that they provided a new and interesting way of discussing all the issues which in an era of 'lifestyle' journalism, could provide new highly visual content to newspaper journalism with so many supplements to fill. From architecture to fiction to fashion, from art works to television programmes, from film to pop video, there was hardly a cultural form which did not display to the journalists the giveaway signs of postmodern sensibility. Jameson's article had the advantage of being an exposition and account as well as a critique from a recognisably left position (as is evidenced in the use of the word 'capitalism' in the title). The article has consequently become, over time, a reference point for the analysis of postmodernism, and has even found itself incorporated (indirectly) into fiction, as Bhabha quoting Rushdie's *The Satanic Verses* reminds us (Bhabha, 1994), and there are also references to the work in Jonathan Franzen's prize-winning novel, *The Corrections* (2002).

Jameson's many examples were familiar to those educated within the framework of North American and European arts and culture. The essay itself is a *tour de force*, it's a confident exuberant piece of writing carried along by the contradictory energies invoked by the depthless and affectless new world of postmodern imagery and style. It possesses a kind of triumphalism. The Marxist critic has risen to the challenge of understanding so many diverse and fragmented strands in contemporary life, whose reality seems to be that they cannot be grasped as a whole, and yet he has managed to achieve this near impossible feat, disproving the claim that we are incapable of grasping these cultural forms as a totality. In the face of various accounts of the end of Marxism, from Baudrillard (on the basis of its productivist core) to Lyotard (for its meta-narrative status), and before that from Foucault (for its 'model of power as an expropriable and transferable commodity' Brown, 1995: 12), Jameson insists on the continuing importance of the Marxist tradition, through the notions of dialectics and historical materialism, and on the basis of capitalism as a universal system. Marxism allows us to think positively and negatively about the new capitalism as a stage of development which will give way to the next and ultimately superior stage, that is, socialism. (Spivak challenges Jameson's use of Marx in this respect, rejecting it as uncharacteristically simplifying, see Spivak, 1999.)

Jameson urges us to follow Marx's lead by recognising the enormous vitality and energy of the new political economy of culture, while simultaneously deploring the devastation it wrecks on its more hidden subjects. That is, one of the most marked features of the new capitalism is that it appears to be clean, shiny and post-industrial (by exporting production and manufacture to the cheap labour zones of the Third World) and it convinces its First World citizens that class divisions no longer exist and that class society is a thing of the past. Now, as it happens these hidden dimensions remain out of sight in Jameson's own account. 'Blood, death and torture' are referred to as the truth of 'late capitalism' but they are not prominent in his own analysis. Of course, as indicated above, Jameson is a literary critic, and what drives the momentum of his analysis is the capacity of the arts to create or render some greater vision beyond itself of a more just society, which in turn has a pedagogic or illuminative function. That said, at least in the extended book length account of postmodernism, there is frequently an unexpected, almost clumsy, lurch from the eloquent and sustained critique of culture to a commentary on the current state of class struggle. For Jameson, culture is now dominant in two senses: not only has it expanded in the sense of sheer volume, more significantly it has achieved a more critical role in the economy as constituting a whole new 'mode of production'. Drawing on the work of Mandel, who following Marx argues that capitalism can be understood as moving by stages from one dominant mode of production to the next (that is, from industrial to monopoly and now to 'late capitalism'), Jameson shows how postmodernism emerges as the logic of cultural capitalism. No longer, then, is the Marxist cultural critic restrained by the fact that 'in the last instance' it is the economy which dictates what occurs in the cultural superstructure; no longer is the world of literature, the arts, images and representations somehow secondary or reflective of the real world of economy and 'base'. In the most recent stage of capitalist development culture is integral to the economy; it provides the economy with a new dynamic, a new source of growth, a new world of possibilities for profit and for control. This more than justifies close attention being paid to the cultural sphere without recourse to rehearsing the grounded economic conditions (for example, labour and production) which no longer underlie it so much as are inscribed within its very movements.

What Jameson can perhaps rightly assume on the part of western readers is a form of almost delightful cultural familiarity. The works which he refers to, the populist architecture of Las Vegas, the films which are remakes of Hollywood film noir, the paintings of Warhol, the new cyberpunk fiction, even the UK punk band The Clash have all achieved a much wider audience than their modernist predecessors. Thus a defining principle of postmodernism is that it articulates with popular culture from the start. Not surprising, then, that Jameson's analysis was so taken up in cultural studies. Jameson, in the later extended version of the essay, concedes that in some circumstances, and he cites the UK, some of the cultural forms he had referred to were indeed more manifestly oppositional to the dominant social order, for example, some punk bands. I shall return to this point at the conclusion of this chapter. It may be worth noting at this stage that 'indie' or alternative subcultural forms, including art works, resonate throughout Jameson's work, although he avoids the critical vocabulary associated with cultural studies.

Postmodernism and Marxism

Jameson's first long essay on postmodernism appeared in 1984 (the same year as *Distinction* by Bourdieu was published in English). Following Mandel he argued that the logic of late capitalism made culture into a new mode of production. The stimulated desire for new goods and services (post-Fordism) meant innovative design-intensive cultural products, but this also entailed a new relation between culture and economy, so much so that it is becoming impossible to prise them apart. There is a 'virtually unmediated' relationship between the two.

> What has happened is that aesthetic production today has become integrated into commodity production generally: the frantic economic urgency of producing fresh waves of ever more novel seeming goods (from clothing to airplanes) at ever greater rates of turnover, now assigns an increasingly structural function and position to aesthetic innovation and experimentation. (Jameson, 1984: 56)

And as he later writes, 'Culture . . . as that which cleaves almost too close to the skin of the economic to be stripped off and inspected in its own right, is itself a postmodern development . . .' (Jameson, 1991: xv). What then is postmodernism? It is not merely a distinctive style, nor is it an aesthetic movement. Instead, for Jameson, it marks a momentous shift as culture becomes a dominant mode of production, and as art is fully commodified, there is a profusion of culture and a repudiation and outstripping of the values of modernism which can be seen across the whole field of arts, media and representation. Postmodernism marks a systematic reconfiguring of the symbolic landscape, where there is also a new kind of subjectivity and an emphasis on the spatial rather than the temporal (or historic). This is a novel situation where nature has gone and is replaced by culture, where everything is commodified, and where there is an aestheticisation of everyday life, and where culture exudes excitement, irony, knowingness. Of course it is connected to an older phase of capitalism, but it represents a new structure of feeling, it is 'historically deaf' to the older order. In the 1984 article, Jameson provides a lucid rationale for the emergence of postmodernism. In architecture there is a rejection of the cold austerity of modernism. The buildings which once seemed so futuristic had become brutalistic, tower blocks were recognised as unlivable and indeed contributed to the decline in urban environment, hence architects began to look to the popular, they developed styles which quoted from different periods, they showed themselves willing to 'learn from Las Vegas'. Postmodernism comes into being and develops as a 'new systematic cultural norm' even as it is defined through its seeming 'sheer heterogeneity'.

Jameson presents this systematicity in terms of new depthlessness and the presence of the simulacrum, the weakening of historicity and the appearance of a new sublime; and of new technologies and new economies. These all gather a particular momentum in the context of the urban experience which dramatises and intensifies the postmodern experience. Depthlessness is explored through an analysis of Andy Warhol's 'Diamond Dust Shoes' in contrast to Van Gogh's peasant shoes. In Van Gogh the intensity of colour is compensatory and utopian, it humanises the poverty, it explodes, and is dramatic. The shoes also speak of a whole way of life, of time and rhythm, the painting draws attention to its own materialism of oils and paints, that is, it proposes the transfigurative, redemptive power of art which is, however, also a human force. Warhol in contrast presents dead objects which are already images twice over: they are photographic negatives, the shoes are deathly and seemingly unpartnered, they suggest a tragic event like Auschwitz, or a fire or other disaster. There is a flatness, a depthlessness here, also a 'waning of affect'. There is a club culture (Studio 54), drug-enhanced intensity about them, a chemical induced high. The Van Gogh shoes seem to speak out to an outside world a 'vaster reality' where the Warhol shoes offer only a 'compensatory exhilaration' and otherwise having nothing to speak of, only 'gratuitous frivolity'.

This superficial quality leads Jameson to describe the breaking down of the old dualisms of modernism, where the depth of the subject revealed an alienation, an inner pain. The 'death of the subject' manifest in both theory and in culture marks the end of this idea that there is an inner as well as an outer self, and with this also disappear other dualisms, those of essence and appearance, authenticity and inauthenticity, the signifier and the signified, and what is left he claims is a kind of flatness, a field of pure artifice. Instead of the deep anxieties portrayed in works of modernism, from Hopper's paintings of 'desolation' to the 'stream of consciousness' of Joyce, there is instead only hallucinatory splendours, and the 'derealisation of the world of everyday reality'. Jameson examines a kind of cultural 'high' a superficial delight, a 'hysterical sublime' which marks a refusal of the natural, as it is transcended, superseded and wholly enculturalised. With this new flattened subject for whom there is no longer an inner consciousness and an outer self, there is also the end of individual uniqueness, that modernist mark of personality or style, nor is there 'solitude', that particular alienated state which is so central to modern art and literature. The figure of Andy Warhol embodies this postmodern subjectivity; in his work as well as his public persona there is a withholding of anything as engaged and embroiled as social critique.

In this terrain of postmodernism there is a 'waning of affect'. Pastiche or blank parody, the version of a familiar style for which in fact there is no original, possesses nothing as forceful as a 'satiric impulse'. And the recycling of older styles, not as copy but as quote, induces a sense of playful irony which once again acts as a foil against history, politics and social critique. History gives way to 'historicism' with the effect that history also becomes a series of signs, marks of 'pastness'. Our image addiction turns history into an endless series of photographic albums, history is subjected to costume dramatisations and the past is a parade of styles, fashions, nostalgia television programmes, period drama. The photographic image, and then in particular the television screen renders the past to an audience hungry for more nostalgia, but in doing so, argues Jameson, the past loses a coherent narrative. Historical time comes to be understood in cultural terms and according to contemporary values, popular history reappears as populist history and the past becomes synonymous with recognisable styles, with a particular wardrobe, a collection of known signs, for example the quiff, the wide skirt, the shoes and so on. In the age of semiology, history means 'pastness'. There is deliberate inter-textuality in cinema and film history itself becomes another rich source to plunder; and how many re-stagings in pop videos, in advertisements, in fashion photographs have there been of key moments in cinema history?

Jameson provides an example of the 'new sublime' in the form of a poem which appears to be about 'China' (its title) but in fact comprises of a series of commentaries by its (non Chinese) author in response to a book of Chinese images found lying on the street. Jameson shows how this mediated poetic discourse is actually about identity and schizophrenia (which he indicates is not a clinical but a cultural term, without 'morbidity') whose lines reach to a sudden euphoria. Instead of the older inner anxieties, such as desperate loneliness or the despair found in works like those of the artist Munch, postmodern aesthetics repudiates the distinction between an inner and an outer self, and produces instead a new kind of subject, alert to new intensities, new exhilarations all of which seem to resonate at a superficial or surface (or street) level. This then becomes entangled with new technologies which in turn produce new bodily excitements, 'hallucinatory splendours'. Jameson refers to cyberpunk, and also films like *Blade Runner*. But perhaps the most lasting of the forms of new technological and hallucinatory subjectivities is one which came into being soon after the publication of Jameson's essay, that is, the rise in 1987 of club culture, raves, drum 'n' bass, and the technological sublime of computer generated musics (acid house/techno) amplified to such a volume that an audience of up to 250,000 dancers at any one time, share in the experience.[1] With Ecstasy taking and clubbing now the norms of leisure activity among young people we might consider the prescience of Jameson's suggestion of new subjectivities (the E generation) along these 'chemical' lines.

Most characteristic of postmodernism is the displacing of the temporal by the spatial. If history has been lost and replaced by signs of 'pastness', it is space which becomes a marked feature of postmodern experience. Architecture itself is one of the first art forms to fully register the break with modernism and the embracing of 'aesthetic populism', and Jameson's reading of an exemplary piece of postmodernism, is frequently cited. This is the Bonaventura Hotel in LA, which features gondolas, lifts, three entrances, escalators and elevators, hanging banners all of which suggest a kind of fake 'going for a walk' with things to look at, but in a closed-off environment. There is no grand entrance, in the traditional style of the great hotels, this in turn reinforces the idea of the hotel as self-encapsulated, not wishing to be of interest to passers-by, never mind street people. The glass walls 'repel the city outside' providing guests with a 'complete world'. But inside the guests get lost, they wander about the place with their luggage, the boutiques for shopping are difficult to find, and hence often empty, there are signposts throughout the various areas but this all adds to an air of 'milling confusion'. Users of this building therefore have difficulty in forming a 'cognitive map' of the area, it is hard or well-nigh impossible unless one is a regular visitor to internalise an overall image of the environment. And in this sense they embody the condition of postmodernity, that is, we are all lost, we no longer have a cognitive map to help us understand the rapid movements and scale of global capitalism.

This leads Jameson to return to questions of cultural politics and to the role of the critic. Where there is a 'prodigious expansion of culture . . . throughout the social realm' with the effect that 'everything has become cultural', it becomes more and more difficult for radicals to sustain themselves with the idea of a separate and distinctive cultural politics or indeed of art as a sphere relatively uncontaminated by the heavy investment of capital (Jameson, 1991: xx). Of course the mainstream high modern art world has long been part of the capitalist economy, so the argument is not that art and culture have been non-capitalised spheres. It is more, I think, that the art and cultural fields associated with radicalism and with Marxist theory retained a more autonomous and fiercely critical identity. Funded by government subsidy and by charitable foundations this independence might well have been an illusion, but somehow there was an ability to keep these more aggressive capitalist forces at bay. By the time Jameson was writing his article, the special place which the arts had occupied for the left on the grounds of this degree of autonomy, or under-capitalisation, was disappearing, and now it no longer exists. How exactly this has happened requires a much more detailed analysis than can be delivered here. But the speed with which seemingly oppositional or even just independent cultural forms are now taken up as innovative and marketed as 'cool', ultimately destroys the possibility of, or indeed desire for, autonomy. Culture now comes into being within an already extended field of hyper-visibility. And critique is almost instantly reabsorbed as style. Independent cultural production as opposition loses its momentum; instead it merely functions as a kind of out-sourcing location for commercial culture and the very existence of radical cultural politics begins to look naïve or misplaced.

Cognitive Mapping

Jameson's answer to this predicament of contemporary culture is to rekindle the arts as a space for the politics of pedagogy. With echoes of

Brecht he wants to explore how pedagogy can provide the cognitive map which has disappeared, and this means emphasising the 'teaching function of art'. He takes up the idea of cognitive mapping from the geographer Kevin Lynch whose ideal of a socially inclusive city space is one where individuals are able to conceptualise the whole city from the viewpoint of their own specific location, rather than only know their own narrow corner or neighbourhood. Jameson describes Lynch's example of Boston's public planning as evidence of how this ideal can be achieved, but he also attaches to his own use of cognitive mapping elements from Althusser's theory of ideology . . . as he puts it in the closing pages of the 1991 book:

> I have always been struck by the way Lynch's conception of the city experience – its dialectic between the here and now of immediate perception and the imaginative or imaginary sense of the city as an absent totality – presents something like a spatial analogue of Althusser's great formulation of ideology itself, as 'the Imaginary representation of the subject's relationship to his or her Real conditions of existence'. Whatever its defects and problems, this positive conception of ideology as a necessary function in any form of social life has the great merit of stressing the gap between the local positioning of the individual subject and the totality of class structures in which he or she is situated. (1991: 415)

For there to be the possibility of radical social change people must be able to grasp the systematic features of the capitalist world they live in so that transformation can be thorough, or total. The great achievement of postmodernism is to totally disguise its own systemic features replacing these with fragments, disconnected impulses, any number of available sensations. Where the great works of modernism dramatised the distance between personal alienation and the possibility of an enlarged emancipatory vision, the opposite is the case with postmodernism. Instead there is a 'barrage of immediacy'. In addition the so-called death of the subject means that the idea of a subject of history (in Marx's terms the working-class) can no longer be rendered as such, or brought into representation. Where once the tools of class struggle, dialectics, historical materialism, imperialism and development could be used to grasp a complex world, that abstract model which Marx so brilliantly produced, is also decentred, challenged from a variety of positions. With Marx seen now by some left intellectuals as the author of a meta-narrative of capital and labour, dependent on a teleology whereby one stage of capital eventually and inexorably gives way to that of socialism, Jameson's task is to not just demonstrate how Marx is still so useful but to renew the conceptual frame of Marx for this particular cultural form of capitalism.

With cognitive mapping we find a fuller exposition of Jameson's attempt to bring together his spatialising account of capitalism with his broader desire to explain political consciousness (or its absence) in such a way as to maintain the centrality of class as the cornerstone for political change. We also find in both the 1988 essay and in the subsequent book (ideas and revisions flow from one to the other) a further development of his thinking on the pedagogic role of art. This is an ambitious attempt to further restore the Marxist tradition. Jameson brings together the role of art with the growth of social and political understanding by showing those points at which historically it became difficult if not impossible to conceptualise global social relations by virtue of being in a specific location in that world. In the age of imperialism, for example, this disparity of connection, this growing difficulty in seeing that what was happening 'at home' was in fact conditional on imperial circumstances elsewhere (the example he gives is the fiction of London in the 19th century) produces, he claims, a focus on 'character' and inner consciousness. Art and writing at the close of the 19th century registers this spatial distance or 'absent cause' he argues, through the pervasive use of irony. At this point character becomes seemingly closed, marked by a turning in on her or himself as in the remarkably interiorised characters in Henry James' novels. One hundred years later, in the third stage of late capitalism, this distance is completely collapsed and replaced by a sense of proximity, there is a 'barrage of immediacy' and yet a frustration in the light of the 'enormous complexity of new international space'. What are needed are new cognitive maps made available through artistic and cultural forms which perform an educative and politicising role. Crude versions of this kind of capacity can be seen, he suggests, in some postmodern works (he cites novels of hi-tech paranoia) but Jameson looks forward to much more substantial works of which Brecht stands as an ideal.

This short article is then more fully extended in the final chapter of the 1991 book. It is I think worth tracing the stages of Jameson's argument here. In some ways it is as though he is addressing his critics, some overtly, others indirectly. For example, some writers (myself included) argued against Jameson that postmodern culture with its breaking down of the distinction between high and low cultural forms, and its eradication of distance and solemnity in favour of 'clash' and simultaneousness, had the effect of being like a 'breath of fresh air': it energised, brought new social groups into a wider cultural space, it seemed to permit or license the activities of a wider group of players for whom serious ideas could be explored in often playful forms and also could be found in new locations including magazines, clubs or discos. Jameson takes this on board, talks about the 'relief' of the postmodern after the too-heavy bureaucratic management of modernism, and recognises that this new tide of energy carried along by new producers does indeed give fresh meaning to arts and culture. But at what cost? It is not just that this transition marks a move away from public subsidy and relatively uncommodified culture to fullblown neo-liberalisation of the cultural economy, but that as Jameson sees it, even the way in which the breaking down of the distinctions between high and low culture allows participation of women, black people, and gays and lesbians, leads only and inexorably to identity politics.

What he claims is that the emergence of groups and associations rather than classes corresponds exactly with the postmodern system of representation as the recent stage of late capitalist development. To be interested in alliances and in the intersection of class politics with those of race and sexuality, is, for Jameson, to be anti-Marxist and complicit with those forces who wish to see the decline if not disappearance of the left. The politics of small groups is that of self-interest, he claims, it artic- ulates exactly with the growth of the media as willing organ for publicising and supporting such fragmented interests and it also feeds directly into processes of marketisation and commodification. Indeed it even allows some of those among the left to pander to some nostalgic desire which envies the 'realer people of the underclass'. This dismissal of inter-class politics of race, reveals the sectarian voice of Jameson. He goes further and says that the left's relation to 'neoethnicities' is one which makes them 'groupies for the real'. We might ponder, in this respect, the full meaning of the word 'real' here. Is this a crude and uncharacteristic swipe? Or is it a fatal attempt to do away with the way- ward politics of groups (and the politics of race)? Classes are in contrast less narcissistic, they are few in number and therefore they are less appealing to those looking for a quasi-political identity. Foolish then are those on the left who mistake social groups, self-organisation, indeed whole new social movements, for what they really are, that is divisive attachments which with various media behind them merely bolster the interests of those who, fearing the emergence of class politics, thrive on the absence of consensus, on difference and diversity of interests.

Jameson denounces those in cultural studies who argue that the media can be a site for various political interventions (for example, through making critical television documentaries or other programmes), and that its seeming monolithic character can be contested so that it becomes a more disputatious space. Instead Jameson reminds us of the Murdoch empire and that the media has to create markets and social groups like yuppies whose sophisticated tastes for luxury goods and whose stylish identity in boardroom dramas or on the stockmarket floors further diminish the possibility of critique, never mind the formation of organised social classes. Jameson in short pours scorn on the reflections of those whose concern is with forms like television, which, from his viewpoint, turns politics into special issues and target markets and which deprives citizens of any suggestion that there might be a 'single sense of domination'. As he comments 'the new representational models also foreclose and exclude any adequate representation of what used to be represented – however imperfectly – as a 'ruling class' (Jameson, 1991: 349). In short, available 'new narratives' are incapable of helping us to understand the basis on which the society operates. The social groups which come into being on the basis of marketisation of media spread these values across the whole society. 'The social climbing of the new yuppie in-group knowledge now spreads slowly downwards, via the media, to the very zoning boundaries of the underclasses themselves' (ibid: 352).

The Anglo-American Axis of Culture?

If for Jameson cognitive mapping is a spatially updated version of class consciousness, then let me illustrate what he seems to mean by this, by imagining how he might approach a recent example of television which not only shows the signs of postmodern affectless sensibility, but also appears to incorporate and take on board into the script itself, aspects of what we might call the academic critique of postmodernism. Let me take the liberty of proposing a Jamesonian reading of the television series *The Sopranos* as a direct counter to his own earlier reading of the film *Dog Day Afternoon*, (see Jameson, 1979). Where a textual analysis of *Dog Day Afternoon* allowed for (or rendered a cognitive map of) 'the political', in *The Sopranos* there is only a disavowal of all readings of class antagonisms in favour of a proliferation of postmodern signifiers of past cinematic pleasures (hence no cognitive map). A Jamesonian account would see Tony Soprano as embodying the redundant (and only to postmodern acolytes, heroic) figure of the working-class male, reduced to relying on the false consciousness of the Mafiosi and the therapist's couch, sinking further into depression and relying on brute force and violence where the cultural values of his own collectivity have now been distorted, co-opted, refracted and mythologised in 'Godfather' film culture played back to Soprano himself directly through the aspirations to Hollywood on the part of the younger Mafioso, his nephew Christopher, and indirectly through his therapist's son who gently upbraids his mother for her liberal middle-class tolerance of Hollywood-inspired images of authentic working-class Italianicity, a justification and romanticisation of violence and brutality. It is the over-abundance of signs of ethnicity (Italian catholicism, Italian food, beautiful women, Mafioso nightlife, restaurants, matriarchs, patriarchs, and so on) flagged up as pleasurable on the basis of the cinematic intertextuality with one of the most popular films ever made (that is, *The Godfather*), along with the postmodern normativity (post-Tarantino) of spectacular and brutish cinematic violence, and nostalgic and ironic gender re-traditionalisation, which provide the conditions of existence of *The Sopranos*. A Jamesonian analysis would see this combination of ethnicity, nostalgia, pleasure and violence as reflecting all that is distracting and diversionary about identity politics, 'libidinal investments of a narrative kind' (Jameson, 1991). The post-Marxist legitimation of the pleasure of difference means that even fellow academics are unable to cognitively map the class relations which underpin the 'tragic' brutality of Tony Soprano on the basis that the text itself refuses, as absurd, such a reading. The playful multi-referentiality of *The Sopranos* precludes any reading other than one based on the superficiality of postmodern style.

Can it be the case that Jameson is right in his account of how the postmodern repudiates the political, but wrong when it comes to class? Wrong on the basis of a hidden class truth underlying the superfluities of ethnic gender and other identities? Whose truth is this? If there are neither clear signs of mobilisation on this mass movement basis on a global scale nor art works widely available which appear to be capable of delivering these cognitive maps, it is difficult to imagine the sources of renewed class politics. And in the absence of these signals of action is Jameson also in error by failing to examine the exact means by which class might 'will' itself through to the surface as a unifying force, a rallying point for re-politicisation? Instead of considering class as embodying a political will in crisis, Jameson launches a sustained attack on new social movements, on what he calls micro-politics, and 'groups'. It is his disparaging comments that this kind of political organisation merely fulfils a narcissistic function providing the 'gratification of psychic identity' which leads Homi Bhabha to put Jameson's Marxism into question as a strategy of power, a 'regulatory spatial dialectic' whose 'pivot is the 'class subject' (Bhabha, 1994).

Bhabha fully appreciates the sophistication of Jameson's reworking of Marx which is now shorn of its strongly teleological momentum. Bhabha points out that what is seen to be beyond grasp, Jameson makes graspable by virtue of the model of capital based on three stages. This analytical move, claims Bhabha, removes or restricts the sheer dynamic of diversity which so unsettled Jameson in the first place, depriving him of understanding. This is, Bhabha continues, the 'West gazing into the broken mirror of its own unconscious'. Why, we might ask? Because what makes the city space incapable of being cognitively mapped is the absence of the comfortable features of a 'knowable community' (as in Williams, 1956) or else the safer confines of an 'imagined nation' (Anderson, 1986). If it is the hordes or migrants with their cultural diversity which transform the knowable space of the city, then what is at stake in Bhabha's critique of Jameson is the political value attached to precisely the 'groups' which are in Jameson's vision driven only by diversionary and 'libidinal' desires. However, if these groups are reconceptualised as minorities, migrants and others, then Bhabha charges Jameson with partaking in his own narcissism whereby he confers on class the role of being the 'glass of history'. By this means the 'sovereignty of class' as a 'superior force' has special powers to see through the distractions of identity politics and emerge as key political instrument. Bhabha urges Jameson to be much more attentive to the 'borderline negotiations of cultural translation', that is, to consider more fully, the discordant, unruly and emergent voices of others, not necessarily as part of postmodernity in its fragmented diversity but as social forces which precipitate Jameson's own panic of postmodernity, pushing him so productively to reinvent Marx to cope

with this intellectual unease of not knowing, of being without the comfort of the cognitive map.

The point at which Bhabha leaves off is exactly where Spivak continues this debate about the residual and emergent 'making their way in
the dominant' (Spivak, 1999). She performs a deconstructive critique of
Jameson which like Bhabha's is also carried out in a spirit of respect and
admiration. In a witty dialogue with Jameson, Spivak nonetheless mercilessly unpicks the flow of his argument and in the process reveals
exactly the difficulties and lack of clarity Spivak describes Jameson's
overtly authoritative mode as a voice which speaks of State, Institution
and Professoriat . . . this voice is troubled and unsettled by heterogeneity but still speaks in terms of 'us' and 'our culture'. (She quotes his
phrases, 'our daily life', 'our psychic experiences', 'our cultural lan-
guages'.) This permits Spivak to suppose the existence of 'underclass
multi-culturalism', which is at least partly the source of such heterogeneity. Thus inevitably Spivak queries the space from which Jameson
speaks. If the new postmodern is the cultural dominant, then, suggests
Spivak, is there not a danger in overlooking those elements which are
not dominant? Where Raymond Williams is more mindful of emergent
or residual cultural forms, Jameson too easily moves onto the terrain of
the dominant and in so doing is ordering (or marshalling) an argument
based on a 'dialectic' which, as Spivak suggests, 'disqualifies and
excludes the inconvenient as its other and vice versa'. This initiates a critique of Jameson for exclusionary practices, for failing to see and thus
articulate that, for example, the micro-electronic transnational capital is
actually also 'supported in the lower ranks by labor practices that would
fit right into old style industrial capitalism'.

Jameson's account disguises the speaking position which he occupies
and also the subject for whom he speaks, which is the 'general US subject', who far from having disappeared is merely feeling an 'old
fashioned' experience, which is 'loss of identity'. It is on this basis that
the subject feels out of control, prompting Jameson to propose the idea
of cognitive mapping. Instead of dabbling with virtual realities of the
computer age, the bewildered subject needs to engage with more political art of the sort Jameson hopes will become available. But this leads
Spivak to rightly reflect on the means by which such elucidation or
clarification will come about. The poem which Jameson offers as a
mark of the postmodern aesthetic is, according to Spivak's reading, an
opportunity to consider the meaning of 'China' (the name of the poem)

in terms of its author's reference to this other space. 'In other words "China" as referent hides the hybrid of Chinatown, hidden in its turn from the culturally unmarked Anglo' (that is, the author Perelman). Spivak continues, 'Perelman has his own place. How does he, as hybrid (because American) force China into the American idiom?' Spivak is therefore asking that we consider the power relations inscribed in the subject position proposed by both Jameson's magisterial analysis of post-modernism and also in one of his key examples, the poem titled 'China'. Jameson mobilises and orchestrates his critique around the category of history (which Spivak argues carries the weight of 'a final author who holds the mysterious name History whose predication is simply "what hurts"', Spivak, 1999: 326). Spivak asks not only that we query this authority of History, but also the process of the dialectic of simultane-ously thinking of the good and bad of late capitalism. She concludes her chapter by reminding the reader that Marx's similar invocation applied only to Europe. 'The point may not be to think well and ill of capitalism at the same time.'

Bhabha and Spivak deliver incisive critical responses to Jameson. In each case they take issue with his reworking of Marx by addressing directly those dynamics in Marxism which, in the light of post-colonial criticism, now are demonstrably weakened and in need of revision. This is more apparent in Spivak's critique for the very reason that she remains herself a Marxist scholar, whose knowledge of Marx's writing she also subjects to her own deconstructive practice. Thus Jameson's making do with Marx's analysis of the stages of capitalism on the basis that it will eventually give way to a higher level of socialist organisation allows him to justify (or overlook) what Spivak calls 'development'. Spivak also takes issue with Jameson's authoritative voice and subject position (US Professor) which allows him to speak and which assumes an attentive reader or student. But more important perhaps are her fleeting engagements with the very concept of culture (or 'our culture') utilised with such ease by Jameson. As she puts it, '"Culture" is also a regulator of how one knows': Foucault's famous capacity-to-know doublet: pou-voir/savoir as the ability to know, is "culture" at ground level' (Spivak, 1999: 356). Is this to charge Jameson with 'knowing too much'? Surely not. Or with too carelessly invoking an assumed consensus when in more conversational mode in the final chapter of the 1991 book he uses phrases like 'our culture'? Perhaps. In conclusion, we might suggest that what is being opposed by Bhabha and Spivak is the sense of holding onto certainty in adverse circumstances which is conveyed in Jameson's incredibly extended reply to his critics. Not because they doubt the value of conviction, and the importance of the Marxist tradition, but because what Jameson takes as his subject matter, what constitutes his field of knowledge (from modern to postmodern culture) they want to re-define as partial, as only having assumed that centrality and value on the basis of the global power of western capitalism.

Notes

1   The annual German Love Parade attracts approximately 3 million party-goers. In the summer of 2002, 250,000 clubbers attended a single party held on Brighton beach hosted by DJ FatBoy Slim.

Extended Notes

Mulholland Drive

Jamesons's writing on postmodernism tends towards the epic in scale. It is grandiose in its breadth, it holds out, maybe against the odds, for a Marxist understanding of the contemporary world, and it is impassioned and immensely erudite. As I have argued here, some of the most incisive critics of Jameson are those who represent post-colonial thinking. And despite their critiques they have quite a lot in common with Jameson, Bhabha is a literary scholar by training (like Spivak) and he also envisages critique as conceivable within the frames of aesthetics, that is, the 'third space' can be that place where artistic endeavours bring into being new kinds of dialogues and communities. Jameson attributes to art a pedagogic function. Bhabha envisages radical social change as a micrological process, in which arts and culture have a key role to play, and where diverse groups and social movements might find solidarity and affinity. Where Bhabha draws on Deleuze's notion of 'becoming minor' by means of inventing new subterfuge means of communication, new elusive modalities embedded within the everyday, and threaded through the social field, Jameson occupies a more traditionally authoritative or 'majoritarian' position as an intellectual. He does not rehearse the politics of pedagogy in more depth, nor has there been, as far as I am aware, a more extended discussion of the possible pathway from Brecht to the contemporary world of arts and culture. If Jameson attributes power to pedagogy as a radical practice then we might want to reflect on the institutional processes of the university, the role of the humanities, the so called 'culture wars', the new place and role for cultural studies and post-colonial theory, and the relation between education and 'cognitive mapping'. I think at this point I can do little more than emphasise the importance of such debates which might follow Jameson's references to these topics.

I hinted at some themes in the above chapter which connect with what we might describe as the legacy of Jameson. While I do not wish to attribute to Jameson alone, the way in which postmodern theory reverberated outside the academy as well as inside, from the mid-1980s onwards, he along with Baudrillard were undoubtedly its best-known exponents. Sometimes this influence is seen as contributing to the so-called institutionalisation of postmodernism within the arts and culture (Roberts, 1998; Stallabrass, 1998). My own preference would be to consider in more depth the way in which this thinking came to shape and influence younger generations of cultural producers, providing them with a brand new toolkit, with the effect of there being an incorporation of postmodern knowingness, even more dramatically present than before, indeed dominant in specific genres of film and TV. While it would be preferable to end this chapter with a wide discussion of a range of these films or programmes (for example, *Magnolia*, *The Truman Show*, *Boogie Nights*, *The End of Violence*, *Being John Malkovich*, *Adaptation*, *The Sopranos*, *Six Feet Under*, of course the Tarantino *oeuvre*, and so on) I am going instead to look a little more closely at David Lynch's 2000 film *Mulholland Drive*, not because it is so close to Jameson's essay, but because the film (originally planned as a television series, and then abandoned for lack of funding) both exemplifies postmodern thinking and also performs a kind of double-take on academic postmodernism. It seems to engage directly with this body of writing and it goes further so that there is an almost total 'derealisation of the world of everyday life' (Jameson, 1991). This is done by fusing the cinematic with the psychoanalytical, the narrative with the anti-narrative, the aesthetic with the unconscious, the landscape of sexual desire with that of dreams and fantasy. *Mulholland Drive* is more than just about cinema, and it is more than a tribute to cinema. The film explores the relation between space, cinema and the unconscious through the psychic, postmodern, geography of Hollywood, a mythic space productive of 'hallucinatory subjectivities'.

Mulholland Drive is a back-to-front film, comprising narrative segments interspersed with anti-narrative devices including dream and hallucinatory sequences as well as dramatic tableaux scenes such as those in the karaoke nightclub. The second half of the film provides an explanatory frame for the first half, and reveals it to be a fantasy, a girlish, semi-erotic mystery narrative, a good deal more innocent, more fresh, more ingénue than is convincing or sustainable within the ruthless political economy of Hollywood cinema, which is the subject of the second half. But already I am extrapolating from a film which intersperses many other short narrative elements in and across both parts of the film as a whole, the overall sense of which attempts to confound audiences. (A succinct synopsis of the film can be found at www.bfi.org.uk/sightandsound/2002-01/mulholland.html.) This film proposes Hollywood as myth, as space of fantasy and of simulacra existing on the basis of there being no underlying reality. In Lynch's account (unlike that of Wenders in *The End Of Violence* (1997)) there is no barely visible, subaltern economy peopled by migrant workers; instead this is a cityscape where everyone is complicit, everyone is looking for a part or has once played a part. The world of the screen (television or film) is now, Lynch suggests, wholly encompassing and definitional. From the opening moment of the film, when the tyres of the limousine make their familiar cinematic low-level, prowling, swishing noise, as the car curls round the sharp corners of the Hollywood hills, what is evoked is that this is a landscape scripted in advance by the history of film and television. Literally every shot in the film asks us to recall a cinematic history. When a young, fresh-faced Betty arrives at Los Angeles airport, excited about pursuing a career as an actress, every camera angle bespeaks hundreds of films, and television programmes which are this film's predecessors. Her sweetness, innocent beauty and good humour seem to belong to a bygone age (the 1950s?). Betty is keen, in a schoolgirlish way, to lend a hand when she finds a seductive, film noir-style figure, who has lost her name and hastily calls herself Rita (reminded by the Gilda poster on the wall) having a shower in her aunt's house and Betty's temporary home. Rita has been involved in a car accident and the girls then embark on an adventure to find out who she is, and what were the circumstances of the accident. Every single location or set in the film is mythical space, the house of Betty's aunt is unmodernised 1930s *film noir*, there are familiar shots from high in the Hollywood hills overlooking the city at night, there is, of course, the Hollywood sign, there are the darkened rooms where movie bosses wrangle, also the diner, the nightclub, the studio set, the streets and driveways. There is the archetypal director's home and pool, perched on the hills. These are locations in quotation marks; far from attempting to create something new visually in terms of landscape David Lynch presents, again and again, only the familiar. Unlike The Bonaventura Hotel, we can't get lost because it is already so well-known as cinematic fiction. The entire urban space is a grand simulacra. Spatiality here is a play of signs, a series of locations. This is a hermetically sealed hyper-reality, a space of accumulated images drawn from the entire history of popular film and television, such that there is no 'outside reality'.

This spatiality of Hollywood produces 'performative subjects', that is, actors, and this in turn works as a model for subjectivity. There is no true self when 'out of character' or off stage. With the play between the first and the second half of the film where we think Betty is a young aspiring actress and we do not know quite who Rita is, and then later on when we find out that Betty is Diane, an embittered, angry actress who is not getting parts, but whose glamorous girlfriend Camille, now rejecting her, is, we can see that Lynch is exploring the idea of acting as subjectivising discourse par excellence. If film, television and celebrity have assumed dominance as hyper-reality, becoming the terms by which we all interpret a good deal of our everyday lives, then the performative effect is to produce normative acting subjects, for whom, following Jameson, there is no longer an inner private self and an outer public self, only a series of shallow, superficial 'B movie' selves. More specifically, Lynch, who has long been fascinated with psychoanalysis, dreams and the unconscious, in *Mulholland Drive* post-modernises psychoanalysis by drawing dream-type materials and fantasies up from underneath, right onto the surface and interspersing these seg-ments with the twists and turns of the fragments of narrative. Instead, then, of there being consciousness and the unconscious, reality and dreams, Lynch does away with this divide, and lets these flow freely into and across each other. The one continually intrudes upon the other; the friendly eld-erly couple who are kind to Betty at the airport reappear later in the film as sinister, indeed malevolent, tiny creatures, so small they scutter across the floor, like microscopic mice. The fiction of the film allows no boundaries between fantasy and reality, so that it is impossible to differentiate between the two. In the first part of the film the scenes of erotic lesbian desire, when Betty is seduced by Rita as they comfort and caress each other, recalls schoolgirl fiction, feminine innocence and beauty transmute into sexual passion, but later in the second part of the film, in the context of hard angry sex between girls, this earlier sequence has to be re-imagined as fantasy. To sum up, almost every feature of postmodern aesthetics as understood by Jameson can be found within the frames of *Mulholland Drive* with the fur-ther dynamic that the postmodern here seems to turn in upon itself, even more so than before, seeking nothing and needing nothing beyond that which is already available within the archives of American film and television.

A Mixed Bag of Misfortune?
Bourdieu's *Weight of the World*

... diverse stories of suffering can be recognised as belonging to anyone who dares to possess them and in good faith employ them as interpretative devices through which we may clarify the limits of our selves, the basis of our solidarities, and perhaps pronounce upon the values of our values. (Gilroy, 2000: 230)

In the last few years, before his death in January 2002, Pierre Bourdieu had become increasingly prominent, not just as an intellectual but for his participation on the wider political stage. His interventions included a series of scathing critiques of French attempts to roll back the state (in fact a cautious dismantling process in contrast to the gung-ho UK privatisation of public services), he had become highly critical of the media (although his analysis of media and journalism was surprisingly one-dimensional), of the vogue for think-tanks, of the ubiquitousness of opinion polls, and he had also accused cultural studies of encouraging the success of global capitalism by describing the pleasures and creativity of multi-culturalism (Bourdieu, 1998; Bourdieu and Wacquant, 1999; Bourdieu and Wacquant, 2001). In a recent piece in *Theory Culture and Society* Bourdieu and Wacquant departed from the norms of polite critique ('Cultural Studies . . . a mongrel . . . discipline') to denounce academic endeavours such as Italian Cultural Studies (Bourdieu and Wacquant, 1999). The seeming absurdity of German-Turkish Cultural Studies also attracted special attention, and the authors blamed such efforts on, among other things, the commercial opportunism of publishers. To most social scientists as well as cultural studies academics the emergence of discussion on 'German Turkish' identity is entirely appropriate, indeed overdue, but to Bourdieu and Wacquant it was somehow scandalous, yet another sign of the diversionary and celebratory impulse of identity politics.[1] Bourdieu and Wacquant also indicated their contempt for the Third Way politics embraced by the UK government, saying of sociologist and political advisor to New Labour, Anthony Giddens 'The masters of the economy . . . can sleep in peace: they have found their Pangloss' (Bourdieu and Wacquant, 2001: 5).

We might consider then the 650 page volume *The Weight of the World* (which appeared in France in 1993 as *La Misère Du Monde*) as a political as well as a sociological reflection on the part of Bourdieu and his team, on the social divisions and sufferings of contemporary France (Bourdieu et al., 1999). It's a departure for Bourdieu for its emphasis on the extensive recording and transcription of spoken voices. Each interview selected and edited for publication is introduced with a short essay written by the interviewer. Layer upon layer of voices, contextual commentary and a concluding section on 'understanding' contribute to an accumulative effect. This is a book which announces itself with a certain *hauteur*. The aim is clearly to pronounce upon the condition of France in a definitive manner. But it can also be seen as contributing to the recent revitalisation of sociology. Although they each occupy quite different positions in the political (left and centre left) spectrum, Beck in Germany, Sennett and Giddens in the UK, and Bourdieu in France have each reinvented sociology as a more critical instrument for the extension of democracy and the politics of social transformation in the post-industrial era. By this means sociology on occasion finds itself in a new proximity to government. Bourdieu makes enormous claims for this particular work, and the question is, are these justified? Are the skills of the team of interviewers and the 'rapport' (a term recently scrutinised by anthropologists including Clifford (1997) and Geertz (2000)) with their interviewees, many of whom they have known intermittently over a lifetime, such that they encourage such heights of self-analysis? Or is there over-statement in the whole project? Is there a sense that in having taken these steps to record ordinary voices of people who are rarely listened to, the team are more overwhelmed by what they have done, and project this sense of wonder (indeed self congratulation) onto the published extracts, many of which might be read as less unique and interesting, more banal, repetitious and aggrieved? Is the denuded (or de-culturalised) effect the outcome of carrying out interviews and relying on voice without the sociological trappings of temporal and spatial specificity, without the boundaries and limits of an urban or community study?

Voice of Pain

Members of Bourdieu's team are, it seems, given a relatively free hand in deciding who to interview. They then embark on interviews with individuals, some of whom are or have been neighbours, others who have no prior contact: all they share is a willingness to testify on their suffering. One interviewer (Rosine Christin) says rather piously that she felt a moment of woman-to-woman communication as she talked over the kitchen table with a 45-year-old supermarket check-out clerk, somebody she had known for years and whose life trajectory was the source of her distress. 'She showed me the life of the worker' (Bourdieu et al., 1999b: 354). But to grant importance to such a moment, so many years after debates in feminist scholarship as well as in anthropology, on the ethics of the research, have well and truly complicated such encounters seems spurious, even gratuitous (McRobbie, 2000 [1981]), see also Pratt (1992) on 'contact zones', Clifford's response to this (1997) and Geertz (2000)). What for the interviewer suggests a quasi-feminist encounter, to the reader could just as easily be seen as a rather sentimental ruse to get the right kind of data. Bourdieu refers to this moment again in his summing up, but we might ask, who gains from gendered recognition of this type?

The proliferation of voices in the book do admittedly fill an absence in current sociological and also social policy writing.[2] But the problem of interpretation without having recourse to historical and cultural context demonstrates that voice of pain is not enough. Without the wider web of social relations in which they are embedded, these testimonies exist merely as the stated truths of personal experience. The Bourdieu team attribute to the transcribed interviews, special, almost transcendental status, but set alongside each other, many readers might ask, is this so very different from the 'clash of viewpoints' which are the subject matter of journalism where 'anti-social neighbours' regularly put their case? Emotion and affect, suffering and trauma are currently the subject of attention in sociology and cultural studies (see for example Berlant, 2001 and Bauman, 2000 among others), more the pity then that Bourdieu and his team did not consider the enactment of grievances and suffering beyond, on the one hand, powerlessness as a result of the structural positions these individuals occupy in social and spatial hierarchies, and on the other hand seemingly irreconcilable conflicts and deep antagonisms.

This laying down of opposing viewpoints from people locked in conflict with each other, evades the issues of power and powerlessness within the poorest sections of the society. And more specifically with the power of racism as articulated by disadvantaged white people over those 'others' whom they perceive as illegitimate in their claims for recognition and already preferred in terms of benefits by a too-liberal state. The spirited and vocal young girl of Arab origin is angered by the barely disguised racism of her French neighbour who so vociferously objects to noises, smells and cats in the communal garden which she claims as her own. There are moments in the interview when the older French woman articulates with utter clarity her objections to others: 'But they are in my home, they are in France, its not me who is in their home'. Might not the interviewer in his introductory preamble have paid more attention to the language of popular racism? Granted then, the substance of the interviews might be important to listen to, but often it is the interviewer's comments which betray a crude and common-sense sociological understanding. All that is said about this woman by her interviewer is that 'this must therefore be understood as the last manifestation of resistance put up by this fraction of the population . . . to contest the process of decline, devaluation and disqualification in which it fears being caught' (Bourdieu et al., 1999: 23). Yes indeed, but this is the kind of point made by sociologists over twenty years ago which Hall et al. (1978) and Gilroy (1987) refuted on the grounds that neither displaced resistance, nor 'false consciousness', nor the attribution of racism as somehow confined to the disenfranchised white working-class, provided sufficient explanation for the circulation throughout the entire social and cultural field (in particular the media) of racialising processes and their subsequent effects.[3]

Time and time again in the interviews we are presented with the confident assumption of knowledge of the other. 'You know how they are' . . . 'they begin to live at ten at night' . . . 'you'd get your throat cut' . . . they keep 'sheep in the balconies', when they first came 'they lived in tents'. As Bhabha argues the racial stereotype works and is sustained by constant repetition like this, over time, of 'knowledge value' which tells 'us' what 'they' are really like. (Bhabha, 1994: 79). And as Said has demonstrated, the power of the West is inextricably linked with the pursuit of knowledge of its others (Said, 1978). In the interviews there is also, on the part of many of the white working-class respondents, a more recent refrain, which is their objection to equal opportunities which they see as inherently opposed to their own interests. They complain about non-whites having access to welfare and forms of social security and they are critical of a too-liberal state which administers such services. They also object to their own prejudices being typecast as racist. Thus they predicate comments with the phrase 'I'm not a racist but' . . . or 'They scream that its racism' . . . 'You would have called me a racist' . . . These disadvantaged whites find some degree of common cause through imagining themselves also to be the victim of racism now practised by a state which positively favours 'others' at their expense.

The interviews do indeed provide an opportunity to consider the prevalence of popular racism in France. In the light of the electoral success in April 2002 of Le Pen and the *Front National* the book will no doubt find itself again in the spotlight, all the more disappointing then that there is no attempt to theorise these social antagonisms. A brief glance in the direction of cultural studies shows that there is no shortage of work which could have been useful to the Bourdieu team in this respect. For instance Back et al.'s research with white working-class parents and children in the East London Isle of Dogs estates, shows the importance of analysing the roots of racist language in white working-class traditions, in the protectionism of trade unionism, in the economic and social history of the specific location, and psycho-analytically in relation to the fear of and fascination for 'the other' (Back et al., 1999). Likewise Back and Ware have more recently provided ethnographic accounts of neo-fascist politics in the context of British white working-class culture (Back and Ware, 2002). This work emerges out of the critiques of anti-racist policies including those of Gilroy (1992), Rattansi (1992), Cohen (1992) and others who challenged the idea that racism could be eradicated by, for example, forbidding offensive language in the school environment. The opportunity to really engage with the various racisms found in *The Weight of the World* are, by such sophisticated sociologists as these, nonetheless refused. Instead the writers are compromised by their own methodologies of intimacy and empathy. We find on one occasion an interviewer, Patrick Champagne, prompting the respondent to follow up racist comments with regard to the appeal of Le Pen . . . he asks 'The solutions posed by Le Pen . . . they must be tempting for some of the people, don't you think?' (Bourdieu et al., 1999: 118). This raises ethical questions of interventionism and direction of the research topics nowhere discussed throughout the book despite the great attention given to the interview situation. Early on in the book, to a white French couple living in a rough housing estate, Bourdieu and Christin ask 'And the neighbourhood, isn't it dangerous for the girls?' (Bourdieu et al., 1999: 20). Such a question presupposes that it might be reasonable to assume that those troublesome people who have just been discussed ('for an Arab he was great') are also likely to be sexually criminal, in fact the woman replies 'No no its fine . . . No its mostly the noise, things like that'.

Bourdieu argues that these individuals can be helped to understand their own structural position, and that what would otherwise be invisible or difficult for them to articulate without prior access to university education, can find expression under interview conditions such as these. The habitus (the terrain of dispositions and routine unthought-about gestures, actions, assumptions) can thus be rendered more malleable and open to change. Once again this attributes enormous weight to the research endeavours of the team, such that this single exercise becomes a kind of pedagogy or even social psychotherapy. But does better understanding necessarily lead to the kind of political or ethical outlook which Bourdieu would endorse? My answer would be that there can be no such guarantees. The direction in which the habitus is shifted by such interventions as these remains uncertain. And, on the impact of 'the interview', who is to know that young disadvantaged people like the two boys Ali and Francois are otherwise incapable of explaining their own circumstances? It would take a different kind of study, one that would entail lengthy periods of 'deep hanging out' (Clifford, 1997) and would involve getting to know not just the boys but the whole cultural environment including their engagement with non-verbal forms such as music, clothes, the objects of the consumer culture, the media they watched or listened to, to be able to develop a full understanding of how social structure including specific location corresponds with individual accounts. Paul Willis succeeded many years ago in producing a complex analysis of working-class lads and the counter-school culture (Willis, 1978). But the capacity of 'the lads' to generate a counter-culture was already there, it certainly did not rely on the 'magical' presence of Paul Willis. Nowadays this kind of research typically attempts to draw in more actively the participation of respondents, providing them with video cameras, bringing them together to report back on their activities, planning follow up events, ending the project with exhibitions, user-group activities and so on, in a bid to create more democratic ethnographic modalities and also to use the process to produce some collaborative outcome (see also Clifford, 1997). The trump card for Bourdieu is clearly the strategy to let the respondents speak out, where editing is done with a light touch. But the work is not to be judged on the truth of the voices, but ultimately on what is done with them. We might surmise that exactly what Bourdieu wanted to avoid was the kind of work associated with Hebdige, whose attention to the signs of the punk subculture produced a textual analysis without any reference to the subjects of punk and their testimony (Hebdige, 1978). Bourdieu in contrast sticks resolutely to the interview format. But surely the effectivity of the interview in provoking self-reflection for social understanding and potentially action for change, is even more problematic (and inflated) as a claim, than the ascription of resistance ever was to the iconography of youth culture?

Allowing the interviewers to find respondents through chains of friends, neighbours or acquaintances sometimes suggests sociological opportunism. Rosine Christin talks with a woman, the daughter of farmer friends of hers, now living in Paris. She persuades the woman to bring her to work on the night shift, once there the interviewer finds an opportunity to talk with a man which she duly reports on. 'Michel B, a short dark man with a moustache, about 60, is the division inspector, a position above TM. He has spent his whole working life in the postal service on the night shift'. '(H)e remembers his arrival in Paris' . . . and so on. It is almost as though the interviewer literally bumped into somebody she thought might have something interesting to say. Consequently the account she offers is sociologically banal, mere reportage of degrees of misfortune, prompting (I am sorry to say) almost the complete opposite effect which Bourdieu claims, a kind of 'so what?' The closing words are a commentary on the failing marriage of the respondent 'things weren't going very well . . . everything had "looked bleak"' (Bourdieu et al., 1999: 308). The emotive tone asks for the reader to respond with empathy, but the seemingly random way in which we are presented with these lives torn from context and lacking in 'thick description' disallows a more engaged response. This then is a mixed bag of misfortunes.

The material includes interviews carried out in the US as well as in France. Loic Wacquant, who has published accounts of boxing and ghetto life in Chicago, contributes sections on hustling in the neighbourhood called The Zone. Bourdieu argues in the preamble for a 'rigorous analysis of the relations between the structures of social space and those of physical space . . . The lack of capital chains one to a place' (Bourdieu et al., 1999: 127) . . . 'Bringing together on a single site a population homogenous in its dispossession strengthens that dispossession, notably with respect to culture and cultural practices . . .' (ibid.: 129). The rationale for including the American material (with sections by Philippe Bourgois taken from his excellent ethnography of crack users) is that the withdrawal of the State from areas of total impoverishment like those described by Bourgois and Wacquant ought to be a warning to the French government seemingly embarking on a similar programme. This is the most engaged section of the book because more time is spent connecting the research with existing debates in American sociology and political debates on race, while also revealing the frenetic 'making do' economy of the area. One respondent called Rickey yearns for a straight job in the Post Office, just as his female counterparts talk about their desire to go back to school. But it is clear that both of these are simply out of reach as possibilities. In an interview with Bourgois a drug dealer describes with some pride that he manages to hold down a day job as a courier, never missing a day. However this is such a low pay activity that he needs to combine this legitimate job with other illegal activities to survive. Thus multi-tasking is as endemic among the poor now forced to live without welfare, as it is for the more affluent middle-classes. The despairing words of Ramon 'That's how life treated me. Life treated me this way so bad that I don't give a fuck no more' (ibid.: 179), are evidently the outcome of the structural forces which lock him into ghetto life, so that death truly is the only escape that can be imagined. These two sections succeed because the writers are able to demonstrate their familiarity with existing scholarship on race and poverty and this makes their arguments more rounded and persuasive.

Other sections of the book where there is little reference to existing work and wider sociological debates, and where instead there is an almost sanctimonious relation to the voice of the speaker, are much less successful. On occasion the respondents appear to be exploited for their own grief. For example the feminist activist tells the life history of her refuge project. Her emotional involvement and her profound distress when the project is taken from the hands of the volunteers and activists and turned into a more professional organisation, is to the reader, less surprising than it is to the professional interviewer/sociologist. Many feminist projects ended in tears, but to print her story in this way where the only visible connection with other stories is that it describes changes in the workplace is of little value to either our understanding of voluntary work, political activism or feminism. The interviewer quotes 'And there are women who claim to be feminists who aren't at all, because they're the ones who did me in' (ibid.: 353). Again, this achieves the exact opposite effect Bourdieu strives for. It personalises, it reduces a serious feminist intervention to a seemingly bitter feud between individuals, it exposes somebody for no obvious purpose other than using her experience for spurious sociological ends. The writer Sandine Garcia quite patronisingly comments on how this feminist is able to 'analyse with great perspicuity just how a bureaucratic world works . . . with its terminology and its abstract impersonal administrative categories' (ibid.: 341). Basically what she is saying is that this woman understands her own working conditions . . . 'she has learnt that social and cultural domination also cuts across feminism, that power exists there too . . .' (ibid.: 341). We might ask, is her learning dependent on the presence and questioning of Garcia, surely not?

In the closing section of the book titled Understanding, Bourdieu eulogises the interviews which are like 'hearing ordinary conversations'. They are, he continues, a 'more accessible equivalent of complex, abstract conceptual analyses' (Bourdieu et al., 1999.: 623), which is to say that they represent a comparable discourse to his own sociology, i.e. the respondents seem to be saying the same thing but in their own words. He asks that we give these interviews the same attention as might be given to 'great philosophical and literary texts' (ibid.: 624). But the failings of the project are directly related to the de-spatialised, culturally anonymous face-to-face encounters with a tape recorder across the kitchen table. In such situations there is little opportunity for any signs of social or cultural vitality to emerge. All the things which co-exist with suffering and disadvantage, the 'syncretic dynamism of contemporary metropolitan life' (Gilroy, 2000.: 245), and which to a certain extent alleviate and also dramatise through collective expression these experiences, in music and art (see Gilroy, 1987, 1993), in language and humour (Willis, 1978), and even just in the 'art of making do' (de Certeau, 1988) are eliminated from Bourdieu's 'world', making it a stark, atrophied place without hope. But even the poor and the dispossessed partake in some forms of cultural enjoyment which are collective resources which make people what they are. This absence is the cost Bourdieu must pay for his antipathy to cultural studies. Indeed one could, without for a moment disputing the prevalence of poverty and hardship, nonetheless suggest that 'misery' is an effect of the utilisation of managed research techniques such as those employed in this project.

Let me conclude this review with a few brief points. First that the world of Bourdieu's sociology and its quite admirable aspiration towards political intervention, in this case, is in fact a self-encapsulated and singular, and thus inevitably a rather self-regarding endeavour. The idea that an interview can effect subjective change is highly questionable. The great efforts his team make to avoid exploiting the privilege of their own education in these exchanges can have the curious effect of gratifying the sociologists on the basis of the 'intellectual love' which emerges from the encounters, and encouraging the team to report that, were they in the same place as their respondents, they would surely have the same opinions. But here identification obscures more intractable political issues. Reading this book it seems as though this is the first time sociology has sought to present itself as political intervention, it also suggests that the aspiration that the academic discipline may have an impact on its subjects (here respondents) of a potentially transformative nature is also unproblematic. In *Weight of the World* Bourdieu is taking his sociology out into the world, transforming it into a form of social pedagogy. This is a brave move, but it stops short at confronting the limits, as well as the basis of our solidarities, and thus the protracted nature of social antagonisms.

Notes

1   For a fuller account of the political context of Bourdieu and his work in France see Wieviorka, 2000.

2   In politics too the idea that 'ordinary people' have not been listened to, has been seen as a reason for the success of the Le Pen vote in April 2002.

3   My own references here are to largely UK studies of race and ethnicity, but as Wieviorka points out, Bourdieu, well aware of fellow sociologists in France and elsewhere working on similar issues, nonetheless studiously disregards these endeavours (see Wieviorka, 2000).

Mothers and Fathers, Who Needs Them? Butler's *Antigone's Claim . . .*

Re-regulating Kinship, Repudiating Feminism

What follows in this essay on *Antigone's Claim* by Judith Butler is a deliberately wide-ranging, even loose, reading of the text, for the very reason that this short book (three lectures given for the prestigious Wellek annual lectures at University of California, Irvine), points to the need for far-reaching feminist re-attention to questions of family and kinship in contemporary political culture (Butler, 2000c). Butler suggests there has been something of a retreat in feminism from fiercely disputing the neo-conservatism of current family policies. There has also been, even within feminism, retrospective self-critique of aspects of so-called 1960s sexual politics (e.g. non-monogamy) which have had the effect of warranting a return to more proprietorial partnerships. Butler's focus is the US, but similar trends exist elsewhere.[1] What marks out the uniqueness of this moment then, is the co-existence of the emphatic endorsement of traditional family values at governmental level (we might add to this George Bush's recent support to the lobby encouraging celibacy among US teenagers), with, at the same time, what looks like a liberalisation, in that there is now great diversity in family life, including gay and lesbian households, reconstituted families, families of choice, and simply ad hoc families-of-sorts. But alongside both of these developments there is 'feminist abeyance', an unwillingness to be positioned back in the firing line by questioning the very existence of the family as was once the norm (Bagguley, quoted in Walby, 2002a). My reading of Butler's *Antigone* is that it encourages us to recognise that this particular entanglement produces new normativities, new fields of interdiction and constraint. In fact there is a double entanglement which Antigone encourages us to confront. The co-existence of neo-liberal with liberal values in relation to families and sexuality, and the co-existence of feminism as that which is reviled or, as I would put it, 'almost hated', and feminism as a political force which has achieved the status of Gramscian common sense, something which is now 'taken into account' (McRobbie, 1999).[2] Moving on from Butler I would suggest that it is in the field of popular culture that some of the most indicative tensions in relation to this double entanglement are played out.

How does Antigone figure in this account? Or rather how does a young woman character from Greek drama precipitate such an analysis? In fact her presence in these lectures marks an absolute continuity in Butler's writing, in that she enables Butler to continue what she boldly set out to do in *Gender Trouble* (see Butler, 1990, Ch. 2) and has subsequently returned to, which is the dislodging of the Oedipus complex from its position of unquestioned authority, on the grounds of its instituting the social (and seemingly universal) mechanisms of patriarchal heterosexuality and reproduction. Antigone is an integral part of the Oedipal scenario, but her presence can be recast, her narrative can be used to produce an alternative threshold of authority. She allows the possibility of envisaging a different modality of kinship, but this requires that the state be challenged, even when it seems to embrace or take on broad feminist concerns. Butler puts Antigone, a girl who in defying the state is seen to act in a manly way, at the threshold of social organisation, at the point where it seems the laws of living a 'culturally intelligible' life are installed. This continues the political project of de-stabilising the seemingly irrevocable 'foundations' of the social and psychic order.

But still, how to move from Greek drama to the contemporary dramas (or soap operas and sit coms) of family life? Butler's route is, not surprisingly given her earlier writing, largely through Hegel and Lacan, with references to feminist philosophers like Irigaray who have also been drawn to Antigone. Let me briefly summarise. Antigone, the offspring of an incestuous liaison and thus symbol of the unimaginable and unintelligible in culture, insists on burying her brother against the instructions of her uncle. Through her defiance (which also emasculates the authority of patriarchy), her perceived gender as a woman is put in question. This de-stabilisation of the foundations of both gender and kinship, is further disturbed by the depth of love for a brother, which results in her death (or self entombment). She chooses death rather than the normativities that might have saved her and re-secured her identity i.e. marriage and motherhood. Butler reminds us that Hegel reads Antigone as making way for the state and patriarchy to replace and supplant matriarchy and kinship, while for Lacan her necessary demise figures the inauguration of the Symbolic which in turn poses certain strict forms of kinship as 'a presupposition of cultural intelligibility'.

The paradox of Antigone is then that she is both kinship gone badly wrong, and kinship itself. She embodies that which the Symbolic casts out, when it asserts the appropriate rules which must prevail between parents and their children. Antigone's defiance stems from a protestation of love for her brother and insistence that he be properly buried. The anxious repetition among any number of writers that there is no incest in Antigone's love for her brother betrays their own fears, hence their anxious citing of the norm, 'no, it isn't incest'. The horror which is unthinkable and repelled is predicated on its proximity, its easy possibility. Lacan drew on Levi Strauss' account of the incest taboo, exogamy and the exchange of women to propose the Symbolic as that horizon of language and kinship which permits access to the cultural, a means for persons to live. It is Symbolic by virtue of being above the specific or particular social realities of family life, this universalism works on the basis that cultures may be very different from each other but they largely obey the requirements of this law. Kinship and language are 'elevated to the status of elementary structures of the intelligible' and for the Lacanians 'language and kinship are not socially alterable institutions – at least not easily altered' (Butler, 2000: 15). But if the Symbolic sanctions while also being unanswerable, is it not a God-like (or as Butler puts it, a theological) thing?

What if the Symbolic is thus nothing other than a threshold of jurisdiction in favour of reproduction and heterosexuality, which is able to evoke the horror of incest to instil fear and anxiety across a much wider field of activities as a way of sending out warnings to its subjects, and thus reining them in, alerting them to the dangers of other irregularities? This idea of wider remit is absolutely crucial to the argument here. The impact of the regulative dynamic is to conjure fear or horror in order to extend a field of jurisdiction in new directions. While able to countenance failure and also diversity and change in kinship, the Symbolic will invariably preside over these changes and insist, in the context of the family, on the need for a mother and a father. For Butler this poses the question of those others whose parental love for a child carries no recognition within the mother–father regime and thus has no 'certainty or durability'. Why must gay families, for instance, with two mothers or two fathers find themselves compromised by the state to operate as if there was a mother and a father? What requires this specific organisation of persons? Does the idea of having two mothers or two fathers, manageable perhaps in the context of everyday life, and a source of comedy in recent popular culture, hold up in law?[3] And what greater warning could there be to those who wish to move away from this norm that they might, in so doing, endanger the life of the child? The figure of Antigone allows Butler to imagine the psychic pain wrought upon the shadowy persons fulfilling 'unauthorised' or irregular kinship roles.

For these reasons Butler challenges psychoanalysis to critically interrogate its 'structuralist presuppositions', i.e. its normative assumptions which even though they troubled Juliet Mitchell many years ago nonetheless remain intact (Mitchell, 1984). She also chastises Lacanians for the authoritative defense of the Symbolic as above social critique, indeed for its function as warning against those who dare to pursue 'utopian efforts'. In a gesture reminiscent of her taking up the position of the 'phallic lesbian' in order to attack the Lacanian Symbolic in *Bodies That Matter* (Butler, 1993), Butler again pushes the Symbolic off its pedestal, reducing it to the status of just another horizon of social norms, 'a form of reification with stark consequences for gendered life'. To uphold the sanctity of the Symbolic as the basis for social and cultural organisation which psychoanalysis plainly does is to retain an inner 'theological' core. That Butler so perseveres (as she has done in earlier work) with this job of prising open the doors of the Symbolic (which she here likens to Antigone's tomb) is testimony to her political commitment to rearranging gender relations, and in this case to question the necessity of mothers and fathers. Of course there is a total logic to this current inquiry, in that having demonstrated in *Gender Trouble* (Butler, 1990) how gender is called into being, and for the sake of heterosexual reproduction is repetitively enacted so as to become the basis for recognition in terms of what it is to be human (i.e. 'being a girl'), Butler now looks to the repeated enactments of kinship ideals when faced with the challenge to social organisation here proposed in the figure of Antigone.

As though aware of the intractable problems in loosening the grip of Oedipus and replacing his authority on how we live, with Antigone's more fluid and uncertain power, Butler's persistence takes on something of Antigone's gesture of defiance. She will not relinquish psychoanalysis in favour of a mere feminist sociology of family life because that would be to let go of understanding desire and its unruly proliferations, the unconscious, fear, trauma, dreams, obsessions, compulsive repetitions, and so on. As Campbell has argued 'Butler's work requires a psychoanalytic account of the social production of the subject' (Campbell, 2001). Psychoanalysis also allows exploration of the whole range of psychic resistances to change which is necessary for political understanding. Antigone stands at the interface between the psychic and the social and through her Butler imagines a revised or re-articulated (let us say a weaker) Symbolic. A 'post-structuralist kinship' of this sort, would allow more diverse 'socially survivable' arrangements, carrying fewer parental warnings about harm to children. Far from saying 'let's relax our attitudes to incest', Butler is showing how the horror and fear of interfering with this foundational stricture becomes a way of refusing to encounter proliferating and irregular relations of love and affiliation beyond those fully sanctioned by the state (see also Bell, 1997).

Antigone is the unimaginable in culture, by virtue of her incestuous parentage, her abject status produces a shudder across the social field, but she also resists this status by defying the state and asserting a human bond which she is not expected to dare to acknowledge. I think Butler asks us to read Antigone as a person who represents the unrepresentable, those various bodies in the body politic denied the status of the fully human and thus who confound and unsettle the principles upon which contemporary sociality is based. She is claimed as a 'not-quite' feminist figure, an 'almost queer heroine'. My reading of Butler here is that Antigone brings to the surface the new, more subtle, exclusions from the status of the 'fully human' which come into being through the changes in gender norms in the postfeminist world. The feminist is always 'old' even 'ugly', she is that which younger women cannot be if they wish to be counted in the wider world.[4] The feminist proposes a presence which is shunned, a feminism which in its repudiation is also, strangely, 'taken into account'. We might ask, what is the political meaning of this spectral existence, to be, as a feminist, that which is granted a presence on the basis of being also reviled? Butler's Antigone also stands as a figure for whom the norms of family relations have been over-turned, she is too attached to her brother, and as a girl she refuses the possibility of regular affiliations. But, we might not ask, is there not something timely in this shadowy existence, are these irregular attachments and 'singularities' (or singledoms) not also played out at this very moment across the 'unconscious' of contemporary popular culture? To explore this more fully requires an intellectual leap from feminist theory to cultural studies, from Antigone to Bridget Jones.[5]

The double entanglement theorised in Butler's Antigone provides ample opportunity for exploring issues which are critical for feminism. While it is impossible in the space of this short piece to engage with these in depth, I will instead propose that we can extract from the abject state to which feminism has been expelled (perhaps a retirement home in an unfashionable rundown holiday resort) and from its status as that which is capable of instilling dread and horror in young women, for fear that they might be mistaken as a 'feminist' and thus robbed of a sexual identity that counts and that has value, a margin of hope through the ambivalence and forcefulness and repetition of these repudiations. At the same time it is the very success of the new right that it has made of feminism such a thing of contempt, and this accounts, I would suggest, for the strain of sadness that runs through Butler's Antigone.

In the light of this, I propose that Antigone provides us with the possibility of developing a socio-cultural analysis of current kinship anxieties influenced as they are by, but now also forced to do without, feminism and the political. While the social and the cultural are inevitably intertwined, for the sake of brevity and by way of a conclusion I will force them apart and rehearse how some of these tensions are manifest first in contemporary family life and second in popular culture. Butler argues that along with families of choice there also comes into being new and expansive forms of constraint, control and surveillance. In passing she also comments on irregular relations (for example fondnesses between 'unrelated' step siblings) which give rise to concern on the part of adults. But what we can surmise is that there has developed a climate where there is a tightening of the boundaries which mark out legitimate and proper relations in the field of attachment, affect, and affiliation.

Undesignated persons, those who can make no official claim in relation to the care or well-being of young persons find themselves, if not considered overtly dangerous, are at least possibly suspicious or with dubious motives. Thus while the appearance in a home of a new stepfather is by and large socially acceptable, the appearance of a caring adult in the guise of an enthusiastic teacher, a too-zealous social worker or youth worker, or simply an adult friend, is now subject to intense social disapprobation.[6] To put it crudely we could say that there is no longer the possibility of being a Miss Jean Brodie.[7] Thus those whose relations with children or teenagers are, as Butler puts it, of uncertain durability, or without the warmth and informality which only kinship now bestows, find themselves cast out in the cold, fearful of the law, and without any possibility of playing a role and of offering things of value in the life and upbringing of the young.

This is a far cry from the radical sexual politics of the family from the mid-1970s, which saw the development of communes, shared child care arrangements and the positive encouragement of involvement on the part of adults with children with whom they had no kinship relation, but for whom they had a social obligation in terms of shared domestic responsibility.[8] The horror now conjured up by the very word 'commune' (though it too can be a source of gentle humour as the Swedish film *Together (Tilsammans)* directed by Lukas Moodysson (2000), demonstrated) is indicative of the end of experimentation in domestic relations, and in many respects this signals again a wider remit of familial conservatism, an impoverishment of community, a turning away from the possibilities of socialised child rearing, this also marks a new modality of social exclusion, a means of creating social outcasts and of further isolating the damaged, the unstable, the loners, the lonely and the childless. The disparaging of the irregular coincides with the pressure on gay families to be exemplary. The recognition of normative kinship within such units, including doting grandparents, loving aunts and kindly uncles, also must come at some cost.

If people and in particular younger people in the western world now live out their kinship relations within this particular regime of double entanglement of liberal choice and neo-liberal family values, feminist common sense and feminist displacement, we might ask how is it done? The field of popular entertainment offers a wide space for the endless and repeated playing out of these anxieties as social comedy. Let me conclude this review by suggesting that Antigone points us directly towards *Bridget Jones* (the book and the film), and the US television series *Friends*, *Ally McBeal* and *Sex and the City*. Writing many years ago about the widely read girls' magazine *Jackie*, I remember analysing how the teenage girl in the magazine was imagined week in week out as someone in search of a boy (McRobbie, 1976; 2000). She could never relax until she had trapped a 'fella' and had a ring on her finger, even then she had to be vigilant in case he found someone else more attractive. These stories were so much the subject of feminist critique that they came to sum up pre-feminist femininity, the desperate, 'always on the look out', search for Mr Right. This way of being a girl was, as many of us argued, a humiliating, subservient indeed unbearable, subject position. During the 1980s this kind of imagery all but disappeared. But this changed with the advent of self-consciously 'politically incorrect' post-feminist popular culture. Suddenly, as though relieved that all that angry feminism has gone, these same narratives reappear with a vengeance, but with an irony that suggested that 'feminism has been taken into account'. Fear of not being married, fear of being left on the shelf, fear of being an old maid, or a spinster, fear of running out of time and of leaving it too late to have babies, indeed fear, dread and the horror of being a woman alone drives each of these girls now unashamedly in search of a man. From *Sex and the*

City to *Ally McBeal*, and then most thoroughly in *Bridget Jones*, feminism has a spectral, shadowy, almost hated existence. They might find themselves having similar concerns on sexual technique as feminists once had (*Sex and the City*), they might find themselves opting for the value of female friendship over unreliable boyfriends, they might consider lesbianism, or have some good lesbian friends, goodness, they might even come close to endorsing sisterhood, but never is the word spoken, they must live out their sexual and emotional lives without recourse to sexual politics. This is the condition of existence of these popular narratives, they must cast the possibility of a new feminism aside, they must muddle through without it.

Despite this, new configurations of kinship do emerge which feminism, now relegated to history, nonetheless makes possible, for example Rachel in *Friends* becomes pregnant by former boyfriend Ross. She decides to have the baby but not to re-start the relationship. Into the pregnancy she continually feels 'horny', goes on dates and reflects on the ethics of having sex with somebody new with a baby by somebody else in her womb. This is a post-feminist dilemma in a culture of female independence and choice, where single motherhood is nothing to be ashamed of. And yet running alongside this narrative in *Friends* is also that of Monica and Chandler whose courtship, engagement, shower party and traditional white wedding offers opportunity for comedy over a period of several months (including the transexual father of Chandler turning up at the wedding in drag).

One of the running jokes in the film *Bridget Jones's Diary* (adapted from the book) is that when she casts her eyes on a suitable man, she finds herself fantasising wedding bells, a white dress and an entourage of bridesmaids. The humour lies in the way in which she indicates that she knows this to be a bad thought, she has the fantasy 'in spite of feminism', and the audience laughs with her because they too know that this is not how girls or women are nowadays meant to be. Feminism is thus the censor, feminism is a psychic policewoman, disallowing girls from the pleasure of imagining the pleasures of pre-feminist womanhood (she also imagines herself at home in the country as wife and mother happily servicing husband and children alike). The film opens with Bridget in her pyjamas facing up to the prospect of going home for Christmas, yet again, without a man, the soundtrack is 'All By Myself', (sung by Jamie McNeal) and the humour emerges from the grimness, the social discomfort, indeed shame, of being unpartnered. The wit and intelligence, the intertextual referencing to *Pride and Prejudice*, the self mocking awareness of the Bridget Jones persona, makes it an exemplary post-feminist text. Its enormous success at the box office, its immediate popularity in gay and lesbian circles,[9] and the social landscape it portrays of confident girls spoilt for choice and enjoying the bright city lights but unable to find the right man and fantasising a life back in the countryside, has made Bridget Jones representative of contemporary femininity. Only the hard-hearted, the too-serious, the earnest, humourless and generationally specific 'feminist' could object, could point to the white Englishness of Bridget Jones, to the voice it gives to the desire for tradition, to its (ironic) celebration of marriage and the assumption of conventional kinship as the solution to the fears and anxieties of being a single girl. In this sense the original newspaper column (upon which the book was based) of *Bridget Jones*, can be seen as a response by a younger woman journalist (Helen Fielding) to her feminist forebearers. It seems to be written as a counter to feminism, Bridget is scatter-brained, rather than too clever, she is interested in calories rather than politics, her career is not her life and she craves the security of a well-qualified husband. Feminism has served its purpose by making various opportunities available, and for this some thanks are due, but now it can be dispensed with: its time is over. Butler's Antigone allows us to reflect on this shadow existence. For feminism to be taken into account it has to be understood as having passed away.

Notes

1   The current New Labour government kindly provides 'handbooks for living' to couples embarking on marriage.

2   Feminism as common sense finds expression across the political spectrum. For New Labour in the UK it has no place in any political vocabulary yet informs many policies (see Walby, 2002a, 2000b), even the word woman is recently excised in favour of the need for 'work–life balance'. The Bush administration justifies aggression with reference to the infringements of women's rights in Muslim states, in both cases the idea that women deserve to be treated as equal to men becomes part of the claim to civilisation and modernity. Outside politics and within the cultural realm this common sense takes a diversity of forms, driving a women's agenda on for example BBC Radio 3 and 4, whose listeners are of an age and social background for whom feminism remains important.

3   In an episode of *Friends* broadcast in the UK (Channel 4) in September, 2002, Phoebe poses as the 'second mother' of the child conceived as a result of Ross donating sperm to allow his ex wife and her girlfriend to have a child. Phoebe does this as a way of bumping

into the popstar Sting whose child attends the same school as the boy. The narrative relies on the school teacher assuming her to be the 'second mum' and the humour of the episode stems partly from Phoebe's clumsy attempts to prove her lesbian status by flirting with the teacher.

4   The BBC Radio 4 programme *Woman's Hour* which carries an overtly feminist brief, ran an item 23rd September 2002 following the success of black UK singer Ms Dynamite winning the prestigious Mercury Prize. With lyrics which refuse the usual female stereotypes of much hip hop and r'n'b music, and by calling herself Ms Dynamite, it is not surprising that she has been labelled as a feminist. The interviewer spoke with groups of North London girls from the area in which Ms Dynamite grew up, asking them what they thought about feminism. The answers were overwhelmingly negative, they said they thought Germaine Greer was 'ugly', followed by all the usual man hating stereotypes (see also Walter, 1996).

5   'Bridget Jones's Diary' was the title of a weekly column which ran in the *Independent* newspaper in the UK from 1996 written by journalist Helen Fielding. Its success led to publication as a book followed by the release of the 'blockbuster' feature film in 2001.

6   Social workers regularly report on how their pastoral roles are now seriously curtailed as a result of publicity about abuse, with the effect that the work of befriending at-risk youngsters, even offering them the occasional bed for the night, and being available at home for informal conversations, all of which have been so effective in the past, are no longer advisable, if not completely forbidden.

7   From deeply anti-feminist, well-nigh misogynist positions, a number of leading novelists (Philip Roth in *The Human Stain*, and also *The Dying Animal*, J.M.Coetzee in *Disgrace*, and Jonathan Franzen in *The Corrections*) explore this terrain in fiction, the extent to which intimate, intense, informal and irregular relationships between academics and their students are now impossible. The rightful highlighting of sexual abuse has nonetheless given rise to a wide climate of fear and suspicion, which in turn reduces the scope of human sociality.

8   I remember while living in Germany in the late 1970s visiting friends who lived in various communal arrangements which in this context developed out of a politics of violently opposing the parenting practices of the older fascistic generation. Children were discouraged to relate with special attachments to biological parents, all adults had a responsibility for care, affection and the more routine tasks of domestic labour. Far from being exceptional or outlandish activities communes were barely remarkable at that time in Germany among left and feminist influenced people.

9   In a feature in the *Observer Magazine* (Sunday 21st April 2002: 35) on gay marriage ceremonies, one young man named Saul Hazan

described the event as follows: 'I had a real *Bridget Jones* moment during the ceremony when I thought, "Oh my God, I've finally got my man!"' In keeping with pre-feminist tradition this couple had adopted the same surname on marriage.

References

Althusser, L. (1971) 'Ideological State Apparatuses', in L. Althusser (ed.), *Lenin and Philosophy and Other Essays*. London: New Left Books. pp. 123–73.

Anderson, B. (1986) *Imagined Communities*. London: Verso.

Appadurai, A. (1990) 'Disjuncture and Difference in the Global Cultural Economy', *Theory, Culture and Society*, 7 (10): 259–310.

Back, L. (1996) *New Ethnicities and Urban Culture: Racisms and Multiculture in Young Lives*. London: UCL Press.

Back, L. and Ware, V. (2002) *Out of Whiteness*. Chicago: University of Chicago Press.

Back, L., Cohen, P., and Keith, M. (1999) 'Between Home and Belonging: Critical Ethnographies of Race, Place, and Identity', CNER Working Paper 2. London: University of East London.

Barthes, R. (1972) *Mythologies*. London: Jonathan Cape.

Barthes, R. (1977) *Image Music Text*. Glasgow: Collins Fontana.

Bauman, Z. (2000) *Liquid Modernity*. Cambridge: Polity Press.

Beauvoir, S. de (1970) *The Second Sex*. New York: New England Press.

Beck, U. (2000) *What is Globalisation?* Cambridge: Polity Press.

Bell, V. (1997) *Interrogating Incest*. London: Routledge.

Benjamin, W. (1973) *Illuminations*. London: New Left Books.

Bennett, T., Martin, G. Mercer, C., and Woollacott, J. (eds) (1981) *Culture, Ideology and Social Process*. London: Batsford Academic.

Berlant, L. (2000) 'The Subject of True Feeling: Pain, Privacy and Politics', in S. Ahmed, C. Lury, M. McNeil, and B. Skeggs (eds), *Transformations: Thinking Through Feminism*. London: Routledge. pp. 33–48.

Bhabha, H. (1994) *The Location of Culture*. London: Routledge.

Bourdieu, P. (1984) *Distinction: A Social Critique of the Judgement of Taste*. London: Routledge.

Bourdieu, P. (1990) *In Other Words: Essays Towards A Reflexive Sociology*. Cambridge: Polity Press.

Bourdieu, P. (1993) *The Field of Cultural Production*. Cambridge: Polity Press.

Bourdieu, P. (1998) *Acts of Resistance*. Cambridge: Polity Press.

Bourdieu, P. and Wacquant, L. (1992) *An Invitation to Reflexive Sociology*. Cambridge: Polity Press.

Bourdieu, P. and Wacquant, L. (1999) 'On the Cunning of Imperialist Reason', in *Theory Culture and Society*, 16 (1): 41–58.

Bourdieu, P. and Wacquant, L. (2001) 'New Liberalspeak: Notes on the Planetary Vulgate', *Radical Philosophy*, 105 (Jan–Feb): 2–6.

Bourdieu, P. et al. (1999) *The Weight of the World: Social Suffering in Contemporary Society*. Cambridge: Polity Press.

Brown, W. (1995) *States of Injury*. Boston: Princeton University Press.

Brown, W. (2000) 'Resisting Left Melancholia', in P. Gilroy, L. Grossberg and A. McRobbie (eds), *Without Guarantees: In Honour of Stuart Hall*. London: Verso. pp. 21–30.

Brown, W. (2004) 'The End of Liberal Democracy', *Theory and Event*, 1 (1): http://muse.jhu.edu/journals/theory_and_event/r007/7.lbrown.html

Brunsdon, C. (2003) 'Lifestyling Britain: The 8–9 Slot on British Television', *International Journal of Cultural Studies*, 6 (1): 5–23.

Butler, J. (1990) *Gender Trouble: Feminism and the Subversion of Identity*. New York: Routledge.

Butler, J. (1992) 'Contingent Foundations: Feminism and the Question of Postmodernism', in J. Butler and J.W. Scott (eds), *Feminists Theorise the Political*. New York: Routledge. pp. 3–22.

Butler, J. (1993) *Bodies That Matter: On the Discursive Limits of Sex*. New York: Routledge.

Butler, J. (1994) 'Gender As Performance: An Interview with Judith Butler' by P. Osborne and L. Segal, *Radical Philosophy*, 67 (Summer): 32–9.

Butler, J. (1999a) *Gender Trouble: Feminism and the Subversion of Identity*, 2nd edition. New York: Routledge.

Butler, J. (1999b) 'Performativity's Social Magic', in R Shusterman (ed.), *Bourdieu: A Critical Reader*. Oxford: Blackwell. pp. 113–28.

Butler, J. (2000a) 'Agencies of Style for a Liminal Subject', in P. Gilroy, L. Grossberg and A. McRobbie (eds), *Without Guarantees: In Honour of Stuart Hall*. London: Verso. pp. 30–8.

Butler, J. (2000b) 'Re Staging the Universal: Hegemony and the Limits of Formalism', in J. Butler, E. Laclau, and S. Zizek (eds), *Contingency, Hegemony and Universality: Contemporary Dialogues on the Left*. London: Verso.

Butler, J. (2000c) *Antigone's Claim: Kinship Between Life and Death*. New York: Columbia University Press.

Calhoun, C. (1993) 'Habitus, Field and Capital: the Question of Historical Specificity', in C. Calhoun, E. Lipuma, and M. Postone (eds), *Bourdieu: Critical Perspectives*. Cambridge: Polity Press. pp. 61–89.

Calhoun, C., Lipuma, E. and Postone, M. (eds) (1993) *Bourdieu: Critical Perspectives*. Cambridge: Polity Press.

Campbell, J. and Harbord, J. (1999) 'Playing It Again: Citation, Reiteration or Circularity?' 'Performativity and Belonging' Special Issue, ed. V. Bell, *Theory, Culture and Society*, 16 (2): 229–41.

Campbell, K. (2001) 'The Plague of the Subject: Psychoanalysis and Judith Butler's Psychic Life of Power', *International Journal of Sexuality and Gender Studies*, 6: 1–2.

Certeau, M. de (1988) *The Practice of Everyday Life*. Berkeley and Los Angeles: University of California Press.

Chrisman, L. (2000) 'Journeying to Death: Gilroy's Black Atlantic', in K. Owusu (ed.) *Black British Culture and Society*. London: Routledge. pp. 453–65.

Clifford, J. (1997) *Routes: Travel and Translation in the Late Twentieth Century*. Cambridge, MA: Harvard University Press.

Coetzee, J.M. (2000) *Disgrace*. London: Vintage.

Cohen, P. (1992) 'Its Racism What Dunnit: Hidden Narratives in Theories of Racism', in J. Donald and A. Rattansi (eds) *'Race' Culture and Difference*. London: Sage. pp. 62–100.

Cohen, S. (1996) *Folk Devils and Moral Panics*, 2nd edition. London: Routledge.

Cohen, S. and Young, J. (1973) *The Manufacture of News*. London: Constable.

Couldry, N. (2003) 'Media Meta-Capital: Extending the Range of Bourdieu's Theory', *Theory and Society*, 25(4): 653–77.

Dreyfus, H. and Rabinow, P. (1993) 'Can There be a Science of Existential Structure and Social Meaning?', in C. Calhoun, E. Lipuma and M. Postone (eds), *Bourdieu: Critical Perspectives*. Cambridge: Polity Press. pp. 35–45.

Du Gay, P. and Pryke, M. (eds) (2002) *Cultural Economy*. London: Sage.

Eagleton, T. (2001) *The Gatekeeper: A Memoir*. London: Penguin.

Enwezor, O. (1997) 'Yinka Shonibare: The Joke is on You', in Flash Art, Nov–Dec, p.96.

Eshun, E. (1998) *More Brilliant Than the Sun: Adventures in Sonic Fiction*. London: Quartet.

Featherstone M. (ed.) (1990) *Global Culture*. London: Sage.

Franks, S. (1999) *Having None of It: Men, Women, and the Future of Work*. London: Granta.

Franzen, J. (2002) *The Corrections*. London: Fourth Estate.

Garnham, N. (1993) 'Bourdieu: The Cultural Arbitrary and Television', in C. Calhoun, E. Lipuma and M. Postone (eds), *Bourdieu: Critical Perspectives*. Cambridge: Polity Press. pp. 178–93.

Geertz, C. (2000) *Available Light*. Cambridge, MA: Harvard University Press.

Giddens, A. (1995) *Beyond Left and Right*. Cambridge: Polity Press.

Giddens, A. (1998) *The Third Way*. Cambridge: Polity Press.

Giddens, A. (2002) 'The Third Way Can Beat the Far Right', in the *Guardian*, 3rd May, p. 21.

Gilroy, P. (1987) *There Ain't No Black in the Union Jack*. London: Hutchinson.

Gilroy, P. (1992) 'The End of Anti Racism?' in J. Donald and A. Rattansi (eds), *'Race', Culture and Difference*. London: Sage. pp. 49–62.

Gilroy, P. (1993) *The Black Atlantic: Modernity and Double Consciousness*. London: Verso.

Gilroy, P. (2000) *Between Camps: Nations, Cultures, and the Allure of Race*. Harmondsworth: Penguin.

Gilroy, P. (2002) *There Ain't No Black in the Union Jack*, 2nd edition. London: Routledge.

Grosz, E. (1997) *Space, Time and Perversion*. New York: Routledge.

Goodhart, D. (2004) 'Too Diverse? Is Britain Becoming too Diverse to Sustain the Mutual Obligations that Underpin a Good Society and a Generous Welfare State?' *Prospect*, 9, 5th February: pp. 30–7.

Hall, S. and Jefferson, T. (eds) (1976) *Resistance Through Rituals*. London: Routledge.

Hall, S., Critcher, C., Jefferson, T., Clarke, J. and Robert, B. (1978) *Policing the Crisis*. London: Hutchinson.

Hall, S. (1988) *The Hard Road to Renewal*. London: Verso.

Hall, S. (1992a) 'New Ethnicities', in J. Donald and A Rattansi (eds) *'Race', Culture and Difference*. London: Sage, pp. 252–60.

Hall, S. (1992b) 'Identity and the black photographic image', *Ten-8*, no. 20: 24–31.

Hall, S. (1998a) 'The Great Moving Nowhere Show', *Marxism Today*, November: 2–11.

Hall, S. (1998b) 'Aspiration and Attitude: Reflections on Black Britain in the 1990s' in *New Formations*, 3 (Spring): 38–46.

Hall, S. (1999) 'Whose Heritage? Unsettling the Inheritance, Re-Imagining the Post-Nation', *Third Text*, 49, winter: 3–13.

Hall, S. (2000a) 'Conclusion: The Multi-cultural Question', in B. Hesse (ed.), *Un/settled Multi-culturalisms: Diasporas, Entanglements Transruptions*. London: Zed Books. pp. 209–41.

Hall, S. (2000b) 'The Multi-cultural Question', Pavis Papers, Faculty of Social Science. Milton Keynes The Open University.

Hall, S. (2003) 'New Labour's Double Shuffle', in *Soundings*, November, pp. 10–24.

Hebdige, D. (1978) *Subculture: the Meaning of Style*. London: Methuen.

Hoggart, R. (1957) *The Uses of Literacy*. Harmondsworth: Penguin.

Jameson, F. (1979) '*Dog Day Afternoon* as a Political Film', *Screen Education*, 30: 75–92.

Jameson, F. (1984) 'Postmodernism or the Cultural Logic of Capital', *New Left Review*, 146: 53–92.

Jameson, F. (1991) *Postmodernism, or, the Cultural Logic of Late Capitalism*. London: Verso.

Jameson, F. (1998) *Brecht and Method*. London: Verso.

Kellner, D. (ed.) (1989) *Postmodernism/Jameson/Critique*. Washington, DC: Maisonneuve Press.

Kim, Y. (2001) 'The Formation of the Black Diaporic Subject', PhD thesis Goldsmiths College, University of London.

Laclau, E. (1990) *Reflections on the Revolutions of Our Times*. London: Verso.

Laclau, E. and Mouffe, C. (1985) *Hegemony and Socialist Strategy*. London: Verso.

Lash, S. (2002) *Critique of Information*. London: Sage.

Lipuma, E. (1993) 'Culture and the Concept of Culture in a Theory of Practice', in C. Calhoun, E. Lipuma and M. Postone (eds) *Bordieu: Cultural Perspectives*. Cambridge: Polity Press. pp. 14–35.

Lloyd, M. (1999) 'Performativity, Parody, Politics', in 'Performativity and Belonging' Special Issue, V. Bell (ed.), *Theory, Culture and Society*, 16: 175–95.

McNay, L. (1999a) 'Subject, Psyche, Agency: The Work of Judith Butler' in V. Bell (ed.) *Theory, Culture and Society*, 16: 175–95.

McNay, L. (1999b) 'Gender Habitus and the Field', *Theory, Culture and Society*, 16 (1): 95–119.

McRobbie, A. (1994) *Postmodernism and Popular Culture*. London: Routledge.

McRobbie, A. (1994 [1989]) 'Second Hand Dresses and the Role of the Ragmarket', in A. McRobbie, *Postmodernism and Popular Culture*. London: Routledge. pp. 135–55.

McRobbie, A. (1998) *British Fashion Design: Rag Trade or Image Industry?* London: Routledge.

McRobbie, A. (1999) *In the Culture Society*. London: Routledge.

McRobbie, A. (2000a) *Feminism and Youth Culture*, 2nd edition. Basingstoke: Macmillan.

McRobbie, A. (2000b [1981]) 'The Politics of Feminist Research: Between Talk Text and Action', in *Feminism and Youth Culture*, 2nd edition. Basingstoke: Macmillan. pp. 118–37.

McRobbie, A. (2002) 'Clubs to Companies: Notes on the Decline of Political Culture in Speeded Up Creative Worlds' in *Cultural Studies* 'Cultural Intermediaries Who Needs Them?' Special Issue, *Cultural Studies*, 16 (4): 516–31.

McRobbie (2004) 'Post Feminism and Popular Culture' in *Feminist Media Studies*, 4(3): 255–64.

McRobbie, A. (forthcoming) *Feminism and the TV Blonde: Essays on the Displacement of Sexual Politics*. London: Sage..

Media Group (Hall, S., Connell, I. and Curti, L.) (1976) 'The "Unity" of Current Affairs Television', CCCS, University of Birmingham, *Working Papers in Cultural Studies* Spring (9): 51–95.

Melville, C. (2004) 'The Roots and Routes of Multi-Cultural London', PhD thesis, Goldsmiths College, University of London.

Mercer, K. (2000) 'A Sociography of Diaspora', in P. Gilroy, L. Grossberg and A. McRobbie (eds), *Without Guarantees: In Honour of Stuart Hall*. London: Verso. pp. 233–65.

Miles, R. (1982) *Racism and Migrant Labour*. London: RKP.

Mitchell, J. (1984) *Psychoanalysis and Feminism*. Harmondsworth: Penguin.

Moore-Gilbert, B. (1997) *Postcolonial Theory*. London: Verso.

Nairn, T. (1979) *The Break Up of Britain*. London: New Left Books.

Odone, C. (2000) 'If High Flyers Refuse to Be Mums', *The New Statesman*, 3rd April, p. 21.

Pratt, M.L. (1992) *Imperial Eyes: Studies in Travel Writing and Transculturation*. New York: Routledge.

Rattansi, A. (1992) 'Changing the Subject: Racism Culture and Education', in J. Donald and A. Rattansi (eds), *'Race', Culture and Difference*. London: Sage. pp. 11–49.

Riley, D. (1988) *Am I That Name? Feminism and the Category of Women in History*. Basingstoke: Macmillan.

Roberts, J. (1998) 'Pop Art, the Popular and British Art of the 1990s', in D. McCorquodale, N. Siderlin and J. Stallabrass (eds), *Occupational Hazard: Critical Writing on Recent British Art*. London: Black Dog. pp. 52–80.

Rose, J. (1987) *Sexuality in the Field of Vision*. London: Verso.

Rose, N. (1999) 'Inventiveness in Politics', *Economy and Society*, 28 (3): 467–93.

Ross, A. (2003) *No Collar: The Humane Workplace and its Hidden Costs*. New York: Basic Books.

Roth, P. (2002) *The Human Stain*. London: Viking.

Roth, P. (1999) *The Dying Animal*. London: Viking.

Rushdie, S. (1988) *The Satanic Verses*. Harmondsworth: Penguin.

Said, E. (1978) *Orientalism*. London: Penguin.

Salih, S. (2002) *Judith Butler*. London: Routledge.

Sassen, S. (1991) *The Global City*. Princeton, NJ: Princeton University Press.

Sassen, S. (2000) 'Analytic Borderlands: Economy and Culture in the Global City', in G. Bridge and S. Watson (eds), *A Companion to the City*. Oxford: Blackwell. pp. 168–81.

Scott, J.W. (1992) 'Experience', in J. Butler and J.W. Scott (eds), *Feminists Theorise the Political*. New York: Routledge. pp. 22–41.

Scott, A.J. and Power, D. (eds) (2004) *The Culture Industries and the Production of Culture*. New York: Routledge.

Sharma, S., Hutnyk, J. and Sharma, A. (eds) (1996) *Dis-orienting Rhythms: The Politics of the New Asian Dance Music*. London: Zed Books.

Shusterman, R. (ed.) (1999) *Bourdieu: A Critical Reader*. Oxford: Blackwell.

Skeggs, B. (1997) *Formations of Class and Gender*. London: Sage.

Spivak, G.C. (1988) 'Can the Subaltern Speak?', in C. Nelson and L. Grossberg (eds), *Marxism and the Interpretation of Culture*. Chicago: University of Illinois Press. pp. 272–313.

Spivak, G.C. (1999) *A Critique of Postcolonial Reason*. Cambridge, MA: Harvard University Press.

Stallabrass, J. (1998) 'A Place of Pleasure', in D. McCorquodale, N. Siderlin and J. Stallabrass (eds) *Occupational Hazard: Critical Writing on Recent British Art*. London: Black Dog. pp. 170–210.

Venn, C. (2004) 'Post-Lacanian Affective Economy, Being-in-the-world, and the Critique of the Present: Lessons from Bracha Ettinger', *Theory, Culture and Society*, 21 (1): 149–59.

Waites, B., Bennett, T. and Martin, G. (eds) (1982) *Popular Culture: Past and*

Present. London: Routledge.
Walby, S. (1997) Gender Transformations. London: Routledge.
Walby, S. (2002a) 'From Community to Coalition: The Politics of Recognition as the Handmaiden of the Politics of Equality in an Era of Globalisation', Theory Culture and Society, 18 (2–3): 113–37.
Walby, S. (2002b) 'Feminism in a Global Era', Economy and Society, 31 (4): 533–57.
Walter, N. (1996) The New Feminism. London: Virago.
Watson, S. (2002) Column in the Guardian, 19th April, G2, p. 16.
Wieviorka, M. (2000) 'Contextualising French Multi-culturalism and Racism', Theory, Culture and Society, 17 (1): 157–63.
Williams, R. (1956) Culture and Society. London: Chatto and Windus.
Willis, P. (1978) Learning to Labour. London: Saxon House.
Young, R. (1990) White Mythologies: Writing History and the West. London: Routledge.
York, P. (1980) Style Wars. London: Sidgwick and Jackson.
Zylinska, J. (2005) The Ethics of Cultural Studies. London: Continuum Books.

Films

Desperately Seeking Susan (1984) dir. Susan Seidelman, Orion.
Dog Day Afternoon (1977), dir. Sydney Lumak, Warner/AEC.
Kids (1995) dir. Larry Clark, Shining Excalibur, Miramax.
Mulholland Drive (2000) dir. David Lynch, The Picture Factory.
Thirteen (2003) dir. Christine Hardewicke, Twentieth Century Fox.
Tilsummans (Together) (2000) dir. Lucas Moodysson, MGM.

Television Programmes

Ally McBeal, created by David E. Kelley. Fox Home Entertainment.
Goodness Gracious Me, written by Richard Pinto and Sharat Sardana with Sanjeev Bhaskar, Kulvinder Ghir and Meera Syral and Nina Wadia, BBC TV.
Father Ted, written by Arthur Matthews and Graham Linehan, Channel 4 TV.
The Kumars at No 42, written by Sanjeev Bhaskar, BBC TV.
Rab C. Nesbit, written by Iain Pattison, BBC TV.
Sex and the City, created by Darren Star. Home Box Office, Inc.
Six Feet Under, created by Alan Ball. Home Box Office, Inc.
The Sopranos, created by David Chase. Home Box Office, Inc.
What Not to Wear, produced by Kaye Godleman, directed by Micci Billinger, David Dehaney, Helen Foulkes, Nicola Silk, Boaz Halaban. BBC TV.
Would Like to Meet, produced by Phillipa Ransford Executive Producer, Daisy Goodwin. Talkback

Index

Present. London: Routledge.

Walby, S. (1997) *Gender Transformations*. London: Routledge.

Walby, S. (2002a) 'From Community to Coalition: The Politics of Recognition as the Handmaiden of the Politics of Equality in an Era of Globalisation', *Theory Culture and Society*, 18 (2–3): 113–37.

Walby, S. (2002b) 'Feminism in a Global Era', *Economy and Society*, 31 (4): 533–57.

Walter, N. (1996) *The New Feminism*. London: Virago.

Watson, S. (2002) Column in the *Guardian*, 19th April, G2, p. 16.

Wieviorka, M. (2000) 'Contextualising French Multi-culturalism and Racism', *Theory, Culture and Society*, 17 (1): 157–63.

Williams, R. (1956) *Culture and Society*. London: Chatto and Windus.

Willis, P. (1978) *Learning to Labour*. London: Saxon House.

Young, R. (1990) *White Mythologies: Writing History and the West*. London: Routledge.

York, P. (1980) *Style Wars*. London: Sidgwick and Jackson.

Zylinska, J. (2005) *The Ethics of Cultural Studies*. London: Continuum Books.

Films

Desperately Seeking Susan (1984) dir. Susan Seidelman, Orion.

Dog Day Afternoon (1977), dir. Sydney Lumak, Warner/AEC.

Kids (1995) dir. Larry Clark, Shining Excalibur, Miramax.

Mulholland Drive (2000) dir. David Lynch, The Picture Factory.

Thirteen (2003) dir. Christine Hardewicke, Twentieth Century Fox.

Tilsummans (Together) (2000) dir. Lucas Moodysson, MGM.

Television Programmes

Ally McBeal, created by David E. Kelley. Fox Home Entertainment.

Goodness Gracious Me, written by Richard Pinto and Sharat Sardana with Sanjeev Bhaskar, Kulvinder Ghir and Meera Syral and Nina Wadia, BBC TV.

Father Ted, written by Arthur Matthews and Graham Linehan, Channel 4 TV.

The Kumars at No 42, written by Sanjeev Bhaskar, BBC TV.

Rab C. Nesbit, written by Iain Pattison, BBC TV.

Sex and the City, created by Darren Star. Home Box Office, Inc.

Six Feet Under, created by Alan Ball. Home Box Office, Inc.

The Sopranos, created by David Chase. Home Box Office, Inc.

What Not to Wear, produced by Kaye Godleman, directed by Micci Billinger, David Dehaney, Helen Foulkes, Nicola Silk, Boaz Halaban. BBC TV.

Would Like to Meet, produced by Phillipa Ransford Executive Producer, Daisy Goodwin. Talkback

Index